EARLY BASEBALL AND
THE RISE OF THE NATIONAL LEAGUE

EARLY BASEBALL AND THE RISE OF THE NATIONAL LEAGUE

by
Tom Melville

McFarland & Company, Inc., Publishers
Jefferson, North Carolina, and London

Library of Congress Cataloguing-in-Publication Data

Melville, Tom.
    Early baseball and the rise of the national league / by Tom
Melville.
      p.   cm.
    Includes bibliographical references and index.
    ISBN 0-7864-0962-2 (softcover : 55# alkaline paper) ∞
    1. Baseball — History — 19th century.   2. Baseball — United
States — History — 19th century.   3. National League of
Professional Baseball Clubs — History — 19th century.   I. Title.
GV875.A1M45   2001
796.357'64'0973 — dc21   2001023077

British Library cataloguing data are available

Manufactured in the United States of America

Cover image ©1997 Wood River Gallery

McFarland & Company, Inc., Publishers
  Box 611, Jefferson, North Carolina 28640
   www.mcfarlandpub.com

To the memory of my parents

Contents

Prologue: Sport as Achievement, Sport as Expression

It's become customary for baseball writers, like ancient poets evoking the muses, to preface their works with inspirational anecdotes or nostalgic reminiscences of their experiences with the game they're covering. Not wanting to spurn this tradition, I'll begin this study as well with a personal testimony, though one, like the work itself, inspired by a recognition of an historical incongruity rather than cultural celebration.

Like many others among the sporting public, I was drawn to the plight of the Florida Marlins baseball club over the 1998 season. Here was a team whose change of fortunes, going from defending World Series champions to dead last place in their league division, had been virtually unprecedented in baseball history. Wide swings in competitive fortunes were certainly not unheard of in pro sports and the Miami public was, as is the case with other developments like this, offered the consolation that their team's precipitous reversal was the result of uncontrollable circumstances: the "business" of the game, high salaries, free agency, etc., and, above all, the arbitrary freedom of the team's owner.

It was, however, the Miami community's complete helplessness and its total lack of control and input over an institution that, like all other pro sports clubs in America, claimed to be so essential to community identity and civic status, that particularly aroused my interest and curiosity.

How was it that communities, which often lavished money and favors upon professional sports clubs on the justification that such institutions were indispensable to community pride and quality of life, held virtually no guiding interest over these clubs, which themselves were under no obligation, beyond economic viability, to remain within the communities in which they were located? Certainly this matter seemed to go beyond

1

the simple economic explanation of a private enterprise offering a community service for compensation. It seemed to indicate a more fundamental social valuation, on the part of the sporting public, of what a culture wants from its competitive structures.

It was during this time that I had the good fortune to come across Eric Leiffer's *Making the Majors: The Transformation of Team Sports in America* (Cambridge: Harvard University Press, 1995), a work that focused and clarified many of these same perplexities with its novel interpretation of how big time American sports developed. Leiffer recognized that the development of pro sports couldn't be adequately explained as a simple economic event, the transformation of sports into "business." It was rooted in deeper, more pervasive social currents actively opposing each other in the demand for and consequences of winning, which Leiffer identified as "cross currents between organizers and enthusiasts." On the one hand sporting publics are incessantly searching for winners, new teams, new champions, excelling under new challenge formats, while, on the other, they are continually abandoning losers and unattractive competitive formats. As Leiffer correctly notes, this is an inherently destructive pattern leading to frequent team failures and instability in competitive structures. Opposed to this are sports organizers who, to eliminate this competitive instability, work to establish uniformity and "sameness" among sports teams and organizations, trying to establish competitive structures which will make winning and losing by the same teams, year after year, acceptable to the sporting public without loss of interest, "to achieve a regularity that is not seriously disrupted by the winning and losing that sporting competition unavoidably involves."[1]

Leiffer's views represent a significant advance over traditional interpretations of how baseball, if not other major American sports, transformed itself into a highly organized professional enterprise. While most other scholars saw only an emerging impulse for profit as the primary force behind pro baseball's historical development, Leiffer recognized that the competitive constructs that arose in professional baseball were in fact reflections of, and determined by, much deeper, broader and apparently even self-conflicting social demands and expectations America's sporting publics entertained about their competitive structures.

Yet this interpretation also contains some problems. Leiffer presents his work as a sociological study, and relies almost exclusively upon secondary sources for his understanding of baseball history — sources which themselves ascribe to and generally support the traditional view that economic forces, the evolution of baseball from "fraternalism" to "business," determined the game's early history. As I was researching my history of

American cricket (*The Tented Field: A History of Cricket in America*), which covered this same critical period of baseball history, I began to question the historical validity of Leiffer's interpretation in the form he had presented it. Specifically, Leiffer puts inordinate emphasis on the influence of early baseball organizers. In their desire to establish "sameness and uniformity" upon sports competition, these organizers, Leiffer seems to believe, were able to personally mold and redirect the sporting public's interests and demands. This would have to assume, however, that organizers not only played a highly influential role at the very beginning of organized baseball, they also displayed a greater personal concern for the well-being of broader competitive structures than they did for the self-interest of their own clubs. As I shall show, neither was necessarily the case during baseball's early history. In fact, the impact of identifiable organizers on early baseball's competitive development was negligible, at least in their ability to influence the sporting public, until the time of William Hulbert and the National League, by which time professional baseball had already reached a mature organizational structure. As I'll also show, the outlook of early baseball organizers was surprisingly narrow and generally limited to the interests of their individual clubs, rather than competitive stability.

In addition, Leiffer's interpretation of the public's "search for winners," from a strictly historical perspective, wasn't nearly as disruptive to competitive stability as he contends. Baseball's early history, it's true, is strewn with failed clubs and an irregular competitive focus, but we must look more closely at what "failure" meant here. As baseball became more popular and better organized, with an ever higher competitive standard, more and more communities wanted to form clubs and gain access to the competitive challenge the game represented. This usually took the form of a local club bringing in outside players and then testing their strength against the country's better teams. If this venture failed, the club didn't necessary disband but simply reverted back to a local, amateur, non-competitive status, which happened to such notable early pro clubs as the Cincinnati Reds, the St. Louis Browns and the Resolutes of New Jersey. The "search for winners," from a strictly historical basis, then, was a vertical dynamic, with some communities always trying to work up to baseball's highest recognized competitive level, while others were always falling back to a lower competitive status.

If my interpretation is correct, then the social cross-currents at work within early baseball were *both* present in the sporting public's search for winners. On the one hand there was a demand, from the sporting public, for competitive integrity, a demand that only "the best compete against the best," which wanted to limit and qualify competitors; on the other hand, there was an equally strong demand to participate in this competitive level with *our* club, *our* team, that strongly resented any attempts to limit or restrict this privilege despite the problems this may have posed to competitive stability.

These are the cross-currents I identify in baseball's early development, both present within the sporting public, which exerted a continual tension and agitation upon the way baseball organized its highest competitive structures. Organizers may have played a role in this process, but only in trying to direct or manipulate these currents. They weren't able to effectively control them.

Which of these demands within the sporting public will determine a particular culture's competitive structures depends on what that society believes to be the social mission of its sporting competitions. The belief that sports organizations strictly reflect "the best against the best" will demand competitive resources be unconditionally utilized towards success (whatever may be the social consequence) while also insisting there be strict limitations and qualification standards for such competition. The term I use for this orientation is "achievement."

The sporting public's demand, on the other hand, that there be open access to the highest achievement level generally reflects a concern with extra-competitive values and expectations, which, historically, have ranged from a concern with moral character, social purpose or ideological identity, but, on the whole, it has been most strongly based upon locality or community. This orientation is willing to compromise competitive standards or requirements for the sake of the right to participate. The term I use for this orientation is "expression."

It must immediately be said that this contrast between "achievement" and "expression" is not simply another way of expressing the alternatives of "playing for fun" and "winning is everything," a common theme for interpreting the history of early baseball. Every sports contest, by its very definition, is concerned with "winning" no matter what the competitive level. What constitutes differing degrees of competitive interest are the social expectations and consequences identified with winning. The sporting public's demand for "achievement" believes that all resources should be unconditionally directed towards maintaining the highest possible competitive level without consideration for social consequences. That segment of the sporting public that, on the other hand, demands "expression" is also concerned with establishing and maintaining a high competitive level and utilizing the resources to this end, but only under certain socially responsible conditions. Both outlooks demand winning, but the former only recognizes winning *for* something, while the latter demands winning *as* something.

This construct also provides a more viable resolution to the "amateur" vs. "professional" dichotomy that has troubled sports historians in their studies of early baseball, typified in Warren Goldstein's otherwise thoughtful work *Playing for Keeps: A History of Early Baseball*. Working on the accepted differentiation that professional baseballers played only for compensation, while amateurs played only "for fun," Goldstein had difficulty understanding clubs like the Easton, Pennsylvania, team of the 1870s, an amateur team strong enough to beat pro clubs of that time. On the basis of competitive results Goldstein couldn't see any difference between the Eastons and regular pro clubs save in their claim to play without pay, leading him to conclude the difference between pros and amateurs, at this stage of baseball history, was largely hypocritical.[2]

The confusion here, though, lies in just looking at competitive status. The fact that the Eastons claimed to be amateurs didn't in any way mean they wouldn't apply all the competitive resources (training, strategy, etc.) utilized by professionals. The Easton club didn't differ from professionals because they represented a lower achievement level, generally assumed for those who didn't play for compensation, but because they freely and voluntarily choose to compete on their own, something not available to professionals who were contractually, and therefore unconditionally, obliged to win. This is a subtle, intangible difference, yet one necessary to those who would know how a society values competitive purpose.

How a society organizes its competitive structures will generally reflect the relative importance it places upon these two competitive orientations, something that involves the interaction of social expectations, traditions and cultural history. For the sake of clarity, the following chart illustrates the competitive characteristics that follow from the relative emphasis placed upon achievement or expression, based upon Leiffer's social categories:

	Expression	*Achievement*
Search for winners	fragmented, focused locally or regionally	national focus
Championship structure	late developing, championship often left undecided	develops early, championship usually the centerpiece of competition
Accommodating losing	results in change of status, usually relegation to lower competitive level, seldom in failure	results in club relocation, reorganization or disbandment
Player mobility	usually restricted by residence	unrestricted

	Expression	*Achievement*
Public mobilization	emphasizes participation, acknowledges obligation to extra-competitive considerations	totally focused on winning, all resources directed towards winning
Amateurs/pros	Suspicious of professionals, wants to subordinate them to amateurs	encourages autonomous professionalism

On the basis of this outline it's tempting to conclude two things: First, that the establishment of highly organized, professional level, sports absolutely requires an achievement orientation. While an expression orientation may properly reflect lower level athletic competitions such as college or school sports, it's structurally incompatible with high level competition. Second, that because America's sporting public has decreed its pro sports be overwhelmingly oriented towards achievement, any countervailing demand for expression has never exerted a formative influence within America's sporting culture. Neither conclusion, however, would be totally correct.

That a society can historically orient its highest competitive standards towards expression is best illustrated with English cricket. Throughout this work I'll occasionally be drawing historical comparisons between the development of baseball in America and professional cricket in England, a consideration some baseball scholars may find irrelevant if not outright offensive. It's extremely important, however, to be aware that another industrial society, sharing many of the same cross-currents within it own sporting public, as well as the same social institutions, could orient the highest competitive demands of its own bat and ball sport very differently than American society did with baseball.

First class (professional) English cricket, for example, has always been rooted in an obligation to geographic location. Such an obligation though present within America's sporting culture, was never able to effectively assert itself during baseball's early development. From the very beginning first class English cricket clubs were identified with counties (not cities) and were established not as business enterprises but organizations dedicated, like the Derbyshire club was on its founding, "to represent the strength of the whole county" in accessing the game's highest competitive challenge. The English sporting public viewed its professional cricket clubs more as "quality of life" institutions rather than economic enterprises, to be supported for their "community service" benefits, like churches or museums. The primary social purpose of these clubs was to provide the cricket talent of the locality a permanent and reliable opportunity to access the game's highest competitive level, a mission that has remained relatively unchanged in English cricket to this day.[3]

Nineteenth century professional cricket clubs were certainly profit-making organizations, but as Sandiford and Vamplew noted, they "took profits rather than actively seeking them," going only to those lengths to secure income without compromising the organization's primary social purpose. Despite the advances in the economics of the game, and the continued pressure to orient themselves more towards profit considerations, pro cricket clubs remain inextricably rooted in their extra-competitive obligations to place and locality. All professional cricket clubs in England are, by charter, inalienable organizations owned by their members, with some having played on the same ground for over 150 years. Even if it would be legally possible to, say, buy and move the Yorkshire County Cricket Club, it would be met with a social outrage in England equal to what one would find in America if someone tried to buy the University of Michigan football program and move it to a Sunbelt state. By the same token, new professional cricket clubs aren't established by awarding a "franchise" to a few enterprising individuals but by elevating long established, competitively proven, local clubs up to the championship competition.[4]

It would also be incorrect to assume that baseball's early and overwhelming orientation towards achievement indicated a weak, or even nonexistent, social concern for the extra-competitive dimension of their sports. Leiffer has convincingly shown that despite its rapid and overwhelming development as a professional sport, baseball wasn't the organizational prototype for the major American team sports that followed, specifically football and basketball. Throughout their early years of development both these sports strongly resisted professionalism, preferring to attach themselves to colleges, universities and athletic clubs while eschewing the establishment of a recognized national championship. The fact that this resistance persisted even within the environment of intensifying sports journalism and technological developments which facilitated competitive contacts certainly seems to indicate there existed a deep and pervasive, if inconsistent, American sporting tradition opposed to an unconditional and comprehensive achievement orientation.[5]

This is not a history of baseball in the traditional sense. Readers won't find here the story of early ballclubs, famous players or historic games. Nor will they find here a work explaining how baseball actually originated, something that has been competently addressed by other scholars. This work represents, instead, an attempt to explain the historical and social forces that determined organized baseball's cultural character. The main

argument of this work is that early baseball, due to the peculiar circumstances of its rapid development in a single city — New York — organized
itself overwhelmingly in response to the American sporting public's
demand for achievement. It was only able to do this, however, by opposing, thwarting, and distorting the American sporting public's equally pervasive demand that baseball's highest achievement level retain an obligation
to, and accessibility from, locality. As I'll try to show, all this transpired
over the first thirty years of baseball's organizational history, resulting in
a competitive incongruity that has effectively remained an integral part of
organized baseball up to the present.

I'd like to express thanks to the many people at the Cedarburg Public Library for all their help and support in gathering the often hard to
obtain resources for this study. A special thanks goes out to Nancy Stecker,
the interlibrary loan director, who once again showed the vast world of
research information can be brought to a small midwestern town.

1

From Winning to Achievement: Baseball and the Spirit of the City

Baseball was born old. Over a mere 15 year period, a game that had been played by only a few local New York clubs in the mid 1850s would become a full-fledged, technically advanced, nationally organized sport played on a professional basis. And if the Civil War had not briefly interrupted this progress, baseball would have reached an advanced stage of development a good five years earlier. Never before or since in history has a team sport progressed so rapidly, so comprehensively, over such a short period of time. Even contemporary observers were struck by this phenomenon, as seen with "old timer" games played between teams merely ten years apart, such as the 1863 vs. 1869 Eckfords, and the pre– and post–Civil War Philadelphia Athletics, which showcased the amazing advances that had been made in technique and playing strategy over this short span. From the very beginning of inter-club organization, baseball seemed to appear pre-formed, exhibiting mature characteristics that were able to carry it rapidly forward without any long, slow period of cultural gestation.[1]

How did baseball, confined to a single American city, catapult itself, virtually overnight, into a "modern," nationally identified sport?

As an organized, permanently structured, institution baseball had existed in New York since the establishment of the Knickerbocker Baseball club in the mid 1840s. After its famous match with the short-lived New York Base Ball Club in 1846 to the early 1850s, the Knickerbockers, however, were virtually the only organized baseball club in New York, and had to limit themselves to playing only intra-squad games.[2]

Part of this was due to the fact that the Knickerbockers could find no opponents in New York, but it also had to do with the club's outlook and purpose. The Knickerbockers were a decidedly "fraternal" organization. Its members played baseball for health, recreation and as an opportunity to socially interact with their peers. "Winning" within such a structure was a purely private affair. Games were got up spontaneously and were played as isolated, single events with no "carry over" effects toward any championship, club standing or player reputations. Anyone who belonged to the club could play, at any time. To the Knickerbockers winning and losing was a private matter and, perhaps for that reason, the team attracted little attention or interest from the sporting public during its early years.[3]

By the early 1850s, however, a number of other baseball clubs had been organized in and around New York, notably the Gotham, Star and Eagle clubs, whose inter-club games marked the first steps in carrying baseball competition beyond a purely private domain. But even these early clubs were organized along much of the same lines as the Knickerbockers. Their primary purpose was to also provide their members with opportunities for recreation and socializing, with competitive success being of secondary importance, as seen in the early accounts of players laying down or smoking on the field during games. In some instances ball playing appeared to be a strictly a peripheral interest, with some club members preferring to spend their practice days fishing or, as was the case with the earliest members of the Athletics, belonging to a musical society.[4]

Nonetheless, as teams began to play more games with outside clubs, rather than restricting themselves to intra-club matches, competitive results began to assume a more cumulative, and therefore objective, importance. Clubs began to establish reputations based upon their competitive success or failure, which in turn began to refocus club purpose more on competitive results than simply recreational enjoyment. "Winning," in short, was beginning to undergo a rapid and critical transformation from being a strictly private, to an openly public, phenomenon.

In order for these early baseball clubs to redirect their social purpose from "winning" (competition as private, with no objective public attention) to "achievement" (competition as public, with cumulative carry-over consequences and expectations) two things, however, were necessary. First, baseball, as a sporting experience, had to be "socialized." It had to develop a format and structure that could be played and accessed by urban adults. Second, there had to be a common ground for extensive inter-club competition, that is, a single, uniform set of rules.

The Knickerbockers had laid much of the groundwork for the first requirement during their "fraternal" years in the 1840s. Whether it was due to Alexander Cartwright or not, the Knickerbockers had settled on a form of baseball more accommodating to urban adult males. Most significantly they had eliminated most forms of physical contact and danger in their play by eliminating "plugging," hitting the player with the ball, a long established feature of "folk" versions of baseball such as townball and the Massachusetts game. Just how important this development was to baseball's success can only be appreciated when it's realized no team sport that utilizes the ball as a personal weapon has developed into a modern, adult sport. With their particular rules, in short, the Knickerbockers had transformed ballplay into "action from a distance," an absolute prerequisite if such a play form was to be accepted by adult urban males.[5]

In addition, the Knickerbocker rules mandating underarm pitching, a designated foul territory and one bounce put-outs all made this type of ball play far more "sociable" for participants, a game that could be enjoyed by individuals of various ages, backgrounds and athletic abilities.

Although the "excitement" associated with this form of play made baseball far "more lively and hilarious" than its strongest competitor of this period, cricket, and therefore more culturally attractive, it's important to understand the "New York" form of baseball was a noticeably altered and "tone-downed" version compared to the "folk" versions of baseball. During its formative years, in fact, the New York game was frequently criticized as a degenerate form of play compared to traditional ball games. Many advocates claimed that the Massachusetts game, with its fly out rule and no foul territory, was not only "more scientific and exciting" than the New York game but the only "genuine" form of ball play.[6]

Just how significant a shift the New York game represented, vis-à-vis America's traditional ball playing culture, could most forcefully be seen in an article that appeared in the Wisconsin *Racine Journal* in 1867. The author, an old townball player who had lost none of his enthusiasm for that game, condemned the New York game as nothing more than a revamped version of townball "shorn of all its life and animation." Compared to traditional townball, with its violent pleasure of plugging, the New York game was "indolent, sickly, puerile, effeminate and disgusting to behold," nothing more than a "'yaller kivered' game to suit the shiftlessness of the age."[7]

And, in the context of the times, this criticism, of course, was quite correct. Townball and other "folk" versions of baseball had been the play form for pre-industrial society, suitable for aggressive, volatile young men to be enjoyed for its spontaneous, if infrequent, emotional release. But this couldn't be the play form of the city, among urban young men, seeking recreation and play on a regular, orderly basis, to be enjoyed as a "manly" display rather than as an outlet for destructive emotions.[8]

Appropriate as the Knickerbocker rules were for the urban male, they were by no means the predominant rules for all New York area clubs. The Knickerbockers, along with the city's other "old line" clubs, the Gotham, Eagle and Star, had, on April 1, 1854, come to an agreement on their own set of rules, the main features of which were nine players per side and games decided by the first team to score 21 runs.[9]

Among the New York area's other baseball clubs, however, there were considerable variations from the Knickerbocker rules, with some clubs fielding teams with anywhere between seven and eleven players and deciding their games over time periods that varied from five to twelve innings. The Putnam club, a prominent organization during that period, even retained a feature of the Massachusetts game, deciding their games on the basis of the first club to reach 62 runs.[10]

Even the Knickerbockers themselves, to accommodate the different clubs they played, had to deviate from their own rules, agreeing to play, in some instances, with eleven players per side in their games with the Putnams. One even gets the impression that one particular club in Newark, which went by the name "Antiquarian Knickerbockers," may have even been organized specifically in protest to the Knickerbocker rules, this club insisting on only playing "old style" baseball, eleven-a-side, with only two innings per game. Clearly, Seymour's contention (which has become standard writ with most baseball historians), that most New York area baseball clubs of this period "aped" the Knickerbocker rules, seems highly questionable.[11]

It was this apparent flux and chaos over specific playing rules that led to the famous baseball meeting of January 27, 1857, among the 14 leading baseball clubs of New York. Just how and who originated the event is not entirely clear, Goldstein claiming the Knickerbockers "issued the call" for the convocation, a claim *Porters Spirit of the Times* seems to support. Peverelley, however, claims the Empire baseball club asked the Knickerbockers to convene the meeting, while *Porters* later gave credit to the four old-line clubs as a whole for initiating the meeting, an indication the Knickerbockers' influence upon baseball, even at this early stage in its history, was on the wane.[12]

Whatever the incentive, as a consequence of this meeting "substantial uniformity" was reached among the attending clubs on playing rules, most significantly in their agreement upon nine players per side and nine innings per game. I've argued elsewhere that an agreement on this type of length determination, that decided games on a total out rather than target run basis, was a prerequisite for baseball's future popularity, for the simple reason that this format made it possible for clubs of differing talent levels to mutually enjoy playing each other. Mismatched teams were guaranteed at least nine innings of continuous participation, a marked improvement over the old Knickerbocker 21-run rule, where a game could be over in as little as two or three innings, something that actually occurred during a Putnam-Astoria game in 1855, the former hitting up the required 23 runs in a mere two innings.[13]

By the same token evenly matched teams were guaranteed a result in no more than nine innings (27 total outs), another improvement over the Knickerbocker rules, in which some games had to be extended to as many as sixteen innings to reach the requisite 21 runs.[14]

It was certainly not completely coincidental that the first great New York baseball boom dates from the time of this agreement on a uniform set of playing rules. Not only did these specific set of rules make it easier for novices to play, they seemed to win over "many old Base Ball players" still committed to the folk versions they were familiar with. By the fall of 1857 the *Brooklyn Times* was already proclaiming "everybody ... who have a due regard for their health should join a base ball club," and, with the playing rules further refined and standardized at a follow up meeting among New York clubs in 1858, the game's popularity had reached such a point that it had become an "epidemic, just now." The *New York Ledger* conveyed the spirit of these times by beseeching New Yorkers to "run out, merchants, lawyers, clergymen, bookkeepers, editors, authors, clerks and everybody else who can, and have half a day of it in the fields every week during the ball season."[15]

This momentum was further reinforced by baseball's first competitive event to attract significant public attention, a series of games between representative teams from New York and Brooklyn played at Brooklyn's Fashion Course racetrack in 1858. Looking back from 1865, *Wilkes* would claim there had been nothing "since to surpass or even equal" that momentous series for attracting popular attention and directly inciting the formation of many new baseball clubs.[16]

This sudden spurt of baseball interest and the resultant proliferation of newly organized clubs, all now playing under a single set of rules, in close proximity, and on a semi-regular basis, also began to noticeably alter the character of the game.

Playing baseball just for the residual benefits of "health and recreation," or as an expression of social standing, "a means of showing off their figures in fancy dress," was now becoming difficult if not impractical. Clubs were now beginning to view their team's competitive results as more important than the social benefits that may be derived from such play. A revealing glimpse of this subtle, yet unmistakable, shift in club purpose can be seen with the Eckfords, one of New York's more prominent working class baseball clubs. The reminiscence of that club's early spirit of play by president Frank Pidgeon, "we had some merry times among ourselves; we would forget business and everything else ... at such times we were boys again," has often been quoted as evidence of baseball's intently "fraternal" character during the game's formative antebellum years. But this was the very same club whose players, in the increasingly competitive environment of New York baseball, also entered into their play with "such a desire to win, and such a dread of defeat" from their very first competitive game.[17]

The changes New York baseball was undergoing during this period, then, is more properly interpreted not as a transition from "fraternal" to "competitive" so much as a transition from "winning" (play as an isolated, private event) to "achievement" (play with cumulative, objective results and expectations). Every sporting event, even those played strictly "for fun," is, almost by definition, concerned with "winning." When winning, however, generates carry-over consequences (status, standing, etc.) which, in turn, generates expectations from an extra-participant public (a "following"), play has been transformed into "achievement." Since they were playing in such close proximity, within a single urban area, something that made competitive comparisons unavoidable, New York area baseball clubs, almost from necessity, had to become more responsive to the expectations of success against outsiders, rather than simply content themselves with providing member satisfaction. As early as 1857 the Eckfords themselves knew they could "never succeed in building up a club" unless they could demonstrate consistent competitive success against other clubs.[18]

With measurable, objective, gauges of success now influencing club purpose, the face of organized baseball began to rapidly change. Recognized ball playing talent began to concentrate within specific clubs, further encouraging players to move from one club to another strictly on the basis of their competitive contributions ("revolving"), something that was easy to do with so many clubs in close proximity to each other. As a result, a number of area clubs began to conspicuously accumulate the area's best ball playing talent such as the Atlantics, Eckfords and Excelsiors. The last mentioned in particular had, by 1860, reached such as state of competitive superiority, at least in playing by the fly out rule, that "no club in existence," it was claimed, "can beat them on the fly." Conversely other clubs, such as the Stars, saw a corresponding loss of status with the defection of their better players. By 1859 the disparity between club status had become so noticeable that the *New York Daily News* was flat out claiming such second tier clubs as the Unions "have no 'business'" playing top-flight teams as the Atlantics.[19]

These developments were further reinforced with the appearance of the "championship game" and the "championship series," a most measurable, objective standard of achievement and success, the traditional best-of-three championship format having appeared as early as 1855. This further polarized club status on the basis of competitive results, with championship contests among top clubs assuming greater importance than other games, something that, by 1859, concerned the *Clipper* insofar as they were drawing interest away from games among average clubs. There was even talk of establishing a handicap system to bridge this widening gulf between the more and less competitively organized ball clubs, with four outs and eleven players being suggested for weaker clubs.[20]

New York baseball's accelerating transition from a primary focus upon winning to achievement became a matter of more public debate during the fly/bound out controversy of the late 1850s. Scholars have traditionally interpreted this episode as a struggle between the "fraternal" community, trying to keep baseball as a game accessible to participants, and baseball "progressives," who wanted to allow baseball to develop into a highly skilled, competitive game.[21]

Such a straightforward interpretation, however, presents several problems. The "old boys" baseball community normally identified with the less competitive clubs such as the Gothams were strongly opposed to any legislation that only recognized outs made by catching the ball on the fly, rather than on the bounce (resistance from the Gothams defeated proposals to this effect at several antebellum baseball conventions). But the Knickerbockers, certainly the most avowedly "fraternal" of baseball clubs, actually championed the fly out rule, while the Mutuals, one of the strongest competitive clubs in the New York area, never played by the fly out rule until it was legalized in 1864. Some observers, in fact, claimed catching a ball on one bounce developed a far wider range of fielding skills than just catching the ball on the fly.[22]

Others claimed a fly out-only rule would result in longer, more protracted games, presumably because it would be much harder to make put outs this way. But as the skill level of New York baseball improved, especially with fielding, it soon became clear this fear was unfounded.[23]

It seemed proponents of the bound out rule didn't oppose the fly out requirement because this would have made baseball harder to play, but because it would further discourage competitive contacts between average and championship caliber clubs. With "the safer and more timid play" of the bound out rule players get a second chance to make put outs, an obvious advantage to less skillful players not available with the fly out rule. The legalization of only fly outs in 1864, therefore, seemed to further reveal baseball's irresistible orientation towards an achievement focus since less skillful clubs were now denied an important equalizer in their games with stronger clubs. This could be seen with the Knickerbockers themselves. With the adoption of the fly out rule some observers felt the Knickerbockers, long time advocates and practitioners of this variation, would become a leading club, when, in fact, they fell further into competitive obscurity. *Porters* suggestion, that a handicap of two outs for a fly catch, one for a bound, made as early as 1856, never seems to have been seriously considered because, like all handicaps, it would have declared handicapped participants, de facto, unworthy of the highest competitive consideration.[24]

Over the span of only a few short years leading up to the Civil War those characteristics most responsible for propelling baseball into a national institution had already coalesced within the urban environment of New York. The "socialized" ball play of the Knickerbockers, that had tempered baseball to the recreational needs of the urban adult, had become "systematized" through a series of conventions, allowing a wide variety of clubs to establish a common ground for competitive comparison and judgment. With so many clubs playing together in close proximity, on a semi-regular basis, under uniform rules, baseball's social focus also began a head long transition from private, indiscriminant, play to publicly supported competition with cumulative expectations and consequences.[25]

Most significantly of all, baseball was rushing towards this development in a relatively free, spontaneous and undirected way. Although a number of influential antebellum figures and personalities stand out during this period of baseball, such as William Van Cott of the Gothams, Frank Pidgeon of the Eckfords and, of course, Henry Chadwick, dean of baseball journalists, none can be said to have shaped or personally directed baseball in its course of development. Baseball wasn't the tool of, nor controlled by, any ideology, ethnic group, or social movement. Even the game's governing body, the National Association of Base Ball Players (NABBP), established in 1858, only had, aside from rule legislation, minimal impact upon the game's social progress. However many promoters, players and organizers that historians may identify as impacting baseball's later development, those scholars who persist in looking to the impact of "cultural leaders" in determining early baseball's character and appeal, must necessarily look in vain.[26]

We must draw a similar conclusion regarding the role of the press, or, more accurately, the lack of it. Though scholars have traditionally emphasized the importance of the sporting press in molding antebellum American athletic tastes and interests, this was an influence, in the case of baseball, that was, on closer inspection, more derivative than formative. If an estimation of baseball's social importance is to be derived from the antebellum New York press, then this importance could said to be even negligible. Most New York dailies virtually ignored baseball, preferring, like the *Evening Express*, to give the preponderance of their sporting coverage to cricket. The most significant antebellum baseball event, the Fashion Course matches, warranted no more than scant notice in the *New York Herald*, a paper that, despite its generous baseball coverage during the mid–1850s, for which the baseball fraternity extended its gratitude for having "brought this game before the public," carried few baseball reports over the latter years of the decade. The best baseball coverage was supplied by the *Sunday Mercury*, and this was a weekly, which, like the major sporting journals, also gave considerable coverage to cricket, the *Clipper* itself not declaring a full-fledged commitment to baseball reporting until its February 18, 1860 issue.[27]

Baseball's early popularity is more properly interpreted as arising concurrent with, not because of, the antebellum press. This we can conjecture from the simple fact that large crowds were already attending baseball games even before the press took notice of them. The very earliest Knickerbocker-Gotham games in 1855 were already "crowded," with large numbers also at the Astoria vs. Putnam and Eagle vs. Empire games that year, all well before the press was giving significant attention to the game. In some instances, games attracted plenty of attention without press notices, as was the case with the Excelsior games of 1858. Even contests among minor clubs, such as the Continental and Harmony, though seldom covered, were attracting significant crowds.[28]

All this seems to indicate baseball was growing, developing and advancing as a social phenomenon because of its own force of appeal, which was percolating through New York neighborhoods by word of mouth and direct, personal contact. All this was no doubt reinforced by the sporting press but it represented more a case of the sporting press discovering baseball, rather than creating it.[29]

The sporting press played a more important role in carrying baseball out and away from its urban environment to other areas of the country, proclaiming and portraying the game as the "only true and legitimate style of Base Ball playing" to Americans that had little more than an arms-length familiarity with the game. It must be remembered that the New York version of baseball was by no means an elevated or "legitimized" form of the many "folk" versions of baseball that had been played in America "since time out of mind." New York baseball was actually a disruptive interloper upon America's bat and ball culture, that displaced the various folk variations played throughout the country. New York baseball was the game of the traveling salesman, the relocated easterner, who transplanted this new version wherever they went, such as Edward Salzman, who formed the first New York style baseball club in Boston, or the transplanted New Yorkers who formed the first clubs in Chicago, Cleveland, San Francisco and Norfolk, Virginia. Above all, baseball was the first game Americans learned principally from print. Whereas townball and other baseball variations had been, as the previously noted Racine critic claimed, "handed down from generation to generation orally, like masonry and many other good things," New York baseball could, for the most part, only be learned by reading about it, which the Janesville, Wisconsin, ballplayers had to do by familiarizing themselves with the "new regulations" of New York baseball, and the Whitewater, Wisconsin, players as well, who learned the game solely by reading the "published regulations."[30]

Far from rising up from the soil of America's national genius, New York baseball was, in fact, an urban peculiarity that proved to be highly successful in appealing to the "urban spirit" of America's sporting tastes, even if it couldn't entirely ingratiate itself to the deep sensitivities rooted in folk ballplay. This could be seen in the sense of discontinuity that persisted, sometimes for decades, after the New York game had established itself. Even during the height of baseball's popularity in New York itself, efforts were made to revive "old fashion base ball," with a few clubs, like the Antiquarian Knickerbockers, noted earlier, steadfastly holding on to their townball as late as 1865. At various times and locations throughout baseball's period of greatest growth the past occasionally reasserted itself, as seen with the Cincinnati supporters who tried to revive townball in 1868 and the old townballers of Dundee, Michigan, who, as late as 1877, wanted to revert to the baseball they played "like 60 years ago."[31]

To some observers of the period, however, the very force of this spontaneous, urban-spawned, sporting obsession was as much a matter of concern as wonder. We must remember that baseball, unlike horse racing, boxing or boating, all popular sports in antebellum America, was the first sport that made it possible for a large number of average Americans to directly participant in the glory and honor of competitive athletics. But sports competition also generates human frustrations and disappointment, and it soon became clear that the socially constructive benefits observers expected from baseball's popularity (improved physical well-being and social harmony), were also beginning to expose the darker side of human nature. The *Clipper*, hoping to see a post-war baseball revival in 1865, may have thought "if anything can be carried to an extreme, base ball is certainly the most harmless," but the publication had earlier expressed concern over the "spirit of faction" that was rapidly infiltrating the game, perhaps the first inkling of that "New York intensity & overinvolvidness" Charles Newcomb found so objectionable in his otherwise favorite game.[32]

There were certainly many objectionable features with baseball's intensifying focus upon all-out achievement, with "petty jealousies, unmanly criticism and childish bickering" appearing in Philadelphia baseball by 1862. The Athletics themselves, against Altoona, a year later, were running into on-field behavior more "fitted for the 'plug uglies' of Baltimore or the 'Dead Rabbits' of New York." By this time the *Clipper* itself was increasingly concerned over the "revengeful retaliation" it was finding too often at New York's major games, such as the "bad feeling" among players of the Putnams and Excelsiors, a deplorable consequence of the overly "ambitious aspirations" of area clubs. It was enough to lead the *Clipper* to openly question the value of championship games, though the criticism was applicable even to minor clubs, like the Nassau and Continentals, whose on field play had become "a little mussey." All this was having carryover effects among non-participants as well, with crowd disturbances becoming a frequent, if unwelcome, accompaniment to more and more major games, such as the Atlantic-Gotham game in 1858 and the Excelsior-Atlantic game in 1860.[33]

Observers, however, had few alternatives to look to. The intense achievement focus that fueled baseball's urban popularity, a focus totally identified with who won, not how or why, left little room for extra-competitive influences. Mid-19th century American culture had no real countervailing tradition to moderate this raw, unchecked, urban achievement drive. American baseball, neither at that time nor in the immediate future, had any developed sporting ethic similar to the one Thomas Hughes portrayed for English cricket in his *Tom Brown's Schooldays*, a competitive outlook which had sublimated this raw competitive drive towards more socially moderate and acceptable expressions, such as institutional loyalty, self sacrifice or character development.

This is why it was so difficult for social observers, throughout baseball's formative years, to find any substantive social worth behind the game's competitive obsession. Those still committed to an anti-sporting "Nanceyish morality" could find in the game nothing more desirable than harmless recreation, while the more disapproving saw behind its emotional intensity nothing more than some "sublimated game of 'tag'" that perpetuated the vices of youth and immaturity.[34]

Two cultural influences could, in theory, have moderated or constructively channeled baseball's achievement drive, but both proved to be weak and culturally ineffective. New York's cultural elite, had they become directly involved with baseball during these formative years, could have possibly given the game some moral underpinning, as it did with such sports as yachting. But as scholars have long known, the character of New York baseball remained overwhelmingly middle and working class. A single club could have possibly stepped forward to exert moral direction and leadership, a role the Knickerbockers, given their seniority and commitment to baseball's "fraternal" mission, seemed, at times, poised to assume. For such a role to be effective, however, the Knickerbockers would have almost certainly had to become a top competitive club, an example of principled athletic accomplishment. For the most part, however, the Knickerbockers, by expressed purpose, never asserted themselves as a competitive club, with the exception of a short period after the Civil War when Asa Brainerd, one the country's top players, was with the club. From the late 1850s on the Knickerbockers were progressively ineffective in their influence upon organized baseball, in all forms. Even the club's influence on rule formulation had slipped away by that time, with the standard printed baseball rules of 1857 following those of the Baltic Club, those of 1858 following the Putnam rules. Nor could the Knickerbockers significantly influence the baseball fraternity's attitude towards adopting the fly ball out rule, which was strongly opposed by the rest of the baseball community until the end of the Civil War.[35]

After the Civil War the Knickerbockers increasingly retreated into competitive isolation, preferring to only play social games where "winning of a trophy is made a secondary consideration ... to the playing of a jolly good game of ball," an attitude "of indifference which party won." Rather than trying to counteract the more objectionable consequences of unchecked competition, the Knickerbockers choose disengagement, content to play informal 10-a-side games with the Excelsiors in 1862 and even taking up some cricket during the 1870s. Little surprise that the baseball fraternity's oldest club was the first to withdraw from the NABPP in protest over the formal recognition of professionalism in 1871.[36]

The other influence that could have possibly moderated New York baseball's accelerating achievement focus was an attachment to geographic or institutional loyalties, in which players and supporters recognized an obligation to place or purpose above and beyond competitive success. This was the pattern first class English cricket followed, with clubs developing inalienable attachments to specific counties, and hence an institutional obligation to geographic locality.

New York baseball did develop as a well-rooted neighborhood game, organized around companies, fraternal associations and professions, but any possibility of developing extra-competitive obligations around a single geographic identity was largely impractical given the close proximity of so many clubs in a single urban area. The demand for winning could be easily satisfied by simply recruiting players from other local clubs, making it virtually impossible to establish any sense of institutional or geographic loyalty. The *National Chronicle*, in 1870, may have led itself to believe "the love these players [the Atlantics] bear the club with which they play, is above all pecuniary considerations" but this was not the reality of New York baseball, as seen in the fact that most of the Atlantic players that year readily joined other clubs.[37]

At no time during baseball's early history, in fact, was a single club ever able to establish an identify as New York's single, dominant club, a point made all too evident from the representative matches arranged between New York and Brooklyn over the years. With the exception of the inaugural series played in 1858 (itself plagued by squabbles over player selection), most of these matches never proved to be very popular with the public and eventually came to be played primarily for charity purposes.[38]

On the whole, New York baseball would be free to develop its achievement focus without regard for social consequences, a development that had already demonstrated the fallacy of *Wilkes'* claim that baseball "depends upon respectability for its popularity, upon the press for its notoriety." An achievement focus was becoming the game's sole organizational mission, with everything else expedient to this purpose. It was a powerful cultural force, rootless, unchecked, and yet, paradoxically, because it identified baseball solely and comprehensively with winning, also surprisingly ephemeral. The strongest evidence for this surprising assertion can be found in the fact that there is no evidence. Unlike English cricket, whose first class clubs have left, in some instances, unbroken records of their activity and existence for over 150 years, a testimony to the durability of their extra-competitive attachment to locality, the great baseball clubs of the mid–19th century have left virtually nothing. Of such once mighty clubs as the Mutuals, Atlantics and Athletics, the last mentioned at one time so heavily patronized it was declared "A Quaker City institution," we have, today, virtually nothing in the way of records, journals or correspondence.[39]

Nor should this be particularly surprising. Like most ball clubs that had built themselves up to a championship status at that time, these organizations had quickly and comprehensively identified themselves with one purpose: reaching baseball's highest possible achievement level. This was their only social mission and once these clubs failed to maintain this objective, as all eventually did, their very existence, at least in the eyes of the sporting public, became purposeless and, consequently, they were all allowed to completely disappear without a trace.

This, then, was the character of early baseball as it developed in New York: a dynamic social phenomenon, centered in and propelled by a naked drive for unconditional achievement, a drive as irresistible in its appeal as it was unstable in its institutional durability. And all this was a social phenomenon that was about to move across the land, organizing and developing itself on a national basis.

2

The Course of Premature Nationality and the Crisis in Localism

Baseball's course of development barely skipped a beat during the Civil War. Although its popular growth was temporarily curtailed during this period, the game also overcame a number of significant cultural obstacles.

It was during these years that baseball firmly established itself in the sporting landscape of Philadelphia, the country's second largest metropolitan area, having "completely overcome" cricket as the city's team sport of choice. In the vanguard of this development was the Athletic baseball club, an organization that saw its membership grow from a modest 100 members in 1860 to nearly 1,000 by the end of the Civil War. The club quickly established itself as the dominant baseball organization in the city, a reputation enhanced by a series of highly publicized inter-city matches with the leading New York clubs during the war, such as the Eckfords, Atlantics and Mutuals. The notoriety attendant on these games certainly boosted the game's popularity even during the war's darkest days to an extent that Philadelphia, a location that had been completely unrepresented at the 1860 NABBP convention, had, by 1866, become a center of urban baseball interest fully equal to New York.[1]

A similar course of events transpired in Boston over these years, with the New York game quietly displacing the Massachusetts game as the dominant bat and ball pastime, to an extent that, by 1863, *Wilkes* could report this once popular local variation had now become "almost obsolete."[2]

By 1865, then, baseball was well positioned for a renewed extension, even explosion, of popularity. While still at a virtual "carnival" level of interest in

23

New York, the game grew so rapidly in Philadelphia that *Fitzgerald's City Item* exclaimed "rarely ... has a pastime leapt so suddenly into public favor as base ball." In Boston as well over the immediate post–Civil War years "ball playing became suddenly popularized," attracting over to its cause, by this time, many of the old-line aficionados of the Massachusetts game.[3]

From the time of its appearance in New York as an organized sport baseball had been an overwhelmingly participant pastime, a characteristic that didn't quickly change in the immediate post–Civil War years. During this period the city's sporting press reveals a proliferation in the growth of social, neighborhood and small town baseball clubs certainly equal to what the game experienced at the height of its antebellum popularity. And even with the game's accelerating shift from a central focus on "winning" to "achievement," baseball, in the immediate post–Civil War period, still maintained a largely participant orientation, with virtually every competitive club supporting second or third "nines" that frequently arranged "muffin" games to attract new members.[4]

But the increasing focus upon competitive success and accomplishment was undoubtedly moving New York baseball towards a structure largely based upon achievement. By the mid–1860s there were fewer and fewer opportunities for competitive contacts between first and second nines, with the practice of actually integrating first and second string players on a competitive basis being looked on as such an "old fogey style" of ball playing by now that the Mutuals had completely discontinued the practice in their own club soon after the end of the Civil War.[5]

In such an environment talent naturally began to concentrate and stratify itself among the more competitive clubs, with the more recognized players freely moving from club to club on the basis of ability or competitive expectations, which they could do with a simple "hop, skip and jump" among the congested landscape of New York baseball. This "revolving" among top clubs, by 1866, had become an accepted feature of New York baseball, with the Atlantics and Mutuals seeing their best players "bought off" that year. The Irvingtons of New Jersey also saw most of their good players move on after 1868 while the Eckfords, almost as a matter of routine, experienced a heavy turnover of their best players every fall. It was during this period as well that players first began to move from city to city, a precedent set by Tom Pratt, who left New York to play for the Athletics in 1866. The Nationals of Washington, D.C., carried this a step further, in 1867, by virtually importing half their team from New York.[6]

All this tended to concentrate talent within a small tier of top class clubs, such as the Atlantics of New York, who claimed to be the champion baseball club for 12 straight years, and the Athletics of Philadelphia, a club that stockpiled so many of that city's top players it had a virtual "monopoly" on local baseball talent.[7]

Logical, even competitively desirable, as these developments were given New York baseball's drift towards an achievement focus, a sense persisted that this represented a compromise of baseball's broader social mission, at least to the extent that these developments were progressively denying the average club and its members access to the game's highest competitive possibilities. It was certainly not the broad, deep, integrated play landscape the *Brooklyn Eagle* envisioned for baseball, which had "hoped that the day is not far distant when there will be so many clubs organized that each and every club, having formed so many friendly attachments, will have their season occupied by playing with their friends. And when such a day does come we may hail it as the day when our manly game was placed on a firm and solid basis."[8]

New York baseball clubs were, by contrast, rapidly becoming command centers for achievement rather than member serving organizations. Instead of developing into a broad network of equally competitive clubs, the landscape of New York city baseball (much to the concern of the *Clipper*) was becoming dominated by two or three top clubs steadily setting themselves above and beyond the baseball fraternity solely on the basis of their competitive standing. It was a concern also shared by Colonel Fitzgerald, one of the founders of the Athletics, this long-time Philadelphia baseball supporter expressing his displeasure in the way his club had, in the course of a few years, fallen into financial mismanagement, factionalism and disruptions from an over-aggressive move to develop a high-caliber club.[9]

Most of the blame for all this was put on the growing attention surrounding "championship games," which, by 1866, had become the focus of so much interest they were forcing clubs to play their more important games within enclosed grounds, something the Atlantics and Athletics, by this time, were doing on a regular basis.[10]

Both the NABBP, which didn't recognize any official "national" baseball championship, and the sporting press became increasingly concerned over this growing trend. The *Brooklyn Eagle* was, in 1867, hopefully predicting these matches "have had their day," a sentiment the *Ball Players Chronicle* also echoed, claiming "we do not think this championship business has any healthy affect on the game."[11]

To properly understand this opposition, which may seem so unusual from a modern perspective, it's important to remember that any mature and established championship structure can only arise by institutionalizing significant competitive discrimination. In a non-championship competitive environment games between clubs carry roughly equal value because nothing definite is at stake. Strong clubs, under this arrangement, are more willing to play weak clubs since the results do not count for anything substantial. The recognition of even an informal championship radically changes all this. Clubs quickly acquire status recognition on the basis of their competitive results in "championship" designated games, whose results tend to further focus attention and expectations upon only games among these clubs. The danger a championship format presents, then, wasn't that weak clubs feared losing to stronger clubs but that stronger clubs would consider weaker clubs competitively unworthy. This could be seen with the Eureka club of Newark, which, despite their loss to the Atlantics in 1865, thought it was "decidedly more honorable to come so near beating the ... champion Atlantics than it would have been actually to win the trophy from two or three less famous clubs."[12]

With good reason then the NABBP strongly resisted any official recognition of a national baseball champion, since it well knew doing so would have sanctioned, if not encouraged, sharp and deep competitive discrimination among the baseball community. So, for the time being, all championship claims would remain "an outside affair," an arrangement the *Ball Players Chronicle* hoped would always stay that way.[13]

Aside from these disruptions to baseball's competitive continuity, observers were also concerned with the broader social consequences of baseball's achievement focus. Since achievement is a public matter, greatly influenced by non-participant interest, especially one that was "prone to go into extremes," observers were upset with the increasing instances of "hippodroming" (losing a game on purpose to set up another) among top clubs, an abuse that was virtually ready made within the traditional best-of-three championship format among top clubs. "Should we be told that fame and honor are not sufficient incitement" for engaging in competitive sports, the *New York Tribune* warned in 1867, "then we answer that sports which cannot be sustained except by gaming should be instantly given up."[14]

Just as disturbing was the way baseball's obsessive focus on competitive results were being manipulated in the interests of third parties. Baseball clubs were, as the *Clipper* noted in 1865, no longer organizations of "no consequence" to public figures working to manipulate popular favor. There's little doubt the publication here had in mind the notoriously corrupt New York city politician William Tweed, who was intimately associated with the Mutuals during the Reconstruction period. Though he never seems to have held an executive position with the Mutuals, Tweed virtually underwrote, during these years, the club's finances and secured its best players phantom positions in the city's street sweeping department all for the sake of local political prominence. Another notorious figure of gilded age corruption, John Morrissey, seems to have been closely associated with the Haymakers baseball club of Troy. His exact relationship with the organization isn't entirely clear, but the ex-boxer-turned-politician's long and unsavory relationship with the New York gambling establishment certainly contributed to that team's reputation as one of the era's most competitively successful, yet organizationally corrupt, baseball clubs, notwithstanding its director's public disavowal of all gambling influences.[15]

By far the most contentious development that arose from New York baseball's accelerating focus upon competitive achievement was professionalism, though not for the reasons traditionally assumed.

The practice of compensating club members to play ball had actually pre-dated the Civil War. And, for the most part, observers, at that time, saw no real issue here since these payments, usually in the form of incentives, like those given to several Mutual players, or benefits, which were extended to such standout players as James Creighton and Dickey Pearce, were seen as rewards for loyalty and individual contributions. The *Clipper*, in 1859, actually took issue with the NABBP over its official stance forbidding any form of compensation, something the publication considered far too "aristocratic" since it denied poorer club members opportunities to play. Frank Pidgeon's frequently quoted objection, that under professionalism players would be "bought up like cattle," only became an issue when compensation began to be extended and exploited as a tool not for strengthening non-competitive ties, but for weakening them.[16]

In a typical "amateur" baseball organization members belonged to a club for purposes other than simply competitive success, such as locality, moral purpose or institutional identity. Team composition in such organizations would usually consist of a few outstanding players intermixed among a majority of mediocre players, with the latter generally enjoying the benefit of sharing in the team's competitive accomplishments though this was generally achieved through the exploits of their team's better players. This seems to have been the arrangement with the Astoria club before the Civil War, a team that, personnel wise, "left most of their playing to be done by two or three members."[17]

Such an arrangement radically changed under professionalism. Talent became a transferable commodity, freeing clubs from the restrictions and limitations of their own local talent resources. Teams willing to hire players could supplement their talent pool while those unwilling were likely to see their local talent base erode. Professionalism, then, didn't represent baseball's transition to "business" (though this would become an important consequence) so much as a crisis in localism. The competitive unity of an amateur system, with good and mediocre members playing together under some common extra-competitive purpose, was no longer becoming tenable in a thoroughly competitive environment. The best players from all clubs were now free to come together and play together, resulting in a pronounced competitive stratification among clubs based upon their ability and willingness to acquire extra-organizational talent.

In the earliest days of professionalism the most common complaint wasn't that baseball was being turned into a "business" but that a progressive and conspicuous concentration of talent was "demoralizing" the rest of the baseball fraternity, and for good reason. Amateur clubs, to retain access to an ever more demanding competitive standard, had to engage in a bidding war to either retain their own local talent or attract outside talent. In either case, this would necessitate a denial of member participation, "the breaking up of all local feeling in regards to base ball" as the *Brooklyn Eagle* put it. Observers had actually seen this danger with English cricket, which had professionalized years earlier, most noticeably in the way these all-professional teams, which contained all the best players, so comprehensively outclassed local amateur cricket sides. It was a system which, if duplicated with baseball, would surely be one that "repels rather than invites the youth of the country to join in the exercise."[18]

This interpretation also means the popular view of baseball's emerging professionalism, that it represented a class issue, the amateur trying to keep down or control talented working class players, is hardly valid. Observers didn't object to the increased enlistment of pro players because they were "from the lower walks of life" but because their mobility, which compensation made possible, meant their relationship to any club was a purely contractual one, for the sole purpose of winning. To all clubs formed on an extra-competitive principle, this was clearly an upsetting development, since it meant "men without social standing, perhaps without character at all, depraved and ignorant, claimed admission and were received into clubs on the single score of being good ball players."[19]

Winning, under the pro system, then, was no longer the expression of local resources that had been developed within a limited organization, but a trait that any club willing to absolve itself from all extra-competitive responsibilities could acquire.

First class English cricket, throughout the 19th century, had found a fairly simple way to avoid such undesirable consequences of professionalism with its residency requirement, which had been instituted to specifically limit talent mobility. Players couldn't join another club unless they had been a resident of that county for a full year (a requirement that was, for a short time, even raised to two years), an arrangement that virtually bound players to their local club for the duration of their careers. In America, with its deep tradition of free labor mobility, such a system was clearly impractical, though observers did suggest other means to minimize professionalism's disruption to the integrity of local competition, to direct it into "legitimate channels" by relegating pros to purely teaching roles, or only allowing them to come together and play as representative sides.[20]

It was largely for this reason that the NABBP, concerned with the "growing evil" of "hiring" after the Civil War, steadfastly opposed sanctioning a system it knew would undermine baseball's very competitive integrity. But in one of those frequently revealing historical instances that demonstrated how "the furor of base ball playing rises superior to all obstacles," the NABBP's opposition to professionalism was as unrealistic as it was out of step with the demands of its own clientele. The obsession with mobilizing whatever competitive resources were available meant, in American baseball, that the professional would never be, like his counterpart in cricket, an ancillary to local resources, but, instead, a replacement for them. He wouldn't be tied to a status of merely helping local playing resources but competing for them as an independent contractor, with all the powers and prerequisites this entailed.[21]

As early as 1868 it was clear professionalism had become "a fixed feature of the game" no matter how many official pronouncements were opposed to this. The achievement standards and competitive expectations of baseball were now so far advanced that the game demanded professionalism to maintain and justify these expectations, no matter what the consequences may be for individual club purpose or member interest. The short-lived sports publication *Bat and Ball*, by 1867, clearly recognized baseball's very popularity and progress now largely depended on the exemplary competitive standard professionalism brought to the game, it being "for them [pro clubs] to set a standard so high that all must attend to the pursuit with diligence to attain even a respectable position. All of this is positively necessary in order to keep up the enthusiasm requisite to make anything popular in this country."[22]

In its recognition of professionalism New York baseball had passed a critical cultural junction. The city's urban culture had now socially accepted that all extra-competitive ties and obligations were to be superseded by a mobilization of all available competitive resources. As *Wilkes* saw it, professionalism had, by 1868, transformed baseball into a game where "now the people go to see the eighteen men who play base ball, and not base ball as played by eighteen men."[23]

As it was, the full implications of this transition, both its possibilities and pitfalls, wouldn't become fully apparent in either New York or Philadelphia but in the emerging baseball frontiers of the Midwest, where, under the urban influence of New York and Philadelphia, baseball was virtually "progressing of itself" during the immediate post–Civil War years.[24]

In Wisconsin, for example, baseball, by 1866, had become a "regular epidemic," and, within a year, its popularity was "raging fearfully" in other areas of the Midwest. Regional and state baseball bodies began to be formed, bodies that further fostered the game's growth by organizing, as Rockford did in 1866, regional tournaments played specifically under the New York rules.[25]

With the New York game, however, western communities were adopting a form of baseball already fairly advanced in technique and skill level. As such, these newly emerging Midwestern baseball clubs were obliged to look to the best eastern clubs for playing standards and comparisons, like the club in Monroe, Wisconsin, whose officers wanted their club to be "modeled upon the experience of the best players in the union." By looking to New York and Philadelphia, however, the western baseball community soon realized they were committing themselves to a baseball variation well beyond the skills nurtured by what ball playing culture they themselves were familiar with.[26]

Some of this, of course, was a matter of demographics, since there simply weren't as many people playing baseball in the Midwest as there were out east. But it was also due to the novelty of New York baseball as a play form. Though seemingly easy to learn and play by modern standards, the New York form of baseball, with its intricacies of fielding and novel rules on fair/foul balls and pitching, presented real challenges to Americans raised on townball or the Massachusetts game.

In some instances demonstrably less talented players familiar with the New York game could actually outplay more talented townballers playing the game for the first time. This is what happened to a team of Delavan, Wisconsin, townballers who had been introduced to the New York game immediately after the Civil War, these newly converted townballers falling victim to a less talented team from Elkhorn simply because the latter had a "superior knowledge of the [New York] game." These same Elkhorn players had, in fact, themselves, a year earlier, "labored under great disadvantages" during their first game under the New York rules against a noticeably weaker, but rule savvy, team from Whitewater. Even the powerful Philadelphia Athletics, in 1860, were outplayed at a game of townball, 45–43, by a team from Mauch Chunk, Pennsylvania, they had previously trounced 34–2 when playing by the New York rules.[27]

In taking up the New York game, then, western communities found themselves not only far behind the east in their technical knowledge of baseball, they also had to completely abandon their own ball playing culture for a new type of ball play. In both instances this resulted in a glaring competitive gap between eastern and western ballplayers, something that was all too evident during the frequent tours top New York and Philadelphian clubs made to other areas of the country during the 1860s.

The motives for these tours were various, some on the expressed purpose of popularizing the game, others to demonstrate modern, urban baseball was no longer simply a "boys game," while still others, like that of the Washington, D.C., Nationals in 1867, the first trans–Appalachian tour by a prominent eastern team, was undertaken simply as a "summer vacation."[28]

Whatever the motive, all these tours by eastern clubs produced the same result, a near clean sweep of even the strongest western opposition, by often discouragingly lopsided scores. Even the Nationals, by no means the east's strongest team, had no difficulty beating Chicago's best team, the Excelsiors, 49–4 during their 1867 tour, a result particularly discouraging to local supporters since the match-up had been specifically arranged to gauge "the relative proficiency attained in the East and West."[29]

All these results, collectively, clearly demonstrated that western communities, left to their own resources, would never be a competitive match for the best eastern baseball, or at least not without a lengthy period of development. The *Chicago Republican*, reflecting the sectional sensitivity of this period, could not avoid the conclusion that the city's reverses against top-caliber eastern clubs "has had the effect of convincing most of the organizers of this section of the country that they really know but very little about ball play." It seemed to be such an unredeemable state of affairs the city's other baseball conscious paper, the *Chicago Tribune*, could only offer the consolation "let us accept the situation gracefully."[30]

But if the west found baseball "dropping in upon [its] people full blown," it had a powerful and readily available tool for satisfying their "extraordinary exertions to catch up to Eastern players": professionalism. With the top eastern ball talent geographically free to seek its most attractive financial opportunities, status hungry western clubs quickly and frequently began to tap into the rich vein of New York/Philadelphia baseball talent. Players from New York's Eckford club, an organization long reputed to be the "training school for the finest players of the country," and a virtual "nursery for good players," were in particularly high demand. So also were players from Philadelphia (a city with such a depth of ballplaying talent it had become, by this period, a "harvest field of baseball" for outside recruiters), many of whom by now were routinely heading west to "the New Eldorado" of baseball opportunism.[31]

For a locality that gave birth to the pro system and which, itself, never had a strong tradition of geographic loyalties, the east was surprisingly critical of the west's aggressive exploitation of this talent mobility. The very principle of complimenting local resources with imported talent was viewed askance, with the success of clubs built up by this practice considered illegitimate since it only represented the success of "picked nines." The east even refused to unconditionally recognize the success of the all-conquering Cincinnati Red Stockings, during that team's *annus mirabilis* of 1869, as entirely creditable because the team was looked on as an "eclectic," not a local, nine. Eastern baseball observers, however, reserved their sharpest ridicule for Chicago, the most shameless and aggressive purveyor of eastern talent, a locality that enrolled so many New York ballplayers it was derisively dubbed "New York's colony on the Lake," or the "Williamsburg and Lansingburg combination" of the Midwest.[32]

It was a competitive dependence even the west itself wasn't entirely comfortable with. Though the radical talent mobility among professional ballplayers made it possible for western communities to achieve competitive parity with the east almost overnight, there always remained a deep and lingering sense of obligation to local talent, the belief that "whatever local glory is worth having only arises from genuine local organization."[33]

If anything, the accelerating talent transfer from one community to another further offended what sense of local obligation there was in other areas of the country. Boston tried to find consolation in the fact that however badly its team lost to Cincinnati in 1869, at least it was a collection of completely local players. Even in Philadelphia there was an underlying sentiment that the national championship its Athletics won in 1871 would have been more satisfying if it would have been achieved with a totally local side.[34]

It was among the more import-laden western clubs, however, that this sense of competitive illegitimacy seemed to be most strongly felt. Though pleased with the almost immediate success of its first pro club, some St. Louis observers still expressed disappointment it didn't represent the accomplishment of a bona fide local side. Even Chicago, reflecting upon a year without pro baseball following the great Chicago fire in 1871, seemed satisfied in thinking "we should have no need to depend upon an Eastern club to afford amusement this summer." And when the city did finalize plans to organize a new pro club, in 1874, the local press still held out hope, however unrealistic, that this team would have no need for "imported" players.[35]

In only one western community was this demand for a nationally competitive standard satisfied through strictly local resources, and this was the Forest City baseball club of Rockford, Illinois, one of the most successful ball clubs of the late 1860s. The local press went to great lengths to assert that Forest City's success was somehow more legitimate, more "real," because it represented the accomplishments of an exclusively local team, whose members "are all original Western men" (though a number of its players, such as Bob Addy, weren't actually born in the Midwest). Even out east *Wilkes* found the home-bred success of the Forest City team somehow more satisfying than that of their more famous rivals, the Cincinnati Red Stockings, declaring "money made the Red Stockings Club, while Rockford muscle made the Forest City Club."[36]

If sports observers sensed some cross-purposes in baseball's social mission — a demand for nationally competitive standards while acknowledging an obligation to local resources — they should have realized this was the direct consequence of baseball's urban origin. In its explosive pre- and immediate post–Civil War periods of growth in New York and Philadelphia, baseball had set upon the nation a premature national standard, "premature" in the sense it had been established and perfected within the limited competitive environment of New York and Philadelphia prior to any other areas of the country. When other localities of the country adopted baseball the competitive deficiencies between their baseball and that played in the east was so great it incited those communities with an inordinate sense of sectional pride to abandon all hopes of expressing their baseball achievement on the basis of local resource development, however strongly it may have acknowledged this obligation. This meant, then, that baseball was forced upon an historically inverted course of development, one in which a high competitive standard actually preceded, chronologically, what normally would have only developed through a process of slow, broadly based, popular interest.

Under an historically linear development sports popularity should grow slowly, but uniformly, in widely dispersed geographic areas. Competitive standards should also rise slowly, but also uniformly, being firmly rooted in local talent development. Following this path of development competitive standards should also rise slowly, but concurrently, as more and more clubs come into competitive contact, gradually building competitive networks up from a local to regional to national basis. Anything approximating a national competitive standard or championship should, under this scheme, be the last stage of development, and one built up "from below" by an expanding and maturing network of locally rooted competitions.

This was the course followed by English cricket in its historical development, with competitive standards and structures slowly developing on a broad geographic front over many decades, from village and country rivalries up to a national competition. If we date the beginning of organized

English cricket from the rudimentary county matches of the early 18th century, no less than 150 years elapsed before anything that could remotely be construed as a recognized national championship structure emerged in 1873. And even for many years after this date the county championship (as it came to be known) remained a loose, largely undefined entity (as late as the early 20th century the championship format didn't even require every pro club to play each other) primarily because traditional local rivalries (such as Yorkshire vs. Lancashire) remained almost as important a competitive focus as any "national" championship.[37]

American baseball, of course, would follow a much different path. With a high competitive standard appearing almost instantaneously during its explosive growth in New York and Philadelphia, early baseball was never able to develop a broad, uniform, locally based competitive network that could slowly build up to a nationally extended standard. Baseball organizers in outlying areas of the country had to abandon and bypass any obligation they may have felt to slowly develop their local ballplaying resources because they were under the much stronger imperative to duplicate, as quickly as possible, the premature competitive standard New York and Philadelphia had established, an objective all localities could potentially accomplish given the unrestricted talent mobility professionalism had made possible.

It was a cultural path contemporary observers weren't entirely comfortable with. The *National Chronicle*, on the eve of all-out professionalism in 1869, still wanted baseball to assert its organizational focus on state and regional, rather than national, championships, an arrangement the *New York Herald* had advocated years earlier, claiming "the arrangement among the leading clubs of the prominent cities being, first, to win the championship of their state ... and then to enter the lists for the United States Championship."[38]

Under professionalism, however, baseball's competitive focus was "leapfrogging" local and regional competitive ties for a free-floating, all-encompassing national standard, the consequences of which were all too apparent for proponents who still hoped baseball's achievement focus would be locally rooted. In New England a highly sophisticated state championship structure, which allowed local clubs to progressively work up through a series of qualifying rounds, was effectively gutted because the state's two strongest clubs, the Lowells and Trimountains, in their orientation towards championship games with the country's leading clubs, didn't bother to participate. In Illinois the divergence between championship aspirations and local obligation was even more telling, when Chicago, in its desire to form a pro team in 1869, effectively abandoned all connections with regional baseball and only focused on beating the top eastern clubs, a decision that soon left the Illinois state baseball association weak, ineffective and "in a wretched condition."[39]

By the late 1860s, then, baseball had evolved into something of a cultural paradox. It had, as a consequence of its New York origins, quickly established a "national" standard (objectively identified in a "national" championship), but this standard had also been virtually imposed upon America's ball playing culture, it hadn't slowly evolved or developed "up" from a broad network of geographically dispersed areas of interest. This path of development would make it possible for communities to quickly access the game's highest achievement level, but to do this they also had to abandon an equally strong, and deeply rooted, obligation that this achievement be an expression of place and locality.

Just how difficult it could be for communities to resolve this cultural contradiction in a workable, sustainable, manner was about to be revealed in its most compelling form in one city: Cincinnati.

3

Cincinnati and the Trauma of Professionalism

The saga of the Cincinnati Red Stockings, and their undefeated season of 1869, is one of the few episodes in sports history in which both baseball popularizers and sports scholars seem to share a consensus of opinion. Both baseball generalists and specialists have consistently supported the interpretation that the Reds were baseball's first openly acknowledged professional team, that "threw down the gauntlet" in defiance of the NABBP's prohibition against professionalism, a development that marked baseball's final transition from the "fraternal" era to the modern era of baseball as big time "business."[1]

If viewed within the full historical context and circumstances that led up to the 1869 Reds this cut-and-dry interpretation, however, raises some problems. Why was it that professional baseball appeared with so much resolution and support in Cincinnati, rather than among the professional clubs in New York or Philadelphia, areas in which baseball had been played longer and on a higher competitive basis? This point becomes more pertinent when it's understood that organized baseball itself was slow to take hold in Cincinnati, a city where cricket "was all the rage" when Harry Wright arrived in 1866 to assume the management of the city's leading sports organization, the Union Cricket Club. In addition to cricket, the first New York–style baseball club organized in Cincinnati, the Live Oaks, also had to compete with a well established townball club, the Buckeyes, for public attention and interest.[2]

How was it that this Cincinnati Base Ball Club, restricted on its inception in 1866 to a mere forty members "to insure exclusiveness," whose chairman, a Dr. May, didn't even know the "first rudiments" of New York style baseball, was able to so remarkably transcend these original limitations and, in a mere three years, become the champion baseball club of America?[3]

Those who only see in the Red Stockings the rise of baseball as "business" also have difficulty explaining why the club abandoned the professional system after only two seasons. We shall discuss the specifics of this in more detail later, but the most widely accepted view, that the inability of the Reds, in 1870, to duplicate their unprecedented record of a year earlier "melted enthusiasm" among local supporters, seems highly unsatisfactory for several reasons. For one thing, it's difficult to reconcile this view with the enthusiasm and interest Cincinnatians continued to show for not only professional baseball but its former players when they returned to play exhibition matches in the city.[4]

It's also difficult to see why Cincinnati, of all the country's urban clubs, so quickly abandoned the pro system, something officers and supporters of such well established pro clubs as the Philadelphia Athletics, the New York Mutuals and Atlantics didn't do despite these clubs' many competitive failures. All in all, it's very puzzling to explain why the Red's unprecedented competitive achievements in 1869 didn't translate into more enduring and resilient support for the instituition of professional baseball.

To begin to answer these questions, we must understand that the Cincinnati baseball club developed under two unusual circumstances. First, the club was, almost from the start, closely associated with the Union Cricket Club. The two organizations shared the same ground and seemed to have some overlapping membership. With the technical and organizational expertise of the Union's player/manager Harry Wright also readily, if not officially, available to their members, the Cincinnati baseball club, as one contemporary observer noted, heavily "leaned" on the Union's resources during its early years.[5]

The other factor that accelerated Cincinnati's rise to a dominant competitive position was its intense rivalry with the city's other prominent baseball club, the Buckeyes. What one would have expected to be little more than a friendly rivalry between neighboring clubs quickly reached a level of almost pathological animosity, a rivalry so intense their games were fought out "not only for supremacy but for existence." Relations between the two clubs became so strained, apparently, that they refused to use the same baseball grounds and even carried their hostility over onto a benefit game for Yellow Fever victims.[6]

The competitive tension between the two organizations further escalated in 1868, the year the Buckeyes "went into the professional system" by bringing into their team three top-caliber eastern players. Cincinnati, faced with this competitive imbalance, quickly countered by hiring the top New York ballplayers John Hatfield, Asa Brainerd and Fred Waterman, whom Harry Wright, now the full time player/manager of the Reds after leaving his position with the Unions, and club president Aaron Champion had recruited during a trip to New York.[7]

The rivalry between Cincinnati and the Buckeyes had now reached such an extraordinarily intense level that on-field confrontations became a regular feature of their games, complimented by off-field accusations of underhanded attempts to drug each other's players. Things came to a head during a critical game between the two sides in September, 1868, won so convincingly by the Reds, 20–12, that it completely "ruined" the Buckeye's hopes of competitive supremacy. Unsuccessful in their efforts to secure local dominance, and financially far over-extended in their attempts, the Buckeyes released their pro players and, by early 1869, had lapsed into bankruptcy.[8]

As things transpired, the Reds indirectly and perhaps unintentionally found themselves with a national caliber team through their battle of attrition with only one local club, the Buckeyes. This had allowed Cincinnati to complete its 1868 season with a highly commendable 41–7 record, that included a number of wins over top eastern clubs during the Red's tour, the first ever by a trans–Appalachian ballclub, to the east coast that season.[9]

Good as the Reds were they still, however, weren't quite up to championship caliber, at least compared to the top eastern ballclubs. The Reds lost at home to both the Unions of Morrisania and the New York Atlantics that year, with the latter beating the home team by such a convincing display of superiority the local press conceded they could have beaten the Reds by 100 runs if they wanted to.[10]

All this indicated the Reds, up to this point in their development, were a very good local semi-pro club, that could go toe-to-toe with the country's top clubs but still couldn't quite match up with them. Why the Reds weren't content with this status, but opted instead, over the winter of 1868-69, to totally divest themselves of the few remaining local players on their roster, and commit themselves to bring in the best available outside talent, isn't entirely clear. Perhaps it was from a sense of sectional insecurity, a desire to achieve "just respect for western talent and skill" as the local press demanded. Whatever the incentive, by the spring of 1869 the Reds had completed their transformation into a fully salaried club with the acquisition of the talented catcher Doug Allison, discovered by Cincinnati manager John Joyce on the local ballfields of Philadelphia, and George Wright, Harry's brother, generally recognized as the country's best shortstop, a more than adequate substitute for Philadelphian John Radcliff, who declined the Reds' contract offer.[11]

Like all other local baseball clubs during this period that set upon the "expensive luxury" of hiring pro players, the Reds soon found themselves more than a little financially over-extended. Already $5,000 in debt as a result of their acquisition of the Union Cricket Club grounds, the Reds saw this indebtedness further increased through their salary obligations to some of the highest paid pro players of that time, all of which lead to such a drain upon the club's financial resources its treasury, by the spring of 1869, had become "flatter than a flounder." Under these conditions of financial duress it's not improbable the Reds undertook their eastern tour in 1869 as a "hard headed business venture," the most logical and realistic plan, after "flying financial kites," to relieve the club's burden of debt, though it was a scheme that sent the Reds east that spring with a financial backing that amounted to little more than "twenty-four dollars in cash and a bottle of arnica."[12]

It was an inauspicious beginning of what would become one of the legendary episodes of baseball history. Not overly heralded (the eastern press felt the Reds would certainly lose some games out east), and only first acknowledged to be an "A no. 1" club after beating the formidable Haymaker team at Troy, the Reds eventually made a clean sweep of all their eastern games, highlighted by an unimaginatively low scoring 4–2 win over the Mutuals, proclaimed by *Wilkes* to have been the "best played game ever witnessed." By tour's end there was no denying Cincinnati had come into its own, going on to finish that season undefeated, with a club ledger largely cleared of debt and even, it was reported, a $1.39 profit to boot.[13]

For the baseball community at large, the consequences of the Red Stockings' unprecedented accomplishments that year were twofold. As the first western club to register more than an incidental success against the top-level eastern clubs, Cincinnati had shattered the complacent confidence that had long characterized the lethargic, in-grown world of top-caliber eastern baseball. No longer was the "hocus pocus" world of New York baseball supportable, with its long history of semi-collusive competitive arrangements among the city's top clubs to ensure no championship claims could be legitimately made by an outside club. It was a long standing scheme even *Wilkes*, by 1868, had condemned as a total sham, though one that wouldn't die easily, as seen with the Atlantic's outrageous claim that they, and not the Reds, were entitled to national championship honors in 1869 for the simple reason that Cincinnati hadn't played them a return game as New York baseball custom demanded.[14]

So comprehensive was its competitive success in 1869 that Cincinnati had, almost single-handedly, raised the achievement level of first class baseball far beyond anything hereto known to the game. From just their impact upon those facets of the game as technique, strategy, organization and training, the Reds' 1869 tour "had done more to elevate the game than any trip of the kind ever before known." The Cincinnati press also proudly pointed out the Reds had "elevated and beautified the national game by making its trials of skill sincere and frank," a gratifying improvement over the underhanded dealings that had characterized professional baseball up to that point.[15]

Observers correctly attributed most of the Reds' success to their captain, Harry Wright, eulogized by the *St. Louis Republican* as a baseball strategist who, though "plain and practical in his operations," was also "a shrewd manager, a superb general and has a power of control over the men placed under him which is simply marvelous."[16]

Talented as the Reds were individually, the *Clipper* felt their success was due far more to Wright's canny ability to mold and adapt his players' personal abilities to the specific situational demands of game-to-game play. To some eastern observers this may have seemed too technical and over-specialized (a criticism frequently leveled at the Reds), with "all such nonsense as Wright indulges in about placing men in positions in the field," but there could be no arguing with the results, which seemed to fully confirm "brains have at last come into the base ball market."[17]

To Cincinnati's strongest rivals, especially those in New York, it could no longer be denied the type of baseball they had played in the past had, for all practical purposes, been eclipsed. The Reds' rampant success had totally exposed the "half-practiced, undisciplined" character of even the best eastern clubs, such as the Atlantics, whose lax, ineffective leadership was notorious for allowing "every man [to do] as he likes."[18]

The Mutuals, whose competitive standing the Reds clearly threatened, were probably most responsive to these new challenges facing top-class baseball. Now fully cognizant that the "carelessness" in which the club had often played their games in the past (against weak clubs the Mutuals would often play in their street clothes and, even against strong clubs, would seldom use the same lineup two games in a row) was the path to baseball mediocrity, the club instituted sweeping changes after the 1869 season.[19]

The Mutual directors gave their newly appointed manager John Wildey much broader authority over player discipline and training, which he used to good effect, instituting a rigorous training regimen for the team. The Atlantics soon followed suit, revamping their training routine and reviving, after a two year absence, mandatory training games.[20]

Collectively this clearly and distinctly set the championship standards of professional baseball far above and beyond the rest of the game. *Wilkes* already knew first class baseball would no longer have a place for the part-timer, as it also knew the intensely discriminating demands of highly skilled baseball play would mean there would be far fewer, but better quality, baseball clubs after 1869.[21]

Whether or not this was a scenario sporting critics desired, it was certainly one the sporting public seemed to want. Attendance at most professional games shot up in 1870, indicating a much more discriminating public demand for meaningful, high quality, baseball play. The *New York Tribune*, by now, could only attribute the poor attendance at an Eckford-Mutual charity game to the now widespread public "indifference to attend a game in which the players are not pecuniarily interested."[22]

The Cincinnati club that began its second season as a fully professional side in 1870, then, found itself in a baseball world that had changed more dramatically over a single year than it had at any other period in its history. With the strategies and techniques developed by Cincinnati now in the public domain, communities far and wide were organizing professional clubs, hoping to duplicate the civic benefits that baseball success had brought to Cincinnati. Cleveland, Baltimore, Chicago and even little Portsmouth, Ohio, fielded professional clubs for the first time that season, while Indianapolis and even far off Omaha, by season's end, were seriously considering getting into pro baseball. Many of these plans were certainly ill-advised, but as the *Clipper* noted, with so many pro players readily available and professional ball playing technique so widely known, any community was justified in thinking they could do what Cincinnati did.[23]

There was certainly no reason why Cincinnati couldn't have continued to prosper in this new baseball world it had effectively created. The club's long winning streak did come to an end that June in New York against the Atlantics, a loss that was probably not felt as badly as those against sectional rival Chicago later that year, but the club still finished the season with only six losses, by any standards an outstanding accomplishment. Yet even before the season was finished the club was experiencing internal discontent and public disapproval, some not always evident and certainly not visibly threatening, but by the end of the year the club's executive committee had voted to release its pro players and revert to a completely amateur status.

The most popular interpretation of Cincinnati's sudden about-face as a professional baseball enterprise usually follows a "victim of success" line of reasoning, claiming the Reds' extraordinary success spawned both unrealistic public expectations and unmanageable financial obligations. When it became evident, in 1870, that these expectations couldn't be realized, public support cooled and attendance dropped, to a point that even the local press began to criticize the club (at one stage even suspecting the Reds of corruption), aggravating internal discontent and eventually leading to the decision to completely disband the team.[24]

The problem with this interpretation, however, is its incompleteness. The difficulties Cincinnati was experiencing as a professional club were certainly nothing unique. First class baseball clubs in other areas of the country experienced the same range of difficulties, yet many of these clubs were able to survive and even prosper. The personnel difficulties Cincinnati experienced, most notable with Charles Sweasy's temporary expulsion for a display of public drunkenness on a riverboat, was relatively insignificant compared to the legacy of disciplinary problems among New York's pro clubs. It may have been unrealistic to think Cincinnati could have maintained its 1869 team for another year (Boston had tried to hire away George Wright at the end of the 1869 season, Troy was after Sweasy and Cal McVey, while Chicago was aggressively pursuing other members of the Reds that year), but turnover was a fact of life in the pro system and Cincinnati should have had no difficulty securing quality replacements.[25]

Public sentiment certainly cooled towards the Reds over their second season, even to the point of inciting open criticism of the team. But the Cincinnati press never became nearly as hostile over unfulfilled expectations of its home team as the Chicago press did with its professional baseball club. From a strictly "bottom line" perspective the Reds were, throughout 1870, under increased financial pressure through a combination of increased salaries (it cost $15,000 to run the club for the seven month season in 1870), and a drop-off in attendance. Yet the club apparently managed to break even that season, a state of affairs that, if disappointing, may have been self-induced since attendance declines were probably due as much to the club's decision to double ticket prices (from 25 to 50 cents) than its competitive reverses. How inconsequential these matters should have been to Cincinnati's financial viability can more fully be appreciated when it's known the Chicago club ended its inaugural year as a pro organization $3,000 in debt, yet the club went from strength to strength the following year.[26]

To correctly understand Cincinnati's path to disbandment it's more important to focus upon the club membership's internal expectations and assumptions about their team's mission and purpose rather than its public difficulties. It must not be overlooked that the Cincinnati club, from start to finish, remained demonstrably "fraternal" in its outlook, an organization that never seemed to abandon its belief the club was to serve the interests of its members. Although the club was nominally organized as a stock issuing body its shares were always undersubscribed, while an attempt to bolster income in 1870 by doubling membership fees from $5 to $10 was received so coolly it resulted in a drop in membership from 490 to 150. On the whole, the club didn't seem to have a clear sense it was organized for, or had any oblilgation as, a profit making undertaking, seen in the fact that what earnings the club did accrue went towards ground improvements, not dividends.[27]

The club also never seemed to be totally comfortable with the consequences of orienting itself towards an achievement focus. From its earliest excursions into top-class baseball, Cincinnati had always expressed displeasure at the win-at-all-cost spirit it found so pervasive in New York baseball, objecting to everything from player conduct to schedule switching to ticket receipt chicanery, as a result of which some Cincinnati supporters were lead to believe it was their club's moral obligation to "teach them [New York clubs] gratuitous lessons in the civilities of polite society." This attitude of moral indignation hadn't completely mellowed even after the team's success in 1869, club management being so disturbed with the relentless pressure for championship results they publicly declared the Reds, for the 1870 season, would only be playing for the "popular verdict of supremacy" not for any championship claim.[28]

With such an outlook it shouldn't be surprising that, over time, a management skeptical of the redeeming qualities of an unconditional achievement focus should run into difficulties supporting and maintaining a collection of players whose actions and behavior must be expendable to this end. Club management soon became frustrated over the moral responsibilities imposed upon them, with director James Joyce having to take it upon himself to keep the players, during their triumphant trek of 1869, "on bread and milk and tucked ... in their little beds at the going down of the sun." Club president Aaron Champion, well versed in the ill-behavior that can result with full-time professionals, was more openly critical of his players, most of whom "not having cultivated tastes, they spend all that they receive and all they can get."[29]

Cincinnati's growing disillusion with the pro system it had adopted became public during the club's fateful annual meeting in December of 1870. Over the course of the meeting, which was occasionally acrimonious and argumentative, a strong sense of frustration and betrayal over the club's social mission became visibly evident. Charges were made that the very idea of hiring a professional team was strictly an executive decision never authorized by the membership at large, who seemed to assume the pro players were to only assist and supplement local playing talent, not take their places, a line of reasoning *Wilkes* itself had expressed a few weeks earlier. The *Cincinnati Times*, even prior to the 1869 season, had felt

Cincinnati could have had a very strong team if only the best amateur players in the city could have all been brought together, a rather ironic and unrealistic idea given the bitter rivalry between the Reds and Buckeyes. In such an atmosphere of disillusion it was certainly no surprise that club members, though wishing to support a championship caliber team in 1871, declined to authorize the $5,000 necessary to maintain such a team, a move that effectively ended the club's professional status.[30]

Ultimately Cincinnati abandoned the pro system because it couldn't reconcile the conditions incumbent upon baseball's highest achievement demands with the social obligation that this achievement be a development of local resources. The Reds had revealed the full potential of the pro system, that the highest achievement levels of eastern baseball could not only be equaled but excelled for those willing to utilize the radical mobility of player talent and management expertise that professionalism made possbile. But Cincinnati also couldn't fully accept that this could only be done at the cost of denying all but nominal organizational control over this achievement. The city's championship status was a result of an arms-length, contractual, arrangement, not a development of local resources, and, for that reason, was no more enduring than any other arrangement of mutual convenience. "They have done well by Cincinnati," new club president A.R. Bonte concluded in the wake of the club's decision to release its pro players, "and we think ... Cincinnati has done well by them."[31]

This point can be more fully illuminated with a comparison with English professional cricket. Throughout the 19th century it wasn't uncommon for wealthy local patrons to bail out county cricket clubs going through periods of financial difficulty. These patrons, many from the local gentry, were willing to extend such generosity because, like a wealthy parishioner propping up his financially strapped church, they knew the "emotional capital" they invested in the club (their interest in, identity with and expectations of, the team) would be stable and secure. There was little likelihood the club would disintegrate from a rapid or wholesale turnover in management or players. This, of course, wasn't the case with professional baseball as it was developing in Cincinnati. There's little doubt Cincinnati supporters could have come up with the funds necessary to maintain a professional team beyond 1870. They choose not to from their frustration and disappointment in knowing the emotional capital they'd invest in the team was now highly insecure and could be quickly lost through the wholesale defection of its players and management once their contractual obligations expired.[32]

Cincinnati was by no means the first community to fall victim to the harsh new realities and requirements of professional baseball. The Unions of Morrisania, whose hiring spree in 1868 had made their club national champions that year, "gave up the professional business" early in 1869 when they were unable to cope with the onerous financial and managerial responsibilities of maintaining a national caliber team. The Haymakers of Troy also briefly reverted to an amateur status before abruptly reversing itself in 1870. Even the mighty Atlantics, overlooked in the notoriety of Cincinnati's disbandment, voted to revert to a co-op status at the end of 1870 after seeing many of its best players hired away by William Tweed for his Mutuals.[33]

In all these instances, however, there was no real community outrage or feeling of betrayal because New York had no single, identifiable, community club. Player turnover and club realignment had long been a fact of life there. The situation was different in a place like Cincinnati. The Reds, by 1868, had become totally and completely identified as the sole baseball representatives of that city. A loss of status under these circumstances was much more traumatic because it meant a complete and total loss of any qualification for championship caliber baseball. The Reds had not been a "last step" in a long, slow, process of building up local talent, an arrangement that would have been much more enduring and stable. Cincinnati's championship status had been acquired, and for that reason, could be just as quickly lost without recourse.

All this, however, represented the peculiar appeals and pitfalls of the emerging world of professional baseball. Here was a sporting institution that could put baseball's highest achievement within reach of every community, but one that exacted the high price of limited control over the means to this end (in the way of talent retention) and an effective abandonment of all obligations that this success be an expression of local resources. Additionally, once a community made the decision to adopt the pro system (hiring outside players, competing nationally) it was rarely able to revert to its former amateur outlook unscathed. Competitive expectations had become so expanded, anticipations so elevated, that even when their pro ventures failed local sporting publics could rarely find interest or satisfaction returning to strictly local competitive horizons.

Some clubs, like the Boston Red Stockings, which Harry Wright and a number of his players joined after their release from Cincinnati, and the Chicago White Stockings, under a communal leadership more comfortable with the calculating power politics of the baseball business than Cincinnati, would prosper in baseball's newly emerging pro system.

Others, however, would suffer from its consequences even more traumatically than Cincinnati did. Fort Wayne, a competitively respectable regional club before 1870, and one, no doubt, incited by Cincinnati's overnight success, decided to form a pro club in 1871, collecting its players, for the most part, from the failed Baltimore pro club. Almost from the start, however, the club showed itself to be completely unequal to the managerial demands of running a nationally focused club, its officers resorting to a draconian "walk or play" personnel policy, not hesitating to jettison players on the basis of just one or two underperforming games. The club quickly fell into disorganization, chaos and financial arrears, forcing directors to disband the club before it had completed its first full season. It was a development that left a deep sense of bitterness and resentment towards this scheme of athletic success by proxy. The *Fort Wayne Daily Gazette*, looking back over the whole incident, declared in a lengthy editorial, "If a town would raise up and send forth its own players it might, perhaps, be entitled to some honor if they should be so fortunate as to win. But where the honor comes in, when a town imports a lot of drunken loafers from all corners of the country to represent it on the contested field, we utterly fail to see."[34]

A similar pattern of over-ambition, failed expectations and sense of frustration was played out during Cleveland's first ventures into professional baseball in 1872, though the local press, in this instance, sensed not so much an organizational failure as much as a sweeping betrayal of local aspirations and identity. After seeing its pro club thrown into mid-season disbandment from the financial and competitive miscalculations of its very first eastern trip, the local press, outraged at a sporting system that had first held the city's civic reputation hostage and then abandoned it in disgrace, summarily proclaimed "Let the national game sink never to rise in this city again."[35]

4

"This Gloriously Demoralizing Game": The National Association and the Failings of Self-Direction

With the Cincinnati Reds and their successor clubs, the landscape of professional baseball had become pretty well settled. A highly developed achievement standard had been established with the best players competing among themselves, one that was geographically transferable but could only be accessed on a contractual basis.

The only thing that was lacking with this arrangement was the recognition of a formal championship structure, which would clearly define the conditions for determining a champion club, something that hereto had been largely a matter "of custom make."[1]

The success of the Reds, especially against New York clubs, along with the proliferation of newly formed professional clubs, all vying with each other in an uncoordinated free-for-all for national championship claims, was now clearly becoming unworkable in resolving the issue of national honors; "as the championship now stands," the *Cincinnati Times* knew, "it is unsatisfactory."[2]

Even with the Reds' demise as a pro club a sense of urgency to resolve this matter continued to persist. In the immediate aftermath of the Reds' 1869 season suggestions for organizing a tournament among the country's top pro clubs to "definitely" determine a championship club was seriously discussed for 1870. The Mutuals actually offered to host such a tournament in New York, but their terms and financial conditions were so blatantly favorable to the host club it was rejected as little more than a "put up job."[3]

For the most part sentiment favored retaining the old "challenge" format, with clubs determining superiority on the basis of which team won the most games in a head-to-head, best-of-three, series against every other contending club. All unofficial standings among the top pro clubs were being routinely reported in this manner by 1870, especially among the most status conscious communities of Chicago and Cincinnati. Suggestions that this format be expanded to a best-of-five series had been suggested at the 1870 NABBP convention, a suggestion the *Clipper* was backing by early 1871.[4]

This was the background for the famous New York meeting on March 17, 1871, arranged among representatives of the "leading" pro clubs to coordinate tours and match series with each other, something the Chicago club had wanted as early as January, and which Nick Young, of the Nationals, had put into motion in February through a formal request for the meeting.[5]

There doesn't seem to have been any premeditated intent, among these clubs, to organize themselves into an official association, but by the time the meeting had adjourned a completely new organization, the National Association of Professional Base Ball Players, composed solely and exclusively of professional clubs, had been formally established. The idea of a strictly pro association was certainly not new. It had been suggested as early as 1868 and seems to have been seriously discussed at the 1870 NABBP convention. The pro clubs that met that March in New York, like others before, actually seemed reluctant to take the final step of formally breaking with the NABBP, whose predominantly amateur membership, not to mention a number of state baseball associations such as New Jersey, were still strongly opposed to professionalism and any recognition of a formal national championship. With revenues generated from playing non-pro teams still a large proportion of their income, few pro clubs probably wanted to risk alienating the amateur baseball community. Only, it appears, when Harry Wright, no doubt confident in the financial leverage he knew professional clubs could exert from his experience with Cincinnati, put his influence behind the idea of a separate association were the more reluctant delegates willing to support the move. The only real opposition seems to have come from the Mutuals, who, perhaps, were concerned New York's monopoly on the national championship would now be a thing of the past.[6]

Like the beginnings of all enduring institutions, the creation of the National Association, which marked the beginning of professional baseball in its modern form, has often been interpreted as a revolutionary event. In fact, the National Association hardly represented any definitive turning point in baseball history save for the recognition of a formal championship. The Association retained the old "challenge" format for determining its championship, the only new stipulation being that the championship series be determined on a best-of-five basis. The Association's contending clubs were all long established and already had extensive competitive networks. Nor was there any public surprise at the Association's formation, as would be the case with the National League's creation. In fact, most sports observers viewed the new association as a logical development, one that spelled the "inaugurating of an era of good feeling" among the leading pro clubs.[7]

It's critically important to understand the National Association wasn't really a "league" in the modern sense at all. It was a loose association of pro clubs whose main, if not sole, purpose was to "authorize a championship title to be contested for by the various professional clubs in the country," something that, as Harry Wright noted, now made it possible for the Athletics, who won the Association's inaugural championship, to put forth the claim as baseball's "first legal and acknowledged champions of the United States."[8]

What's more, the National Association, despite its title, represented only a small segment of baseball's competitive spectrum, even among National Association clubs themselves. Most of the National Association members continued to play the majority of their games against amateur or semi-pro clubs. Chicago, for instance, only played four of the 11 games on its eastern tour, in 1871, against Association clubs, while Boston, in 1873, played fully half of its 110 games that season against non–National Association teams. Association clubs even arranged extra-championship games against each other, the Bostons, Mutuals and Athletics, in 1872, getting together for a triangular tournament in New York, these games being played above and beyond these club's regular championship matches.[9]

Like other loosely organized bodies, most of the authority in the National Association was vested in its members. Teams scheduled games among each other on an individual basis "at such time and place as they may agree upon," with the only stipulation, after 1871, that a five day notice be given for official championship games. Such wide latitude gave clubs like Boston the flexibility of playing one of their games against the Athletics at the College Regatta in Springfield in 1873, another one against the Mutuals at the Weymouth Agricultural Exposition in 1872, though this scheduling self-reliance also resulted in mistakenly bringing the Resolutes to Middletown on July 4, 1872, for a game with the Mansfields that had never been scheduled.[10]

Routine Association business such as finances and personnel matters were also highly decentralized. The treasurer's report at the 1872 Association meeting noted his office "have received nothing, paid nothing, and have got nothing." Bob Ferguson articulated the Association's hands-off policy on the important matters of enforcing contractual obligations and player misbehavior when he asserted, as player-president, that these were matters to be strictly handled by individual clubs.[11]

Probably the National Association's most important provision, the one that would represent both its greatest strength and most glaring weakness, was its open membership policy. Any pro club could join the Association and enter the championship race by simply paying a nominal $10 fee (raised briefly to $15 in 1874), a policy that effectively delegated, to individual clubs, the authority to self-determine their qualifications and worthiness to compete.[12]

Because of this, and other reasons, scholars have not been kind to the National Association, which they have repeatedly criticized, if not outright condemned, for its inefficiency and organizational backwardness. From the perspective of modern, highly centralized, restricted membership, sports leagues much of this criticism would be valid. But if the National Association is more properly viewed from the perspective of its intended purpose, and within the context of its historical antecedents, it also becomes evident the organization wasn't nearly as ineffective and inexpedient as commonly portrayed, and was certainly no "baseball Frankenstein's monster" as one scholar imaginatively described the Association.[13]

The National Association's most widely perceived weakness, its open admission policy, was certainly a matter of concern even to member clubs. Some of the country's newly aspiring pro clubs, such as the Mansfields, had clearly joined on a premise of "misplaced self-confidence" and, in fact, the membership of this Middletown, Connecticut, club had been specifically opposed at several National Association meetings by Boston. Yet the policy also revealed the National Association's sensitivity towards public opinion. The organization, after all, had, as its founding principle, authorized a championship format open to all professional clubs, a policy it knew would turn "public feeling" against them if clubs like the Mansfields were denied admission.[14]

In any event, admission to the National Association didn't by any means imply equal competitive consideration. From the very beginning there had always been an unofficial distinction between "regular" stock-company professional baseball clubs (those with full salaried players) and weaker co-op clubs (who paid their players from club earnings on an as-you-go basis). These two classes of pro clubs had, by 1875, become so competitively distinct that they were routinely being listed separately in championship standings. Whatever official status these weaker, mostly small town, co-op clubs could claim as members of the National Association, the stronger "old line" stock clubs always looked on them as the "little fry" of the baseball fraternity. New Haven was never considered anything more than a "pro forma" pro club, as was the weak Maryland club. Some of the more nondescript clubs, like the New York Atlantics, were generally looked on as doing little more than "humbugging the public" in their championship pretensions, a class of pro clubs the *St. Louis Republican*, by 1875, was condemning wholesale as "an infernal set of asses."[15]

If getting into the National Association was easy, gaining competitive attention was not. The Association was definitely not a mutual support system for member clubs. Teams could freely enter but they were also freely allowed to fail within the Association's "swim or sink" outlook. Although the stronger National Association clubs were, constitutionally, obliged to schedule games with all members, strong as well as weak, this was seldom followed in practice. Most co-op clubs had been strong local or regional teams with national aspirations, like the Mansfields, a club "of no mean order of ability" when it joined the National Association in 1872, or the Westerns of Keokuk, Iowa, who had been "something of a sensation," drawing as many as 3,000 spectators to their games the year before they joined the National Association.[16]

Once in the National Association, however, most of these teams fared poorly against the stronger, more established, stock clubs and soon realized they didn't have the financial resources to endure extensive travel obligations. Old line stock clubs would routinely shun the Association's weaker members, such as the St. Louis Reds, which a number of stock clubs, such as Boston, outright refused to play on the road. The St. Louis Browns, the city's stronger stock club, also refused to play the weak and unremunerative New Haven team. Usually the stock clubs would schedule a few early season games with newcomer clubs to test their markets and then simply ignore them the rest of the season if the financial returns from their games proved insufficient. So it was that Baltimore didn't even bother to show up for one of its appointed game with the Mansfields, and the Philadelphia club was a no-show for one of its games with the Resolutes of Elizabethtown, New Jersey. Boston, rather than waste another day in Keokuk, simply forfeited its second scheduled game and left town, leaving the Iowa ballclub with no recourse to such "shabby treatment" from the Association's top club.[17]

This policy of benign neglect did result in a high casualty rate among National Association members, but it was viewed as a normal course of events without any particular discredit to the Association itself. Seldom was remorse shown for failed clubs, the *Philadelphia Times* even looking on the disbandment of their home town Centennials as a welcome development "to clear the course of minor clubs." For the most part the major stock clubs went through their seasons pretty much unaffected by the carnage of failed clubs that lay about them, since all the games they had completed against failed clubs were simply thrown out of the championship standings. By 1875, in fact, the Association's stock clubs had come to so anticipate the failings of their weaker brethren that they decided, even before the season had begun, to increase the number of scheduled games among each other to ten that year.[18]

It also shouldn't be overlooked that the National Association's open admission policy contributed to a number of notable successes. The Philadelphia club, which entered the championship in 1873, was "a hit from the very start." This club, proclaimed by some as the "coming champions," made a strong run for the pennant that year before fading late in the season to Boston, whose manager, Harry Wright, was the first to admit his team's games with the Philadelphians "pay better than with any other club." The Association's unscreened admission procedure also made it possible for Chicago to reenter professional play in 1874 and St. Louis to enter the following year, both of whom proved to be strong competitors and profitable adversaries for the Association's other "old line" members, particularly Boston.[19]

And it's been precisely this, Boston's competitive dominance of the National Association (the team won four of the Association's five pennants), that's led many scholars to condemn the organization for its "lack of balance," a criticism that perhaps more than any other reveals the injustice of comparing the National Association with modern sports leagues.[20]

It was, in fact, Boston's year-to-year dominance that secured the National Association's appeal and standing with the general public. The club represented everything positive and desirable about championship baseball, not only in the consistency of their success but the integrity of their play, a combination that made the club so popular it received invitations to play against local teams from as far away as Dallas.[21]

There could be little argument Boston was the best managed club within the National Association. The founding principle of its first president, Ives Charles, that this team would represent honesty in baseball, was closely adhered to under Wright's tenure as manager, reflecting such a sensitivity to public perception that Wright once strongly rebuked the Philadelphia team because their failure to show up for a scheduled game in 1874 had "shaken the confidence of the public in our management." Within such an environment of respectful support and dedicated purpose it should probably come as no surprise that Wright could openly declare the management of his particular club was "the most reliable and as capable of supporting a professional club as any in the states." All this is what probably kept Wright in Boston for so many years, even when the club was threatened with disbandment after the great Boston fire of 1872, and despite the many attractive offers Wright received to manage elsewhere.[22]

Boston's continual and consistent success, then, was the result of a well coordinated combination of organizational purpose and Wright's managerial expertise, the "Boston plan" of running a ball club, which observers defined as "training, temperance, and discipline, and strict integrity of character."[23]

Much of this, of course, was, in a more mature and developed form, the discipline and regime Wright had developed in Cincinnati, where all resources had been directed towards "earnest and united efforts to win." According to contemporary accounts it was a remarkably advanced and conscientious regimen that combined the physical theory of the country's leading physical educator, Dio Lewis (whom Wright, at one time, asked to help train his team), with highly practical applications. Tolerating "no shirking or loafing" at any time from his players, Wright conducted his practice sessions with great vigor and intensity, running his team through all "points of play likely to occur in a game" day after day, from 9:00 to 11:00 in the morning and again from 2:00 to 4:00 in the afternoon.[24]

And it would be a great mistake to imagine that because his Boston team was a collection of talented, successful, professionals Wright was dealing with a team of self-motivated, like-minded young men working in close harmony. In a revealing letter to Henry Chadwick, Wright made it quite clear his championship team of 1875, for all their talent, was a collection of irascible, egoistic and frequently undermotivated athletes who consistently resisted his authority and ballplaying philosophy. Ross Barnes was "continually finding fault" with his teammates, while James O'Rourke exhibited such a "stubborn disposition" towards anyone daring to criticize his play at first base that Wright frequently had to threaten to send him off the field. Andy Leonard and Cal McVey were just as uncooperative over Wright's cricket inspired fielding strategies, often openly disagreeing with their manager over "your cricket notions you never see of done by any other club." Of all his players only Harry Schafer, the team's third baseman, according to Wright, could be counted on as someone who "plays his best at all times."[25]

If Wright seemed to have a knack of getting the most out of players not always motivated to perform their best, he also seems to have had an eye for talent that could contribute to this end. In an era with no amateur draft or cadre of minor league scouts to prequalify playing talent, this proved to be a valuable skill, allowing Wright, during his wide-ranging baseball travels, to scout out and scoop up promising baseball talent from all around the country. Aggressively pursuing talent wherever he saw it, even to the point of enticing non–National Association players to break contracts, Wright was usually able to keep a step ahead of other pro clubs in the recruiting wars, though not without earning for himself a reputation as "a kind of pirate on the high seas."[26]

Wright's club completely ran away with the National Association pennants in 1872 and 1875, winning, in the latter year, with a club so dominant observers proclaimed it was "immensely superior to anything we have ever before seen in the way of a base-ball nine." Of all Wright's Boston teams this one was certainly the most professionally minded, going through the entire season without a single stretch of competitive laxity, despite the fact that four of its star players had, at midseason, already signed to play with Chicago the following year, a development the *Clipper* felt may have been the only way to break Boston's stranglehold on the Association championship.[27]

With the exception of these two seasons, however, Boston's baseball supremacy was never a foregone conclusion and, at times, even in doubt. Both Baltimore and Philadelphia pushed Boston hard in 1873, making the National Association race that year "pregnant with excitement." A similar scenario unfolded during 1874, with the Mutuals challenging the Bostons for the pennant well into September. In both years only a round of late season wins against the league's weaker teams, the Nationals in 1873 and the Baltimores in 1874, was able to see the Bostons safely home to the championship.[28]

The relatively free mobility of playing talent, along with a largely nonexistent central authority, has given rise to the most pervasive misconception about the National Association, that it was a "player controlled" organization, run by and for the players themselves, rather than in the interests of individual clubs. Professional ballplayers during the National Association era were probably as aggressive in their use of free market opportunities for determining their market value as any period in baseball history, but this is a far cry from actually controlling a competitive structure. Most National Association players were independent practitioners contracted to individual clubs. Few had an equity stake in their clubs or held any positions that could directly influence club policies.[29]

Those who claim the National Association was a "player's league" have traditionally based this assertion on Bob Ferguson's tenure as the Association's president in 1873. This, however, overlooks the fact that the Association presidency was a largely figurehead position in an organization with largely powerless executive officers. And if Ferguson's position itself doesn't argue against this claim, his personality certainly did. Though a very talented ballplayer, Ferguson was widely reputed to have been "probably the worst tempered man playing ball," a "nervous and quick tempered" player who, as captain of the Atlantic team, dealt with his players by brute force. Any "spirit of fairness" towards colleagues, a trait Harry Wright was well known for, was clearly something "which Ferguson has yet to attain." His ambitions for the National Association presidency, like other positions of responsibility he would seek over the years, from his plot to influence the International Association to his plans to run for a Brooklyn aldermanic seat, seemed to reveal an individual who entertained grossly exaggerated estimates of his leadership abilities. He evidently didn't take the presidency of the National Association seriously enough to even bother attending its special meeting in 1873.[30]

In only one sense could it be said the National Association was a "workers paradise," and this was in the matter of player workload. Though the professional baseball season was fairly long during this period, from May to October, most clubs didn't play an exceptionally large number of games over this stretch of time, and many of these were against amateur clubs, which hardly brought out the best in the pro players, who, like the Bostons, often pulled back and played the "letting up" game against weak non-pro clubs.[31]

With the Association's go-as-you-please scheduling policy, players often found themselves with plenty of spare time on their hands, with the Athletics, at one point, "whiling away the time" in Cleveland for two full days between games, which was probably a more productive use of time than the Mutuals were accustomed to, a team notorious for loafing around on their off days.[32]

As a generality, National Association clubs didn't seem to view their work obligations any differently than other secular occupations at that time. With spectator interest "one of complete stagnation" during the late summer vacation months clubs routinely planned light schedules during this period, especially in August, traditionally "a dull month in base ball." During the 1873 season Boston only played three games against Association clubs during August, the Athletics only four that same year and, a year earlier, had scheduled no league games at all from August 7–21.[33]

What baseball the Association clubs did play that month was effectively working vacations, with many teams touring the country playing amateur teams, which Boston did over the entire month of August in 1875. This, in fact, had become a well established tradition at Boston, with the club spending August of 1872 on a long trip to Canada, which it repeated the following year, a twenty day excursion through the Dominion that even included some cricket. The practice also seemed to set a pattern for other pro clubs, with Baltimore, in 1873, spending most of that August playing non–National Association clubs, and St. Louis, in 1875, spending most of that August on a far-flung tour through Kansas.[34]

In some instances clubs preferred to play no baseball at all. Following a custom he had established with his Reds at Cincinnati, Wright allowed his Boston team, in 1872, to take a break from ballplaying altogether during their excursion to Cape Cod where the players "had a high old time among the fish, oysters and clams" and "felt slightly disinclined to work" when they were recalled to the rigors of competitive play. The Philadelphia club took a similar vacation at Cape May in 1873, from which they weren't as successful in regaining their top-class form, the team proceeding to rapidly throw away an apparently insurmountable lead in the championship that year.[35]

A proper understanding of this traditionally "soft" period in the National Association schedule also makes it possible to more correctly access the famous baseball tour to England undertaken by Boston and the Athletics in 1874. Given the fact that the National Association, as the main purviewer of professional baseball, was frequently beset by image problems with the American sporting public, the decision by the officers of these two clubs to spend that August playing overseas seems best interpreted as baseball's attempt to assert its domestic standing by establishing legitimacy abroad. Like other status insecure American institutions at that time, baseball seeming to assume the attention of a foreign culture was somehow the most authoritative way to ensure its "establishment ... as the legitimate national game of America." And even if this didn't succeed Wright felt confident the venture would at least give "notoriety" to the participating clubs.[36]

The idea of legitimizing baseball domestically by exhibiting the game internationally had actually been broached as early as 1860 and again in 1867, with the suggestion, that latter year, that a fund be established to finance the scheme. Plans for such an undertaking were again discussed in 1871 but it was left to Wright and his ambitious minded pitcher, Albert Spalding, to eventually push the plan into motion.[37]

What scholars have criticized as an ill-fated junket that led to a serious disruption of the National Association season amounted to, in fact, little more than having the Boston and Athletic clubs spend their traditional baseball holiday month of August abroad. The Athletics had expressed some reservations about the financial viability of the whole scheme, and the *Boston Globe* even feared their team's long absence would "kill" baseball in Boston. Both concerns proved to be largely unfounded, with the Hartford and Philadelphia clubs actually filling the local baseball void with a game in Boston during the Reds' absence. Though slightly pressured to get their late season games in, both clubs also had little trouble finishing out their National Association schedules once they returned home that fall.[38]

If a more quantifiable claim for the National Association's overall viability is required, probably the best would be the the sporting public's overall demand for the type of baseball the Association played, and on this basis there doesn't seem to be much room for skepticism. With a clearly defined championship now in place, attendance at professional games during the National Association's very first season was reportedly twice that of the previous season.[39]

This interest was strong enough to carry well into 1872, Wright observing there was still "a good deal of enthusiasm in base ball" at the beginning of that season, an interest that also seemed to hold up despite a lopsided pennant race that year. A much closer pennant race kept up public interest throughout the 1874 season, and even during the National Association's final season, a time when many scholars believed the organization was on the verge of collapse, the *Clipper* found pro baseball "was never more popular than it is the present season."[40]

At least some of these rather anecdotal generalizations can be confirmed through specific attendance figures, especially for games among traditional, local or sectional rivals. The Athletics-Philadelphia rivalry drew over 6,000 spectators to their 1873 series, while over 15,000 reportedly attended the series between the arch western rivals, Chicago and St. Louis, in 1875. The long-standing rivalry between the Atlantics and Mutuals, despite the former's competitive decline, could still bring out 5,000 fans to their 1873 series, with 6,000 alone attending the July 4, 1874, game between these clubs, all evidence enough, to the *Clipper*, that pro baseball certainly "wasn't played out."[41]

The professional baseball of this era, of course, was a profit-making enterprise where success is very precisely defined in terms of dollars and cents. On this criterion the National Association may not have been uniformly profitable to all its members at all times, but the organization showed itself to be far more financially resilient than often portrayed.

The demands of running a nationally focused club as a profit-making operation during these early years were never fully mastered even by such clubs as the Athletics, who, as a result of "loose management," couldn't even turn a profit during their championship year despite total revenues reportedly in excess of $50,000. Other clubs had to operate under special financial constraints, such as the Mutuals and Atlantics, whose rental agreements with the Union and Capitoline grounds (where they, respectively, played) took fully one third of their game receipts.[42]

But the National Association's overall financial picture at the end of its inaugural season was evidently strong enough to induce a slew of weaker clubs to try their luck as professionals the following year. The baseball business was particularly robust during 1873, with so many fans drawn to the Association's close and protracted pennant race the season ended, by general consensus, as a "great success financially," especially among the top contending clubs, Boston, the Athletics and Philadelphia.[43]

Even amid the carnage and debris of their failed brethren, both large and small, a number of National Association clubs sailed along surprisingly and, at times, impressively profitable. The Philadelphia club had such a strong cash flow during its inaugural season in 1873 (the team took in $5,000 from just one game with the Athletics that year) it ended the year with a "plethoric treasury," more than enough to show a positive balance on its books at year's end, even after distributing a 100 percent dividend return to its investors. The St. Louis Browns told a similar story of success their first year in the National Association, ending their 1875 season with a healthy $3,000 surplus.[44]

As would be expected Boston was, by far and away, the National Association's outstanding financial success story. Leveraging his club's championship reputation to great effect, Wright routinely required guarantees as high as 60 percent of gate receipts from non–National Association clubs who wanted to play Boston, and this was above and beyond the $300 guarantee he also demanded to cover his team's expenses. With Wright further insisting on 50 cent admission fees for all the games it played, whether against pros or amateurs, the Reds developed into a consistently strong profit center, taking in an unprecedented $31,000 in 1874. Yet within a year even this figure was eclipsed, the club generating over $17,000 alone from its trip west that fall, making it possible for the team to end its season with a clear $3,000 profit as well as some agitation from stockholders for a dividend distribution. So profitable were the Reds that season that they wouldn't match these figures for another three years. It could even be said that Boston's persistent success actually turns Leiffer's claim — that National Association teams were no better off than independent clubs— on its head. Far from just "gathering crowds" in their wide ranging travels, the Reds were actually able to establish a national following that, at least within the technological constraints of that era, wasn't at all unlike the way baseball clubs were to establish national publics in the TV era.[45]

The National Association openly and unabashedly had put the baseball business before the sporting public, but it also brought the darker side of professional baseball, specifically its gambling and corruption, squarely into public view. This was certainly not an inconsequential consideration considering that the American public had long viewed professional baseball with suspicion, many looking on it more as a tool to manipulate public interest, an enterprise "to be used like a race horse or a bull terrier in the hands of experienced sportsmen" rather than a pastime for exhibiting skillful play.[46]

This had always been professional baseball's greatest danger, that it was appealing to a public highly skeptical of a sporting system whose practitioners were demonstrably vulnerable to ulterior motives. The *New York Tribune*, during the emerging years of professionalism, articulated this stern social watchfulness over the game, "should we be told that fame and honor are not sufficient enticement" the paper declared, "then we answer that sports which cannot be sustained except by gaming should be instantly given up."[47]

With its championship determined on a total win, rather than individual series, basis after 1871, the National Association was able to structurally eliminate some of the most egregious opportunities for "hippodroming," a practice the Atlantics and Mutuals had long been known for during their pre–Association days.[48]

But there's little doubt games continued to be thrown during the National Association era, and in this case the practice had more sinister consequences since an entire season could be bartered away in a few games, something the Philadelphia club was suspected of during their rapid fade from championship contention in 1873, just as the Mutuals, at a critical stage in their championship run during the 1874 season, were strongly suspected of throwing games to Chicago.[49]

The National Association structure of cumulative wins also carried the seeds of its own corruption during uncompetitive seasons, such as 1875, Boston's early and secure lock on the championship giving non-contenders little incentive to use their games as anything except gambling opportunities. As a result the *Clipper* had to conclude "the campaign ended disastrously" for the Association that year, an embarrassing refutation of the paper's early season proclamation that "no sign of hippodroming has yet been seen" in Association games.[50]

The National Association format could also induce more tailor-made forms of corruption, seen in the rumors that the Centennials and Philadelphia clubs were conspiring to lose games on purpose to help the cross-town Athletics gain ground on Boston.[51]

Here was perhaps the greatest drawback to the National Association's decentralized organization. The league simply couldn't present a unified front to counter gambling influences, which found it easy to infiltrate these single, autonomous, clubs. The Union Grounds in New York, home of the Mutuals, permitted pool room operators and gamblers to openly ply their trade on a specially located area in the stands during scheduled games, a corner of activity that quickly became known as "the gold room." It was widely known that some clubs, like Troy, were being used "like loaded dice and marked cards" by the gambling fraternity, while still others, like the Philadelphia club, were rumored to have officers who bet heavily on their own team. It was this practice in particular, notwithstanding their director's hypocritical requirement that all club officers disavow gambling, that most contributed to the Philadelphia club's standing reputation as a refuge for "the most graceless scalawags on the turf."[52]

Gambling, however, couldn't have made inroads into pro baseball to this extent without the willing collusion of the players themselves. Even those observers of this period prone to skepticism regarding the extent of player corruption couldn't avoid being highly suspicious of the all too frequent occasions "where one player in a nine plays badly the remaining eight are apt to follow suit."[53]

The magnitude of this problem during the National Association years was hard to determine, even for contemporary observers. The *Clipper* thought there were 10 corrupt players within the professional ranks, Ferguson said there were six. Whatever its extent, corruption took various forms, from John Radcliffe's attempt to bribe umpire William McLean, one of the most highly publicized instances of attempted bribery, to the duo of Hartford players who reportedly received $1,000 to throw games against the Athletics in 1875. There was even one bizarre instance where corruption seems to have canceled itself out, when a Chicago player, in 1875, dissatisfied he wasn't in on a fix by several Philadelphia players to throw the game, tried to upset this scheme by sabotaging his own team's play, all leading to the ludicrous spectacle of both teams trying to throw the game to each other.[54]

If the National Association itself assumed a "let things work themselves out" attitude towards corruption, the sporting press couldn't, with *Wilkes*, in 1873, advocating the league initiate more active measures so that "this cheating and thieving [can] be broken up and rooted out root and branch." By 1875 the *Chicago Tribune* had reached such a point of frustration over this persistent blight upon the game it declared "it would be better for the game if the crowd would tear down the fence and stands rather than suffer another player to be bought and sold."[55]

Confronted with such expressions of public outrage, even the Association itself could hardly sit on its hands. Secretary Nick Young had called for a ban on ballfield pool selling in 1873, a measure that was eventually adopted a year later. For the most part, however, reform measures remained largely symbolic, such as the Chicago club's $500 offer, in 1875, to anyone who could prove any of its players were corrupt, or the *Clippers'* fanciful hope that William Tweed's conviction for corruption while in public office would somehow be a deterrent for all ballplayers also tempted to go afoul. As a consequence, the National Association was never able to completely shrug off its reputation as an organization with a very weak and passive reform bent, something that would pave the way for its eventual successor, the National League.[56]

But I don't believe it was the National Association's reputation for tolerating corruption that posed the greatest danger to the organization's viability. Corruption, on both a collective and individual level, was, after all, part and parcel of the baseball business as it was in so many other lines of business in Gilded Age America. Here, as elsewhere, there was always an underlying tolerance that "human nature is human nature," with baseballers no more susceptible to the temptations of greed than any other segment of society.[57]

Far more significant for the National Association was the general perception that the entire pro system, as it was developing and working itself out, was betraying baseball's more fundamental social mission. Significant because it was a sentiment that touched those segments of American society that had no direct contact with nor interest in the game.

As baseball continued to grow after the Civil War, with increased participation and an ever increasing level of skill and expertise, it was assumed this reflected an overall elevation in the moral character of those who were involved in the game. In a lengthy editorial on the social benefits of sports, the *Clipper*, on the eve of openly professional baseball, was hoping this meant there would be "a vast improvement in the character of the race now coming upon the carpet to assume control of affairs. The people are growing more liberal in their views, more fearless and independent in action, and more deserving the reputation for intelligence and ability which has always been their boast." The *Chicago Tribune* was somewhat more *quid pro quo* regarding the social benefits of professional sports, demanding, with the city's decision to re-establish a pro team, that "an institution which demands such a pecuniary outlay ought to make a corresponding return in moral and physical culture."[58]

As a city without a long standing tradition of intense, high-caliber, urban baseball, Chicago didn't seem to sense the rising criticism over professional baseball's social worth that was developing in New York, a place where years of unchecked, cut-throat competition for championship claims had, as the *New York Times* saw it by 1870, distorted both spectator and participant involvement in baseball "ludicrously disproportionate to the subject." [59]

Far from uplifting and ennobling those who came into contact with baseball, far from drawing out their higher sentiments and best character, high-caliber baseball seemed to be bringing out the worst of those involved with the game. By the late 1860s the character of the typical pro baseball crowd, consumed by an increasingly intense competitive identity, seemed to be noticeably deteriorating, if the ones Charles Newcomb was finding at championship games in Philadelphia are any indication, the morally sensitive Newcomb finding, among these gatherings, individuals of "vulgarity, imbecility, as creatures, vermin-like, of ill breeding."[60]

A number of urban clubs were particularly notorious for the type of supporters they attracted, such as the Irvingtons of New Jersey, whose games, during the late 1860s, were routinely attended by thugs and pickpockets. Followers of the Mutual Club had to fend off hostile and threatening Irvington supporters with bats and fists during one game with the Irvingtons in 1867, a not uncommon precaution since supporters of this club, when aggravated, were known to draw knives on their opponents during games.[61]

Spectator abuse and crowd disruptions were by no means limited to New York or Philadelphia. The Athletics were roundly abused by the "white trash" they found in the stands at Rochester, while the Washington Nationals ran into an equally abusive, rowdy, crowd during their game at St. Louis in 1867. Even in Chicago, a city that would later pride itself on the orderly character of its baseball crowds, a visiting Forest City club from Cleveland, in 1871, found that "the average Chicago baseball crowd affords strong evidence in favor of Darwin's theory of the descent of man, with the alternation that he came from an animal having much longer ears and much less sense than the monkey tribe."[62]

Nor did spectator quality at professional ballgames appreciably improve during the National Association years. Crowd disruptions did appear to be less frequent, but also more violent, during National Association games, probably the most bloody outbreak occurring during a Mutuals-Troy game in 1871, leaving fans, players and even Mutuals manager John Wildey bloodied and bruised. As far as rowdy followers went, there wasn't much to choose from between the Mutuals and Troys during these years, but the latter was widely reputed to be the worst for visiting teams, acting as perfect hosts before and after, but ruthless hucksters during, every game, "like the South Sea islander, who fattens his victims and then eats him, the Trojan has always allowed the base-ball visitor to be cordially treated prior to a game, and then to be artistically flayed."[63]

Spectator violence, however, seemed to be a highly democratic phenomenon during the National Association period, showing no regard for location or participants. Not content with stoning the Baltimore players themselves, one Philadelphia crowd, in 1872, spat tobacco on the team's followers and insulted their wives. The more uncontrollable spectators at a St. Louis game three years later nearly provoked a riot in the stands when they got into a fist fight with fans from arch rival Chicago. Even baseball crowds in staid New England were, if less violent, hardly more well behaved than elsewhere, as Mark Twain discovered when his umbrella was purloined during a game at Hartford.[64]

Disturbingly visible as these incidents were to baseball's image, they weren't the main focus of social concern. This was centered around individual players. Professionalism had made it possible for a small, elite, cadre of well paid, highly skilled players to move to the center of the sporting public's attention and adulation. Did all this represent a benefit for individual players? Did it represent a benefit to society? These were especially pertinent concerns because the breakdown of the fraternal structure, with its extra-competitive ties, meant baseball's achievement focus had almost exclusively become a matter of contractual obligation. Unlike the amateur ballplayer, who played baseball as an expression of some social obligation or identity, the professional had no real obligation to himself or his club save the requirement to win. Given nineteenth-century America's association of physical superiority with moral character, this put the professional in an unusual obligation of moral self reliance. On the one hand society demanded the professional ballplayer be a "gentleman" in his competitive pursuit while, on the other, it also acknowledged that, because the pro player was, in effect, an independent practitioner, "this must be obtained," as *DeWitt's Base Ball Guide* put it, "in obedience to a players' own mind."[65]

If a status induced, self-imposed, sense of moral responsibility was the ideal society wanted from the professional baseballer, it was hard to find this within the professional ranks itself. Throughout the early years of professionalism irresponsible self interest was generally the norm. In its most benign form this took the shape of persistent revolving and shirking of stated obligations, along the line of William Craver's self-serving decisions, in 1870, to first renege on an expressed commitment to play for the Trimountains of Boston (who had even set him up with an off-season saloon business), sign on with Troy, and then promptly walk away from these obligations to sign with Chicago, all in the span of a few months. Not as complex, but equally as offensive, was Columbus, Ohio, J. W. Freed's deft move, in 1875, to abandon his club and sign on with Philadelphia, taking with him his former club's advance but leaving behind his unpaid bills.[66]

More public, and therefore more vulnerable to social criticism, was the ruthlessly unsportsmanlike behavior of many players under game situations. This varied from the jeering, loafing and generally obnoxious behavior of the New Haven players in their game with Syracuse in 1875, to such disconcerting practices as shouting to confuse opposing fielders trying to catch fly balls (a practice Mike "King" Kelly excelled at), to intentionally laying bats where the opposing catcher would trip over them, a practice that persisted until it was officially outlawed in 1881.[67]

To the game's one figure of authority, the umpire, the professional ballplaying fraternity virtually scorned the "silent acquiescence" observers demanded they unquestioningly assume before all his decisions. From the earliest years of professionalism the umpire was looked on as an obstacle to, even intruder upon, the ballplayer's right to manipulate every available resource to his advantage, making the umpire's role probably the most abused and reviled in all of baseball, by spectators, managers and players alike, such as Chicago's Cap Anson, who so perfected the art of umpire intimidation he earned the nickname "Associate Umpire." Those few umpires unaccepting of this treatment had little recourse except retaliation in kind, which former-ballplayer-turned-umpire Dicky Pearce once did by personally assaulting an especially abusive player, Ezra Sutton.[68]

All things considered, there seemed nothing remotely in the cards to support Albert Spalding's contention, perhaps unrealistically over-influenced from his recent baseball trip to England in 1874, that baseball was fast becoming a "gentleman's game" just like cricket. The professional baseballer was a specialist, the practitioner of a highly demanding skill and, probably for that reason, someone whose character was developing in a narrow and one-sided manner. "There is a power there, and a certain kind of mechanical skill," the *Chicago Times* observed with its local professionals when playing against Harvard in 1870, "but no brains and none of that irresistible will that is the accompaniment only of cultured minds."[69]

The very demands and requirements for success in professional baseball, with its amazing exhibitions of skill in otherwise long periods of total nonproductivety, just wasn't like the success known to conventional American society. The professional baseballer was a strange, contradictory social phenomenon, who came "from the idle, shiftless and yet ambitious class of mortals who are ready to work with the energy of giants one day in the week ... provided they have the privilege of lounging about the other six days, boasting of their feats and basking in the admiration of the little boys of the neighborhood."[70]

Post-Reconstruction America was slow to accommodate this relatively intangible phenomenon of athletic achievement into its traditional social views of success as a reward for productive work, a perspective that would naturally show up the professional baseballer and his calling to be "ridiculous in the eyes of all sensible folks," and, in his most morally directionless expressions, "an eminently undesirable person, [who] ought to be peremptorily and completely suppressed."[71]

With their insistence that physical skill be a complimentary expression of a whole, morally directed, personality, 19th century American observers felt they could find this in amateur baseball, provided this segment of the baseball fraternity could display a corresponding level of athletic excellence. There were a number of amateur ballclubs during the National Association years that were nearly as strong as professional clubs, such as the Stars of New York and Eastons of Pennsylvania, but, for the most part, social critics, going on the assumption that "the student and athlete combined should make the perfect man," looked to college teams as the most desirable social model for baseball.[72]

Observers had a ready-made champion for this sporting philosophy in the Harvard baseball club, whose president, in 1867, claimed their members only "play ball for pleasure and exercise," with an understanding that when "the game becomes so exacting in its claims upon our time as business, it loses its interest and value." It was a fitting and desirable countervailing stance to the rising phenomenon of professionalism, and one bolstered by Harvard's notable successes during the late 1860s. The 1869 varsity team could hold its own with virtually any pro club of that period, claiming, during a successful national tour that summer, wins over the Athletics and Eckfords.[73]

Instances like this gave rise to the recurring expectation that American college baseball teams would develop like gentleman cricket teams in England, competitively equal to the best pro clubs without any denigration of moral character. The analogy, unfortunately, was neither correct nor realistic. In English cricket the best amateur players, usually drawn from the ranks of the gentry or professions, had a clearly defined relationship with the professionals on their respective teams. Amateur players almost always captained English professional cricket teams, enabling them, without the obligation of performing for remuneration, to independently assert direct moral leadership upon their professional teammates.[74]

This, of course, would never be the case with college baseballers. Not only was the social bias against professional baseball playing still prevalent enough to prevent the outstanding Yale pitcher Ham Avery from accepting an offer to play for the Hartfords, those college players who decided to join the professional ranks did so as simple co-workers, on an equal footing with their pro teammates without any special right or claim to team leadership.[75]

And even if some right to moral leadership had been asserted, America's traditional cynicism toward unmerited privileges would have opposed it. Observers were too well aware that a good college education didn't in any way ensure a good quality of character, as the Athletics realized in their game at Harvard in 1867, the professionals finding in the rowdy, offensive, student crowd "such narrow minded, selfish and ungentlemenly specimens of unfinished humanity."[76]

The *Chicago Tribune*, long the advocate of the professional system, was far more cynical about the moral purity of the student athlete, sarcastically declaring, in response to Harvard president Charles Eliot's widely publicized demand, in 1882, that college teams cut off all competitive contacts with pro clubs, "This is as it should be. The professional players are none too moral now, and if they associate much with the rat-killing, cock-fighting college students ... they would rapidly sink into the lowest depths of depravity."[77]

All said, there were few cultural traditions that could provide any substantive moral direction or moral guidance to the professional fraternity, and certainly nothing in the traditions of the game itself that could do this. The professional player, being a freely mobile private practitioner, as Chicago manager Jimmy Wood noted, had to make themselves respectable, they were individuals that "have their character in their own hands."[78]

If these were the years when Americans were vaguely beginning to sense the social importance of the "role model" within the highest levels of athleticism, they encountered mostly frustration and disappointment in the professional baseballer. Even among his peers, the pro player was rarely able to assume responsibility for self-leadership and direction, seen in those instances when players were delegated managerial, or, more correctly, "player-coach" duties. In most instances the arrangement ended disastrously, as it did with the Indianapolis and Baltimore clubs. In the latter case, captain/manager Cal McVey proved to be an especially ineffective leader though it's not known if he was of the breed of player/manager who abused his authority to the point of treating his teammates "as if they were so many slaves."[79]

Off the playing field as well the typical pro baseballer of the National Association era rarely evidenced what Charles Newcomb termed a "collateral scope of life," or revealed themselves as personalities "who have other aims in life than to get a few thousand dollars and then die."[80]

Here perhaps was the most palpable evidence for any social condemnation of the pro system, it being an enterprise with no real corresponding carry-over into the sphere of normal social worth. On the basis of its own extensive examination of professionalism *Wilkes* could only conclude that "excellence in the professional player tends to unfit him for any useful sphere hereafter," a disturbing generalization all too often confirmed by the professional fraternity of that period.[81]

Many pro ballplayers fell onto hard times or were unable to productively fit into society once their playing days were over, the *Clipper* sadly noting how most members of the once famous Haymaker club of Troy fell into dissipation and died prematurely. The history of these early days of professional baseball is peppered with similar stories of rapid individual descent from stardom to personal misfortune, such as the standout New York baseballer John Hatfield, record holder for the longest baseball throw, whose domestic life sank into such chaos the *Cincinnati Enquirer* sarcastically noted "our report from New York says John Hatfield has not whipped a woman for ten days." Other players such as John Glenn and Henry Wheeler ran afoul of the law once their playing days were over.[82]

Given the professional baseball fraternity's less than shining reputation, individuals such as Henry Luff must have appeared to be not only a rarity but, as the *Cincinnati Enquirer* noted, "a decidedly peculiar fellow, a character rarely met with in the profession, a college graduate, highly connected and of good means, [who] has played ball simply out of love for it."[83]

Of all the traditional weaknesses noted in the National Association, it was this failure to establish a sound and socially acceptable moral foundation for the professional system that stands as the most glaring. Since its earliest days, with its focus centered in a rootless achievement drive, baseball had difficulty attaching its heightened skill level, playing technique and mass appeal to an acceptable social morality or purpose. And if the National Association, in its decentralized organization, felt that the glory and spectacle of highly specialized, amazingly skillful play, in itself, could offset this need, it was sadly mistaken.

It should be no surprise that a subdued, yet persistent, undercurrent of skepticism towards professional baseball's social value shadowed the game throughout the National Association period. The era that saw such an astonishing growth in baseball's popularity and skill level also brought forth some of the most impassioned criticism against the game from some of the country's most influential publications, such as the *New York Times* and *Forest and Stream*.[84]

Typical of these protests, in tone as well as content, was the editorial that appeared in the January 7, 1873, issue of the *Hartford Daily Courant*. Hartford itself wouldn't have a professional club for another year and, as such, hadn't directly experienced the abuses of the professional system, which is why the social indignation is even more telling, a foreboding sense of how professionalism had disengaged baseball from all social responsibility normally associated with ties to locality. "Instead of the best youths of the land striving in honest rivalry with parents and friends as witnesses of their skill," the paper lamented, "hired hands of trained players scour the country, followed by crowds of gamblers and pick pockets."[85]

This sense that the pro system represented something of a betrayal of the game's obligation to locality and its resources, had, of course, been articulated since the earliest days of professionalism at Cincinnati. The *Courant*, however, was outraged at how radical a course this had taken, with success at the game now largely the consequence of a reshuffling of transferable resources. "What do the highest baseball honors now signify?" it queried. "Simply that Boston last year was willing to pay professionals more than any other club." With criticism like this, the *Courant* may have been the voice of baseball's social conscience, but it couldn't do anything to constructively alter the achievement orientation the game had been following since its New York origins. Because this was a course American society itself had set for baseball, the course the National Association had only followed, it was impossible for the paper to deny the consequences, admitting "with the lowering of the moral of the base ball field, however, the proficiency of the players has increased amazingly."[86]

In its five year existence the National Association brought to maturity all of baseball's social characteristics that had begun in New York. It had completed the game's progressive achievement orientation by formalizing a championship structure that competitively recognized, even if it didn't always ensure, that only the best played against the best, something that, it believed, could be best served with the free mobility of talent and autonomy of individual clubs.

If the National Association had a weakness it was its willingness to allow this course to develop freely and without internal regulation. It was unable to provide a workable qualification system within an otherwise *laisse-aller* competitive structure, or, most importantly, to ameliorate the impressions of social or personal abuses such a free and open competitive system generated.

As a functioning organization, however, it must be said the National Association performed tolerably well, trying to strike, with its open championship policy, a workable balance between the sporting public's intensifying demand for the integrity of competitive standards and general society's insistence that the game's highest achievement level remain accessible and responsive to social expectations. But as the Association entered what would be its final year, in 1875, pressure from numerous quarters was pushing for change, by no means to an imminent collapse, as scholars routinely claim, but a self-transformation from where it had already taken baseball. "We have the vitality that is rising supreme to bad government and dishonesty of supreme factions," the Philadelphia *Sunday Mercury* optimistically declared at the conclusion of what would be the Association's final season. "Who shall say we may not have to survive even that gloriously demoralizing game — Base Ball?"[87]

5

Chicago and the Making of the National League

For much of its history the National Association was a cozy east coast corridor league, with most member clubs located in the large Atlantic coast cities between Boston and Washington, D.C. With the disbandment of Rockford and Ft. Wayne at the end of the Association's first season, Chicago's withdrawal that same year because of the great fire, and Cleveland's withdrawal a year later, the remaining National Association clubs usually had to go no further west than Troy nor further south than Baltimore for championship games.

This arrangement had a significant bearing on the Association's character. Many championship road games could be completed on a "day trip" basis, minimizing per game expenses. Such geographic compactness consequently encouraged several co-op clubs situated in such mid-sized railroad corridor cities as Middletown and New Haven, Connecticut, to join the National Association in the hope of picking up "whistle stop" games from the organization's stock clubs as they passed through town, something the large city clubs were usually willing to do because of the minimal expenses this entailed.

All this changed when Chicago re-entered the National Association in 1874. The Association immediately became far more geographically extended, escalating travel costs and outlays since the number of scheduled National Association games now required each club to make at least two road trips to far off Chicago each season.

This also meant the competitive status of each Association club became far more important. Clubs that weren't strong enough to attract large crowds to their road games were reluctant to undertake long, expensive, trips. Chicago, by the same token, was reluctant to come east to play small, poorly drawing, co-op clubs. Such a scenario actually unfolded after 1874, with the National Association's smaller co-op clubs, like New Haven and the Atlantics, simply refusing to travel west and the western co-op clubs from St. Louis and Keokuk, which had been organized, for the most part, to arrange side games with clubs coming to Chicago, refusing to go east.[1]

The increased sense of economic injustice over this system, with the larger stock clubs "subsidizing" weaker co-op clubs by making long trips to co-op towns, but rarely vise-versa, developed into a full-fledged reform movement, especially when rumors began to circulate that as many as sixteen (some sources said eighteen) clubs would be in the National Association in 1876, the majority co-op clubs from small or mid-sized towns. This organizational tension between stock and co-op clubs was certainly nothing new. The *Chicago Tribune*, as far back as 1873, wanted the National Association to limit itself to one stock club per city and, by the spring of 1875, calls for more meaningful reform were being heard from other quarters. The Association's western stock clubs in Chicago and St. Louis (which joined the National Association in 1875) were hinting they might simply refuse to play the Association's eastern co-op clubs while, in Boston, the *Globe* was openly declaring, on the eve of the 1875 season, "the fact is people are getting tired of seeing these one-horse clubs play, and the sooner the leading clubs of the country devise some means to bar the weak clubs from entering the championship arena, the better it will be for their interest and the game generally."[2]

The eastern stock clubs may have been dissatisfied with the Association's co-op clubs, but it was unlikely they themselves would initiate any meaningful reform. These particular clubs, Boston, the Mutuals and the Athletics, still heavily depended upon revenues from their games with smaller co-op clubs and weren't overly inconvenienced with clubs they only had to go short distances to play. It was left to the western stock clubs to form the catalyst for change in the National Association since they were the ones that suffered the greatest financial consequences of the Association's two-tier arrangement. But even then sympathy for their plight wouldn't come easily. The eastern stock clubs had been doing quite well playing local co-op clubs for years. To implement a system whereby the eastern stock clubs, for the benefit of some distant western clubs, would unilaterally cut themselves off from this network of close, inexpensive, co-op competition, would require a persuasive force based upon extraordinary financial and organizational leverage.[3]

Only one city in America, Chicago, was in a position to exert such leverage on organized baseball, and for reasons that reflected not only the

city's growing economic and social force at that time, but also its obsessive, almost pathological fixation upon its perceived rights to this status.

Like other midwestern cities of the immediate post–Civil War period,
Chicago had latched onto baseball as an inextricable symbol of its civic
grandeur and status, seen with its obsessive desire to dethrone Cincinnati
as the region's top baseball city. Chicago's infatuation with its baseball,
however, far from being just a consolation for local supremacy, developed
into a symbol of self-expectation. "Not failure but low aim is a crime,"
was the motto Chicago baseball organizers set for themselves when plotting their re-entry into professional baseball in 1873. This, in itself, was
little more than a resurgence of an almost morbid self-judgment the city
had always seemed to see in its baseball club at every turn and challenge,
once asking, after losing to the semi-pro Clinton, Iowa, club in 1871, "is
our civilization a failure?"[4]

It would hardly be expected that the city's baseball organizers would
ever be content to let Chicago, baseball wise, "play second fiddle" to any
other city, always fixing before their eyes, year in and year out, nothing
less than what it would take to ensure "Chicago leads the world in base
ball."[5]

Certainly the Chicago sporting press kept these expectations continually before the public in all their inflammatory and impulsive appeal. All
the city's major dailies, the *Times, Inter-Ocean*, but especially the *Tribune*,
like biblical prophets castigating a wayward Israel, would ruthlessly criticize every failure, rhapsodize every success, and never for a moment let
its readership forget Chicago's destined greatness in baseball. Both players and officials, from all areas of the country, had to heed these declarations and penetrating observations, not least the Chicago players
themselves, especially those who didn't come up to expectations, to a point
that Davy Force, standout shortstop of that era, didn't want to play in
Chicago, despite its lucrative salary offers, out of personal fear he'd have
to "run the gauntlet" of a vindictive Chicago sporting press.[6]

If the local press was articulating and popularizing a perception of
Chicago's grand baseball destiny, it was an image the Chicago sporting
public willingly supported. From its earliest days, the city's professional
baseball club, the White Stockings, enjoyed extraordinary local fan support, in both number and enthusiasm. During its first year in the National
Association, Chicago routinely outdrew every other Association club,
upwards of 10,000 spectators turning out for the team's more important
games, a vast crowd by the standards of the era. Chicago crowds were
intense, enthusiastic, demanding and, apparently, widely appreciated, to
an extend that even *Wilkes* had to concede, after the great Chicago fire of

1871 had forced the White Stockings to disband, that the National Association just wasn't the same without the zeal of Chicago baseball.[7]

All this provided Chicago with tremendous financial leverage in its relations with the rest of organized baseball, far more than even New York or Philadelphia could exert upon the game. With its club organized as a closely controlled stock issuing corporation, a far more suitable and efficient, if publicly unresponsive, structure for the demands of professional baseball than Cincinnati had with its club, Chicago was able to preside over one of the most lucrative and popular clubs in the National Association. Perhaps not as lucrative as "all of the other professional clubs put together," something the *Chicago Tribune* claimed at the end of the 1875 season (Boston certainly grossed more that year), but the White Stockings were probably the most consistent in maximizing total returns from its baseball operations.[8]

Chicago baseball organizers showed no reservations in aggressively leveraging their economic strength to acquire championship caliber teams. Confirming a perception in baseball circles that "Chicago generally buys a thing if she wants it, no matter what the price is," club officials took maximum advantage of the talent mobility within the pro system. To form the nucleus of its first professional club, in 1870, club officers would openly "forage the Atlantic clubs for good players," hiring away from New York a large contingent of the Eckford club by paying them "fancy Western prices," salaries reportedly twice that of comparable eastern clubs. Fully content with a personnel policy of "talent selected from its victims," club officers also hired and instructed manager Tom Foley to aggressively scout and recruit appropriate talent from other National Association teams, by whatever means necessary.[9]

When Chicago returned to the National Association in 1874 it renewed this same aggressive and financially extravagant policy in collecting a championship caliber team, even to the point of courting controversy. Frustrated in their efforts to get Davy Force from the Athletics when the National Association judiciary committee voided their backdated contract with him, Chicago officers further aggravated public opinion and Association members by trying, in a less publicized but no less brazen way, to get Jack Burdock to break his contract. This was something that even angered Harry Wright, who sensed Chicago was overstepping even the free and easy rules of National Association recruiting, warning Chicago president William Hulbert "can you blame the players for not respecting the rules when the club managers do not?"[10]

More legitimate in its execution, if not acceptable in its public perception, was Chicago's greatest recruiting "coup," the signing away from

Boston itself, in 1875, four players who made up the nucleus of that championship team, Albert Spalding, Ross Barnes, Cal McVey and Deacon White. It was clear officers had willingly "spent money like water" to get the players it felt would make Chicago a baseball champion. Spalding in particular got an amazingly generous package, with full managerial powers plus 25 percent of the club's profits, all above and beyond his salary, something that didn't seem to overtax the club treasury, which had, at the end of 1874, a $7,000 cash balance.[11]

Even to those parties within the eastern baseball establishment quite familiar with the intensely competitive world of professional baseball during this period, the cold, premeditated and calculating way Chicago used its economic strength to achieve its supremacy aroused animosity. *Wilkes* well knew that under Chicago's grand baseball plan, "New York was to be wiped from the map of the United States in the matter of playing base ball, as it had been commercially and socially long ago by the Garden City." Chicago itself certainly never did anything to disavow these intentions with its baseball, the *Chicago Tribune* claiming the city was specifically rejoining the National Association in 1874 to bring down its "haughty and complacent rivals" within eastern baseball.[12]

Behind all this was the unmistakable impression that Chicago was willing to secure the resources necessary for establishing a championship caliber team anywhere it could find them, a policy that, in the eyes of eastern baseball, rendered Chicago baseball wholly illegitimate, in both success and failure. The White Stocking's unofficial championship claims in 1870 were met, in the East, by derisive "sneers" because this team of mostly eastern ballplayers (all lured to Chicago solely for "filthy lucre") was perceived to be "more of a credit to Brooklyn, Philadelphia and Troy than to Chicago."[13]

The White Stockings were also openly ridiculed as "montebank muffins" following their disastrous eastern tour in 1870, as a result of which its management came under severe criticism for bankrolling a team of ill-disciplined and poorly managed imports, "base ball hacks who have been floating about Williamsburg for some years past, and who never were anything more than third rate players until they took the notion of going to Chicago and coming back as representatives of the West."[14]

With no better results to show for its collection of highly paid easterners, sporting expensive, custom made uniforms, when they returned to the National Association in 1874, particularly after a humiliating 38–1 loss to the Mutuals in New York, Chicago was again savaged by the eastern press for its almost total dependence upon imported talent, which didn't show the slightest respect for local personnel. "The president, however, is a

Chicagoan," the eastern press scoffed, "and so, we are given to understand, is one of the ticket-sellers at the gate."[15]

The weight of this sectional animosity, this almost paranoiac belief that the "East was against [Chicago]," cannot be underestimated in understanding the course of Chicago baseball. From the time it first organized a club with championship aspirations, Chicago believed "the eastern sports [papers] ... pursue the Chicago club with the relentlessness of hate," inciting Chicago organizers to move and work at very turn to justify and legitimize itself against what it believed was the unmerited status of eastern baseball, which "Like all New Yorkers ... believe that there is nothing worthy of consideration beyond the confines of Manhattan Island, and they treat us Western people as if we were a community of idiots."[16]

But behind all this vitriolic rhetoric and animosity, there was also a strange, almost symbiotic, dependence between Chicago and eastern baseball. The east may have despised the way Chicago used its wealth to acquire status, but it also needed this wealth for the very health and vitality of its own baseball. Despite Chicago's relative distance from other professional baseball centers, the eastern baseball fraternity knew from the start that "it pays out there the boys say." Over the years games in Chicago routinely drew the largest crowds and consistently paid visiting teams the best returns. The Olympics of Washington, D.C., not a particularly strong team, made $3,500 from their three trips to Chicago in 1871, while the Baltimore club, another non-contender, was guaranteed $700 for their three Chicago games in 1874. When these games involved marquee teams the returns could be even more impressive, with Boston clearing $3,000 from its three Chicago games in 1875, $1,100 from one game alone. In some instances clubs like Hartford actually made more money playing in Chicago, despite heavy travel expenses, than they did playing pro clubs much closer to home.[17]

Only Chicago, then, had the financial leverage to bend eastern baseball to its specific needs and requirements, especially by 1875, when Chicago's financial benefit to visiting clubs had become so substantial the White Stockings claimed they were virtually subsidizing some eastern ballclubs. This was critically important if Chicago was to have more reliable, closer ties with non–Midwest clubs. Unlike eastern baseball, Chicago was a monolithic power in a relatively barren baseball landscape. It had no real network of good local college, amateur or semi-pro clubs that could satisfy its competitive claims as other National Association clubs had throughout their history. Chicago could only secure a national status against distant eastern clubs, and for this it had to have a reliably functioning national competitive structure. An obsession with championship status was almost incumbent upon Chicago baseball, because without an out-standing, well supported, financially lucrative club the city couldn't attract eastern interest to such a far-off island of professional baseball. Anything less than consistent championship caliber results would mean virtual extinction for Chicago baseball, because it would almost certainly relegate the city to a regional, not national, power. The *Boston Herald,* speaking years later, knew full well that "nothing can save [Chicago baseball] but continued success."[18]

Only from the perspective of western baseball did the inadequacies of the National Association fully appear, and only from the West could any meaningful and active reform of the Association originate.

Chicago's influence on any potential reform plans was further bolstered with the formation of several other trans–Appalachian professional clubs. St. Louis entered the National Association in 1875, while Cincinnati and Louisville planned to form their own pro clubs and enter the following year. Though the *Clipper* welcomed these additions for expanding the championship into a more truly national scope, there was also an uneasy sense that with this "coarse of base ball empire ... toward the Pacific" the four western pro clubs, fully half the stock clubs of the National Association, "will monopolize the sport" in players, talent and organization influence.[19]

And, in fact, by the late summer of 1875 rumors were beginning to circulate that the western clubs were forming a "clique" that would "take matters into their own hands" if meaningful reform to the National Association wasn't initiated. By that October the *Boston Globe* was listing only stock clubs for the National Association's upcoming season, while, at the very same time, a "curious story" was coming out of St. Louis on October 3 hinting that co-op clubs were to be excluded from the Association. A month later the *Sunday Mercury* was more openly explicit about this, declaring "no more shyster clubs, no more gate money, catchpenny humbugs" were to be in the National Association, "as they are vampires," *Field and Stream* further added in December, "thriving upon the blood of solid organizations."[20]

Just who originated the idea of reforming the National Association, and when, isn't entirely clear. A number of western baseball officers certainly contributed to the plan, among them Charles Fowle of St. Louis (the *St. Louis Republican* would later claim the whole plan was "his idea"), but as is the case with so many other influential movements, success was not so much a matter of origination but execution, and there was little doubt this was largely the result of one man, Chicago president William A. Hulbert.[21]

Born in upstate New York, Hulbert was brought to Chicago at an early age where he became a successful coal merchant and respected member of the city's board of trade. Though it doesn't appear he was ever directly involved with baseball as a player Hulbert clearly recognized the game's importance as a tool for civic prestige and standing. He first appears as a director of the Chicago club in 1872, became its secretary in 1874 and finally its president in October, 1875, a position he would hold until his death.[22]

Certainly no other figure did as much to establish the White Stocking's identity with the drive, aspirations and expectations of Chicago's growing national stature as an urban center. Throughout his tenure as club president Hulbert aggressively, forcefully, even outrageously, pushed his club to its highest competitive potential, never tolerating anything except absolute championship expectations. Fully reflective of the city he loved, Hulbert's style was confrontational, uncompromising and uninhibited, highly indicative of this man who was known for an "overbearing" and relentlessly "bull dozer" attitude in all his personal dealings. The personality that comes through his correspondence is hard-charging, calculating and relentless but also surprisingly deficient in judgment, especially with non-transparent individuals (he once believed James Devlin, later implicated in the notorious Louisville scandal, was "honest and square"). Rough and unhewn, he had little of the urbane sophistication and liveliness of intellect characteristic of such eastern baseball figures as Boston's N.T. Appolonio. Yet he was without doubt the first figure in baseball history to exert a deep and lasting imprint upon the game solely from the force of his personality.[23]

Just how this vague and unorganized dissatisfaction with co-op clubs progressed from a simple reform movement to the outright replacement of the National Association with an entirely new professional baseball organization is not entirely clear and probably never will be. From the records of the Chicago baseball club, though, it seems clear that this entire development unfolded as a progressively more precise and radical plan of Hulbert himself, who, working in close conjunction with officers from the other western clubs, hammered out the blueprint for a completely new professional organization, the National League.

At first it didn't appear that Hulbert envisioned anything more than a revamping of the National Association. In September, 1875, he told Campbell Bishop of the St. Louis club that pro baseball needed a "new association" of "first class clubs," with no details of who or what would be the arrangements for this new organization. Within a month, however, Hulbert seems to have carried this basic idea much further, demanding an exclusion of co-op clubs, with only one pro club per city. These were the plans detailed in the well known *Chicago Tribune* article of October 24, 1875, generally looked on by scholars as something of a manifesto of the coming National League. Hulbert himself confirmed the *Tribune* article "reflects my views" on the matter of baseball reform, though he seemed to leave the impression changes still be carried out within the existing structure of the National Association.[24]

This also marked the beginning of a long and close relation between Hulbert and the article's author, *Chicago Tribune* baseball reporter Lewis Meacham. Under Meacham's editorial hand, the *Tribune's* baseball columns, from this point on, virtually became the mouthpiece for Hulbert's policies and positions. Though Hulbert persistently claimed he was "in no way committed to Meacham," there's little doubt he gave the sportswriter preferential treatment, offering him "an inside view" into many of the Chicago club and league plans (the *Tribune* was also the only paper permitted to attend the National League's closed door meetings). Little wonder that the rest of the sporting press viewed the *Tribune's* baseball department, headed by a reporter it dubbed "Chadwick Jr.," who "sits on his stool in the *Tribune* office three hours every day," as little more than the National League "organ" that slavishly expounded the league line and philosophy.[25]

Even as late as November Hulbert didn't seem to be completely set on the idea of an entirely new baseball organization. In a letter to Charles Chase of St. Louis he certainly wanted "to give the governing and playing rules [of the National Association] a thorough overhauling — they sadly need it," but only to protect stock clubs from "the hordes of dead beats who infest the present national association." Within a few weeks of this letter, however, Hulbert seems to have finally decided that the National Association had to be completely replaced, now demanding there be a "*new* association" more restrictive and self-limited in its scope and based upon the principle "one-club-to-the-city."[26]

The actual plans for implementing such a scheme were finalized at a meeting between officers of the Chicago, St. Louis, Louisville and Cincinnati clubs held at Louisville in early December. The meeting, which had apparently been kept under wraps for sometime (Hulbert had told Bishop, as early as September, "don't say a word" about the meeting), was clearly intended to solidify western baseball interests, to make sure its participants would "pull together, work in concert and secure our share" of the benefits of organized baseball.[27]

Confident as Chicago and the rest of the western clubs were in the success of their plans, there was probably little chance it would succeed without at least tacit support from the most powerful baseball club in the

National Association, Boston, a consent that, for a number of reasons, wouldn't be hard to obtain.

Boston did represent eastern interests in pro baseball as well as a long-standing obstacle to Chicago's championship aspirations. Boston was also quite wary of Chicago's calculating ambitions, which provided the eastern club with many opportunities for annually "starting a war upon the Chicago club" in the way of recruiting battles, schedule preferences and league policies. But this rivalry should not obscure the more important fact that the two clubs shared a close like-mindedness in outlook and objectives for organized baseball. As the two strongest, most financially viable, clubs within pro baseball, Boston and Chicago knew their destinies were closely tied, a claim amply supported by the degree of confidentiality Hulbert expressed in his letters to Harry Wright and other Boston officers, at one point even reassuring Boston president N.T. Appolonio Chicago would always be Boston's "western home."[28]

Boston, like Chicago, had also been hurt financially by the instability of the National Association's co-op members, through non-returns, poor attendance and even outright forfeits, all of which certainly made Boston sympathetic towards, if not outright supportive of, Chicago's plans for overthrowing the National Association structure. At least this can be surmised from the fact that Wright, as early as February, 1875, had confided to Hulbert his own concern over the best way to weed out the Association's weaker clubs. Wright also seems to have had an advance notice about the secret Louisville meeting and its purpose.[29]

So it came about that Hulbert, at the very time he was scheming to push through his plans for a new baseball organization, was also ensuring its long term success by solidifying a Boston-Chicago baseball axis, a like-mindedness in purpose and outlook between baseball's two strongest organizations that would transcend any specific competitive differences these clubs may have within the new organization.[30]

With a united front of western clubs to support him and the tacit approval of Boston, Hulbert was finally able to present his scheme for an entirely new governing body for professional baseball, the National League, to the rest of the eastern stock clubs in New York during early February, 1876. What exactly transpired at this historically significant meeting seems to have been neither as dramatic nor astonishing to its attendees as tradition would have us believe. Spalding's account, which has been uncritically accepted by most scholars, tells us that Hulbert, after dramatically locking the meeting room door and pocketing the key, arm twisted and cajoled recalcitrant eastern clubs into abandoning the National Association for the new National League arrangement. Contemporary accounts of the meeting, however, seem to indicate matters transpired in a much more mundane manner. Most attendees, "almost spellbound" by Hulbert's proposal, seemed quite receptive to the idea, allowing Hulbert and his western representatives to return home content in their knowledge that "we had an easy time, for none of our Eastern friends were in condition to make effective resistance."[31]

Only the new league's territoriality provision — permitting only one National League club per city — seemed to present problems, as Hulbert correctly anticipated. "Once get Boston, Hartford, Mutuals and Athletics to agree to *that*" he was sure, "and the rest is easy." Given their long traditions of intra-city rivalries, especially in New York and Philadelphia, a number of eastern clubs were understandably uncomfortable with this provision, especially the Athletics, who would have to abandon a lucrative rivalry with the cross-town Philadelphia club, a rivalry that had earned the Athletics close to $15,000 over the past three years. The temptation and promise of monopoly income, however, seemed to eventually sway all doubters, Hulbert reminding William Cammeyer, manager of the Mutuals, that, within the National League arrangement, "you have a monopoly of profitable play in Brooklyn," while also promising Morgan Bulkeley, president of the Hartford club, "your club will have earned *more* money (much more) by Aug. 1" if it followed the new National League scheme. Even the reluctant Athletics came to be convinced excluding all local rivals would create "a proprietary right that will certainly result in a pecuniary advantage."[32]

The "coup" that led to the formation of the National League was certainly a watershed event in baseball history but it was hardly any "revolution in baseball." More properly, it was a self-transformation undertaken by the National Association's larger stock companies on their own initiative that established new conditions for cooperation and interaction while unilaterally restricting the championship format to a small closed circuit of stock clubs.[33]

Only to those parties, both clubs and individuals, who hadn't been privy to all this did the National League "coup" come as "the Confederate attack on Ft. Sumter," and only among those co-op clubs now excluded from championship consideration did it cause anything like "a bombshell of confusion." And even their criticism and outrage was due more to the way the stock clubs went about creating the new league rather than the actual results. The *Clipper*, which had been excluded from the behind-the-scenes dealings that led up to the National League's formation, didn't at all like the stock clubs' "anti–American methods of doing their business reform," while New Haven, the most vocal of the excluded co-op clubs, charged "there is a 'nigger on the fence' in this movement."[34]

In truth, the stock clubs probably had little other option than to cloak their plans in secrecy, given their intention to exclude all non-stock clubs, especially since the 1876 National Association meeting was to be held in New Haven, hardly a comfortable environment to be debating the expulsion of your host club. Nonetheless, it was from this point that the National League acquired its long-standing reputation as "sort of a secret society" that conducted its important business behind closed doors and far away from public scrutiny.[35]

From a publicity standpoint the most serious consequence of the National League's secret and unilateral reform methods was a rift with the country's most respected sports journalist, Henry Chadwick. The long time baseball editor of the *Clipper* always believed whatever changes were needed in pro baseball could have been openly worked out through the National Association itself, a far more effective method than the repeated "blunders" he found with its successor organization.[36]

Seeing in all this nothing more than resentment from "a played out and passed by man" in the changing world of pro baseball, the *Chicago Tribune* became openly hostile towards Chadwick, whom it dismissed as a no longer effective sports figure "limping around in the wreck of the old National Association" like "Marius wandering in the ruins of Carthage." Most of this was a straight out public declaration of Hulbert's own animosity towards Chadwick, the Chicago president at one point declaring to Harry Wright "personally I so dislike Mr. Chadwick" that he even tried to convince his Boston colleague to offer *Forest & Stream* preferential baseball information in order to undermine the *Clipper's* authority as a baseball publication.[37]

From a more substantive perspective, the main criticism of the National League was its closed circuit format, the self-appointed right, among League members, to designate which club was entitled to compete for the national championship. Even as the earliest rumors of such an arrangement were beginning to surface the New Havens objected that "no club has the right to assume to itself the power to judge the status of another club."[38]

The criticism was well founded, for the policy effectively ended the last vestige of local access to baseball's highest achievement level. No longer would clubs or communities, on the basis of their own qualification assessment, be entitled to championship competition. This prerogative was now exclusively in the hands of the "charmed circle" of National League participants, derisively dubbed the "Great I ams" by the Philadelphia *City Item.*[39]

Why the stock clubs settled upon such an exclusion policy, rather than some less draconian qualifying policy (something *Forest & Stream* had advocated, and the *Clipper* felt would immediately "disarm all opposition" to the National League) isn't entirely clear, but it would represent one of the most critical junctures in the history of organized baseball.[40]

Alternatives were certainly available. Hulbert and Wright, in their correspondence, had bantered around the problem of maintaining a competitive continuity without compromising championship standards well before the idea of a closed circuit had taken form. Wright wanted the stronger stock clubs to have an "option" of playing weaker co-op clubs, that would "let them [co-op clubs] slide" either succeeding or failing through competitive attrition. Also worth considering was Wright's idea, made a year earlier, that the National Association establish a formal admission policy for all new clubs, and the *Sunday Mercury*'s suggestion, made a year later, that the country's pro clubs all be divided into three classes with handicaps for the weaker clubs.[41]

We can only conjecture why all these ideas, which certainly seemed viable at the beginning of 1875, were rejected over the course of the National Association's final season by the stock clubs, especially Chicago, which may have believed the failure of so many co-op clubs, so early, that year, left them with no alternative than to simply deny these clubs any unapproved access to championship competition.

In restricting the national baseball championship to a closed circuit of stock clubs, the National League certainly settled upon an organizational structure more financially and competitively beneficial to its members, but it also put itself, with the implied claim to represent the highest expression of American baseball, under a number of unprecedented cultural obligations. First, to uphold its image and claim as representing the best in baseball despite being a very narrow niche in the vast spectrum of competitive baseball, the National League had to make sure it retained the best talent, the best managers and perfected the most competitive play. Secondly, to ensure reliable and consistent delivery of a high quality product (good baseball playing) it had to extend a common, unified set of standards and expectations on all its members at the expense of their individual autonomy. Thirdly, under an expressed constitutional obligation to "elevate" all baseball in general, the National League had to acknowledge a self-imposed moral accountability upon its personnel and policies, the absence of which had been so damaging to the National Association.

As the National League began to find its way and solidify its position on the baseball landscape over its first few years, however, it encountered severe challenges to its ability to meet these obligations.

Though the National League's eight stock clubs claimed to represent baseball's highest competitive echelon, their competitive record against non–National League clubs over the 1876 season raised serious doubts about this. National League teams lost no less than 37 times to outside clubs that year, six in one week during September, strong evidence that "science and skill exists outside, as well as inside, the League." The litany of losses became so embarrassing even the *Chicago Tribune* could hardly deny the fact that "some of the Leaguers have been beaten so often by semi-professionals and amateurs that it seems doubtful whether they had any business in the League in the first place."[42]

It's unclear if this run of success by outside clubs directly led to the formation of a rival league, but it certainly provided the competitive confidence to counter the National League's perceived attempts "to monopolize baseball patronage in this country." The idea of bringing together the best pro clubs outside the National League had been floated about by the end of the 1876 season, largely on the initiative of L.C. Waite, president of the old St. Louis Reds ballclub of the National Association.[43]

Coming together in a collective protest against the National League's restrictive entrance policies, 13 of these clubs met in Pittsburgh in February of 1877 and officially established the International Association, an organization structurally more sensitive towards individual club autonomy and "not run on the interest of any club or clique."[44]

Geographically dispersed as far west as St. Louis and Columbus, Ohio, and as far north as London, Ontario, the International Association was largely a collection of semi-pro clubs from the mid-sized industrial cities of New England and upstate New York. Competitively speaking, most members of the International Association were, like its Springfield, Massachusetts, club an "uneven mixture of good and bad players," but their experience and standard of play had certainly benefited from their success against the National League the year before.[45]

With the expulsion of the Mutuals and Athletics, at the end of 1876, releasing more players onto a market in which "the woods are full" of unemployed pro baseballers, many of these former National League players readily made their way to the International Association, enough to give the new league, some claimed, fielding talent actually superior to the National League.[46]

Largely dismissed by the National League as no more than a "wild cat" organization, which Spalding believed "will not survive the first three months of the season," the International Association, in fact, developed into a formidable rival. Of the 72 games the National League lost to outside clubs in 1877 (thirteen of which were lost by the League champion that year, Boston) most were to International Association clubs. A number of International Association teams were particularly troublesome to the National League, such as the Tecumsehs of London, the International Association champion that year, which beat Chicago several times that season, the Lowells who had an impressive 9–5 record against National League clubs that year, and Pittsburgh, which won seven of its thirteen games against National League clubs. More significantly, the International Association seemed to be establishing that intangible, yet important, ability to attract public interest and respect, with some sports observers noting how the Association's pennant race was becoming "now quite as interesting as the League pennant struggle."[47]

For the first time in history organized baseball's achievement center seemed to be in danger of fragmenting into multiple competitions, with no assurance the National League would be able to prevent this, something the *Chicago Tribune* feared even before the 1877 season had ended.[48]

To maintain the integrity and stability of its closed circuit format, the National League also had to impose stricter standards of mutual obligation upon member clubs. Initially this took the shape of a fixed, predetermined schedule, which the League first put into effect during its 1877 season, largely through Hulbert's initiate but also supported by Harry Wright, who felt a set schedule would be a "decided improvement over the old plan" of the National Association with its "as-you-go-scheduling."[49]

It was certainly no surprise that Chicago and Boston favored a fixed schedule. As the National League's two strongest teams, able to attract the largest crowds and most public interest, both clubs would greatly benefit from an arrangement that ensured their opponents were clear and certain about their scheduling obligations. Such an arrangement, however, wasn't as warmly received by the National League's other members, long accustomed to the flexibility and freedom of the old National Association scheduling policies. Other League clubs were specifically upset with the "arrogant" way Hulbert tried to force upon them a schedule that was perceived to be favorable to Chicago and Boston, with Bob Ferguson, manager of the Brooklyn club, in particular, complaining how "Chicago and Boston wants [sic] all the cream, the rest of the clubs take water."[50]

Even before the National League implemented its fixed schedule it was clear some member clubs were finding it hard to abandon the rather casual attitude towards scheduling they had become accustomed to in the National Association. The Mutuals and Athletics, both pleading financial hardship, refused to go west and finish their scheduled games with Chicago and St. Louis during the National League's inaugural season, a practice both clubs carried over from their days in the National Association. The Athletics hadn't completed its obligatory end-of-season trip to Chicago in

1874, while the Mutuals passed up on their final western trip a year later, a practice even Hulbert seemed to tolerate at that time, advising Charles Fowle, angry over the Mutuals' refusal to visit St. Louis, to "let him [Cammeyer, the Mutuals manager] off gracefully" on this occasion.[51]

Hulbert was no longer so forgiving of wayward members under the new National League format. Under his initiative the League extended disciplinary action against both the Athletics and Mutuals, eventually resulting in their expulsions from the League at the end of 1876. Scholars have traditionally interpreted this bold and unprecedented move to expell clubs from the League's two largest markets as proof the National League was committed to putting principle squarely before profits. Such an interpretation, however, is far too simplistic, overlooking a complex array of factors, from economic opportunism to personality clashes.

In the Mutuals case it must be remembered that William "Smiling Billy" Cammeyer was primarily the manager of a ball park, the Union Grounds, with the Mutuals being his major tenant. His commitment to the Mutuals went only as far as the team contributed to his business, which, by the latter years of the National Association, had considerably declined. By 1875 rumors even had it the Mutuals wouldn't be in the National Association, and the club that Cammeyer eventually did put together that year, and during its first year in the National League, was a hybrid stock/co-op team, with only four of its players on full salaries.[52]

A variety of other problems plagued the Mutuals during their first year in the National League. The team personnel was a varied collection of questionable personalities, in both ability and character, "a sort of infirmary for the refuge of players whose lack of reputation or ability ... have shut them out from other clubs." Long known as the one pro baseball team that "requires more iron ruling than any other club in the county," the Mutuals were continually beset with disciplinary problems and suspicions of player corruption, to a point that even Cammeyer had become "tired about this sort of thing." All in all, the Mutuals, as a club, had, by this time, simply become "a drag" on the National League.[53]

Faced with all these troubles, Cammeyer was evidently planning, barely half way through the 1876 season, to abandon the Mutuals and relocate the Hartford club to his grounds, a team that itself had a large contingent of Brooklyn players. Cammeyer's decision not to complete the Mutuals schedule seems to have been an intentional, if not premeditated, move, something that caused considerable problems for Hulbert. With the expulsion of the Athletics imminent, the Chicago president certainly didn't want to see two League clubs thrown out in one year, even going out of his way to offer the Mutuals generous financial incentives if they would complete their last western trip, so that "we should not have more than one club (if any) to discipline for defaulting."[54]

By now, however, Cammeyer had completely turned his back on the Mutuals, not only refusing to take his club west, but not even bothering to contest their expulsion. He didn't attend the National League meeting that year and virtually endorsed the Mutuals' expulsion by notifying Hulbert "it is no use for the League to have rules if it did not enforce them." As it all worked out, the Mutuals' expulsion gave the League what it wanted, an opportunity to collectively assert its authority over individual members, while giving Cammeyer what he wanted, a new (presumably more financially viable) National League tenant for his ground.[55]

Although one always has to be cautious about interpreting historical events solely on the basis of personality conflicts this seems to be the most valid explanation for the Athletics' expulsion, which transpired as the final act of a long standing personal feud between Hulbert and the Athletic management.

From the very earliest days of professional baseball Chicago had routinely looked on Philadelphia as prime recruiting ground, a posture Philadelphia baseball organizers came to openly resent and resist. During the National Association's very first meeting in 1871 both the White Stockings and Athletics claimed the services of Ned Cuthbert, who had complicated matters by signing with Chicago and then trying to jump to the Athletics. A similar dispute arose over Levi Meyerle who, as one of the Philadelphia club players Chicago secretly signed in 1873 when the city was relaunching a pro club, tried to renege on his obligations and return to Philadelphia. Collectively, incidents like these left Chicago baseball organizers with a deep-seated belief their city had "always been cordially hated in Philadelphia."[56]

Tension and hostility between the two clubs further escalated with the Davy Force case, another instance of what the Athletics perceived to be Chicago's relentlessly underhanded attempts to sign away its best players, in this case by backdating a contract with their star shortstop in 1875. The matter took a more troublesome turn when the contract, which had been upheld by the National Association's outgoing judiciary committee, was overturned by the Association's newly elected committee, one that was controlled by Philadelphia baseball officers, among them the Athletics' highly detested president, Charles Spering.[57]

At one time desiring "harmony and good will" between his club and the Athletics, even to the point of suggesting a trade for the Athletics' talented young infielder, Cap Anson, Hulbert, as a consequence of this incident, seemed convinced the Athletics would never be a compatible member of the National Association nor any other pro league. Even during the National League's earliest stages of planning, Hulbert confided to Campbell Bishop of St. Louis he wouldn't admit the Athletics into his planned league "until Philadelphia overthrows Spering, McBride ... et al."[58]

Hulbert eventually got his wish, the Athletic membership itself voting Spering out of the presidency at the end of 1875, "for which the western clubs," the *Chicago Tribune* reported, "will raise up their thanks." But this didn't in any way alter Chicago's belief (also shared by Harry Wright) that the Athletics were the most uncooperative and unsportsmanlike club in professional baseball. The club routinely perpetrated so much on-field trickery, intimidation and, above all, blatantly biased umpiring, that Hulbert had long ago resigned himself to the fact that in his games with the Athletics "I don't think *we* can win from Philadelphia."[59]

As was so often the case with pro baseball clubs of this period, on field corruption were signs of a weak and ineffective organization, which was certainly the case with the Athletics during its first year in the National League. By this time the Athletics were one of the League's weaker clubs, heavily in debt and drawing so poorly the *Cincinnati Enquirer* was claiming "this city is almost dead as regards base ball." Club officers had tried to convert the organization into a full fledged stock company at the end of 1875 but they underpriced the shares and allowed stockholders free season tickets, a major financial blunder for an organization that had already assumed the $5,000 debt of its predecessor. By mid-season the Athletics were clearly disintegrating as a viable club and by September were considered "as good as disbanded," leaving no hope whatsoever the club could complete its schedule.[60]

It was all developing into an ideal opportunity for Hulbert to finally rid Chicago and other western clubs of "Philadelphia 'boss' rule," and one he was ready to exploit even before the Athletics had finished their season, declaring to Charles Fowle "I for one should be glad to bid adieu to the Athletics. From my first experience they have always been a double dealing set of *bastards*."[61]

Hulbert took care that the Athletics' expulsion, which he vigorously pushed through despite the personal pleas, at the National League meeting, from Athletic officer George Thompson, be viewed strictly as a matter of principle, claiming the integrity of the League would be as "dead as Judas" if the expulsion wasn't upheld.[62]

Aside from the significant competitive benefits of securing, for Chicago, the services of Cap Anson and, for St. Louis, those of George Bradley, both of whose contracts with the Athletics were invalidated with the expulsion, Hulbert had, with the Mutuals' and Athletics' expulsion, also established the important precedent of claiming it was the League, ultimately, that had jurisdiction over member clubs.[63]

No longer would National League clubs be allowed to follow their own practices freely and without regard for their consequences upon the organization as a whole. In the old National Association it could only be hoped that uncooperative or disruptive clubs would fail or resign on their own. With the National League, as Hulbert envisioned it, the League now reserved the right to outright expel members deemed inappropriate to its objectives and policies.

The National League also soon realized this assertion of a unified authority would have to extend well beyond the matter of policing League policies to the actual enforcement of a recognized moral mission. As a closed circuit competition that self-designated the competitive worthiness of its members, the National League was virtually obliged to impose upon itself a collective moral standard. The corruption of the National Association, after all, had only been a matter of individual, highly autonomous, clubs that came and went. The National League, on the other hand, had to project an image that such a restrictive organization as theirs could not only be collectively free of suspicion, but that these moral obligations would extend to everyone involved with the organization.

From the time the very first rumors of the National League's formation were circulating, the eastern press was expecting a moral re-direction for baseball, transforming it into an institution that "ought to assume the standing of a national game ... and become an influence on the formation of the Anglo-Saxon traits that have so successfully asserted themselves in higher forms of achievement than sports of the field."[64]

Though not expressed in such sweepingly abstract terms, the National League did openly acknowledge an obligation to eliminate the "abuses of public confidence" that pro baseball had so often brought upon itself, to make itself, instead, into an organization as "honorably managed as a bank" so that the public could be assured every time they came to a League park they would see a "good game and an honest game."[65]

As a matter of policy the National League's sincerity on this point shouldn't be doubted, as seen in the many ways the organization was able to present matters of self-interest in a morally contributing light.

The most prominent example here was the League's long standing policy of requiring an unusually high 50 cent admission fee to all its games, a practice it inherited from the National Association but presented to the public as a tool for patron selectivity. The idea of charging above average prices for important games (in most cases 25 cents instead of the usual ten cents) had become common practice soon after the Civil War. Ticket prices for the more decisive Atlantic-Athletic games of this period reportedly ran as high as a dollar, with some going as high as $5 for an especially crucial game between these two clubs in 1868. The standard practice of charging 50 cents for all regular professional games was established by Harry Wright in the wake of his Cincinnati team's success in 1869, the club not only doubling its ticket prices from twenty-five to fifty cents for all home games the following year, but also requiring a similar fare from all clubs it played on the road.[66]

Fifty cent ticket prices weren't popular with all pro clubs, especially those in New York, who felt it put their games beyond the reach of many working class patrons. The historic game between the Atlantics and Cincinnati in 1870, that ended the Reds long winning streak, came off only at the last minute when Wright prevailed upon the Atlantics to raise their ticket prices for that game to 50 cents. Backed by the influence and prestige of his Boston club, Wright, by 1872, was also able to establish 50 cents as the prevailing ticket price in the National Association, a fare even adopted by the Association's weaker clubs, such as the Westerns of Keokuk.[67]

Wright himself seemed convinced the unusually high 50 cent price was absolutely essential to maintain pro baseball's image as a high-quality, and therefore eminently desirable, commodity, warning that when "the public refuse [sic] to pay that [50 cents] then good bye base-ball."[68]

Adopting uniformly high ticket prices to all games assumes a consistently high caliber of play from all clubs on all occasions, something the National League, like its predecessor, the National Association, could hardly assure. From the earliest days of professionalism the integrity of pre-priced games were always vulnerable to the more glaring revelations of ineptitude, such as the 50 cent game between the Atlantics and Athletics in 1869, a game so poorly played the Philadelphia *Age* exclaimed "a few more exhibitions of the sort and the 'National Game' will have a very 'potent and sudden conclusion' in this vicinity." With such poor quality clubs as the Mutuals, Athletics and Cincinnati within its ranks during its first year, it was generally believed the National League's quality of play simply didn't justify their high ticket prices, an example being the game between the Athletics and Cincinnati, so poor a contest the *Hartford Daily Times* felt those who attended the game had paid "about 49 cents too much" for their tickets.[69]

If the National League couldn't indisputably justify its 50 cent ticket prices on the grounds of product quality it could do so as a tool to ensure its quality of patronage.

The idea of using high ticket prices to screen out undesirable patrons had been put forward during baseball's pre-professional days, the *Ball Players Chronicle* advocating, as early as 1867, 25 cent ticket prices to keep rowdies out of important games. Such a practice certainly complimented the National League's professed intent to "elevate" baseball very nicely, since the policy supposedly "lent dignity to League games" by attracting orderly, high quality patrons, of the type that one normally found at the "opera house, the lyceum or the public garden." As a result of the policy, League supporters repeatedly claimed "the character of the [baseball] audience has been revolutionized." Chicago, the strongest advocate of the 50 cent fee, in particular, always proclaimed such ticket prices were attracting only high class, orderly crowds to its games.[70]

First hand accounts from this period, however, seem to indicate the National League had no real assurance crowds at its games could be "made to behave" because of such a ticket policy. Rowdy, disruptive fans, "the imperfect civilization of the masses," could still be found attending National League games in St. Louis, nor was such behavior unknown even among "respectable" patrons. The *Cleveland Plain Dealer* was surprised to find that, at its National League games, "young men who belong to good families sometimes join in the rabble of ruffians who indulge in ungentlemenly demonstrations." Crowds at Buffalo were so persistently abusive, especially towards umpires, that the *Boston Post* sarcastically suggested the worst punishment for Charles Guiteau (the soon to be hanged assassin of president Garfield), "would be to make him umpire a game of ball at Buffalo."[71]

The National League found the going even harder when trying to extend a moralizing influence over its own personnel, particularly its players. From the very beginning there was widespread skepticism about both the National League's sincerity and ability to ensure every one of its ballplayers was a "good and true man." If anything, the National League, with its small circuit of evenly matched ball clubs, was probably more structurally vulnerable to the corrupting influence of gamblers and pool sellers than the National Association. Nor did the National League's open declarations to actively oppose these influences convey a great deal of confidence to the sporting public. "The habitués of the various city pool rooms of New York, Chicago, St. Louis and Philadelphia," *Forest and Stream* skeptically noted, "will smile in their sleeves at this."[72]

The general consensus among sports observers seemed to indicate corruption was just as rampant in the National League during its first year as it had been in the old National Association, even to the point of engulfing, it was claimed, entire clubs. In addition to the always suspect Mutuals, teams such as the St. Louis Brown Stockings, which suspiciously lost critical games to arch rival Chicago, were also believed to be infiltrated by gambling interests. Others even saw a suspicious pattern in the way the League's moral pillar, Chicago, always seemed to lose the first game of all its series with other clubs that year.[73]

On an individual basis as well rumor, innuendo and gossip implicated numerous National League players with gambling interests during the National League's inaugural season, with evidence of suspiciously unreliable play often glaringly evident. "The people are no fools," the *Hartford Times* noted, "they can tell when a man tries to play well and when he doesn't." Throughout the season rumors, of varying degrees of credibility, implicated numerous League players with game selling, among them Bobby Matthews of the Mutuals and Mike McGeary of St. Louis. Even Spalding and Cammeyer weren't beyond the pale of suspicion during the League's darkest days of corruption.[74]

And, like its predecessor organization, the National League found itself frustrated and virtually helpless in its battle against incipient corruption. In an era of primitive investigative techniques and surveillance methods, even the *Clipper* conceded it was virtually impossible to prove or substantiate accusations of game selling, as was evident enough during the highly publicized McManus-Devinny scandal. After weeks of highly detailed press exposés, affidavits, accusations and counter-accusations, umpire Dan Devinny's charge that St. Louis manager George McManus had blatantly tried to bribe him were never substantiated, leaving critics like the *Chicago Tribune* (which deplored the whole affair as "dirty and disgraceful from end to end") frustrated and disappointed.[75]

Even in the face of apparently irrefutable evidence suspected players were often able to avoid conviction. Louisville's George Bechtel simply denounced as a forgery a telegram in his name offering a bribe to teammate James Devlin, a denial Hulbert himself also had to make to a letter forged in his name. Confident in their knowlege that their detractors had little to go on except weak evidence and testimony usually no more substantive than "your word against mine," corrupt baseball players knew they had little to fear in the way of detection, something the *Chicago Tribune* was well aware of, going so far as to admit that had the infamous Louisville foursome, expelled for selling games, simply "locked their jaws" and withheld their confessions, it would have been virtually impossible to convict them.[76]

Faced with the prospect that "two thirds" of the public's interest in pro baseball was being jeopardized by its do-nothing stance against corruption, the National League came under severe pressure to undertake some decisive and effective counter measures. The League did uphold the expulsion of one player, William Boyd of the Mutuals, in 1876, on charges of corruption, but it didn't expel anyone else, a lack of decisiveness that was strongly criticized by the *Clipper* and other eastern papers.[77]

All told, the National League seemed incapable of waging its war against corruption on anything more than a symbolic front, as seen with the highly tokenistic $2,000 reward offer by Hartford and League president Morgan Bulkeley for certain proof of player corruption, a reward offer also made by Cammeyer. It was a neat little public relations game that even suspect players like James Devlin got into. In a gesture almost contemptuous in its sincerity, the soon to be implicated ringleader of the Louisville scandal personally offered a $500 reward to anyone "who knew me do a wrong action in my life."[78]

As it turned out, Devlin and his Louisville club presented the National League with the first real opportunity to rehabilitate its public standing at the end of the 1877 season.

Going into the last month of the season with a comfortable lead in the pennant race, the League's Louisville franchise suddenly had "a terrible cave in," losing game after game during its late season eastern swing until Boston overtook the club and eventually went on to win the pennant.[79]

Rumors soon began to circulate that many of these games had been lost on purpose, to such an extent that even Hulbert was sure some form of "shameless corruption of players are rife in the East."[80]

Louisville officials investigated the matter and were eventually able to extract full confessions from three of its players, James Devlin, Al Nichols and George Bechtel, with a fourth, William Craver, implicated on strong circumstantial evidence. The four players were summarily expelled from the club, a move that was upheld by the National League at its annual meeting.[81]

As stunning a development as this was at the time, the Louisville scandal had been, in actuality, a crisis long in the making. Three of the convicted players had long histories of suspicious behavior. Craver had been expelled from both Chicago in 1870 and Baltimore in 1873 for behavioral problems, while Bechtel had been temporarily suspended by Louisville itself in 1876 for an alleged bribery attempt. Chicago officers had become so suspicious of Devlin when he was with the club in 1874 that they kept him on the bench during several important games.[82]

Whether Devlin was the actual ringleader of the bribery plot is not entirely certain, but his past history certainly points to that conclusion. The Philadelphia born pitcher had been "a source of almost constant trouble" from the time he first joined the Louisville club, once even petitioning the League itself to get his release from the club on the grounds it reneged on a promised advance. Not wanting to lose its standout pitcher, the club stubbornly declared that Devlin "will play in Louisville whether he wants to or not," a hard line stance that certainly must have provided Devlin with a strong incentive to betray his club.[83]

Faced with such undeniable evidence of corruption within its ranks, evidence that could potentially, it was claimed, kill pro baseball "deader than a mackerel," Hulbert knew bold and decisive action was necessary to turn this incident to the League's advantage, to "strike an effective blow" once and for all against corruption and henceforth "open a new era of prosperity and popularity" for pro baseball.[84]

This essentially took the form of a harsh and totally unforgiving stance against the expelled players. The League steadfastly denied all their appeals for reinstatement, uninfluenced even by Craver's personal appeal to Harry Wright and Devlin's often told personal plea to Hulbert himself. At its 1880 meeting the League declared it would no longer hear any more appeals from the expelled players, a decision that effectively banned them from ever playing professional baseball again.[85]

The favorable publicity that resulted from this hard line stance was also, no doubt, further reinforced by the personal misery it inflicted on the culprits themselves. All the expelled players made repeated attempts to get back into pro baseball, with either International Association or other independent clubs, but the stigma of their offense was so deep and the weight of the National League ban so effective (League clubs refused to play with any team that either enrolled an expelled player or played against one that did) that none were ever able to resume their careers on anything more than a temporary basis.[86]

And of the four, Devlin seems to have been hit the hardest. In trying to get back into baseball rumors had him playing in Canada for $15 a week in 1878, at Easton, Pennsylvania, in 1879, in California in 1880 and even in Trenton, New Jersey, in 1882. For a while he even tried to play under an assumed name.[87]

With his already precarious financial situation fast deteriorating, he briefly tried to umpire for the International Association and made an impassioned plea to the American Association, on its formation in 1882, for reinstatement, an appeal that had, like all his previous attempts, as much chance of success, according to the *Cincinnati Enquirer*, as "trying to teach a dog how to talk."[88]

As a result of the Louisville scandal the National League had established the right to assert its moral authority over every one of its players. But the League wasn't about to limit this authority strictly to individuals.

For all the assistance it rendered in exposing this scandal, Louisville was a club that, itself, reputedly operated under a veneer of moral hypocrisy. The rest of the League always looked slightly askance at the "high toned wealthy gentlemen" who directed the club from afar while its players conducted themselves in a "wild and unmanageable" manner on a day-to-day basis. Here also were baseball officers who, on the one hand, condemned the unprincipled "Everyone for himself and may the devil take the hind most" attitude they found in New England society, while, on the other hand, refused to give their catcher, Charles Snyder, his backpay until the League forced them to.[89]

More acute observers were also perturbed in the way Louisville was willing to accept Devlin's testimony implicating his teammates while suppressing equally credible evidence that the club had, in fact, unduly influenced their appointed umpire, Dan Devinny. It was a shady arrangement the *Chicago Tribune* had, earlier, mockingly criticized for having made a sham of "Kentucky chivalry."[90]

As things unfolded it became clear the Louisville scandal would not only destroy the careers of four ballplayers but the viability of an entire club. In early July Hulbert already had a sense Louisville would "go to the wall" by season's end, which it did, burdened by an increasing indebtedness and inability to resurrect its reputation among League players or colleagues. Their director's decision, after considerable vacillation, to disband the club and drop out of the National League was, consequently, received not with remorse or regret but a sense of relief that the League's "dead branch," as Harry Wright put it, had finally been discarded.[91]

If, with the Mutuals/Athletics' expulsion, the National League had asserted its right to discipline member clubs for policy violations, with the Louisville scandal the League had now asserted its right to discipline these same clubs on purely moral grounds, an explicit declaration that, as an organization, "the league can no more stand a defaulting and dishonest club than can the club stand a dishonest player."[92]

The League also exercised this prerogative with the expulsion of its St. Louis franchise at the end of that same season, an incident that's been widely misinterpreted by scholars. With three of the Louisville ballplayers, at the time of their expulsion, already contracted to play for the Brown Stockings in 1878, the Louisville scandal certainly weakened St. Louis' competitive prospects for that year, but this alone was hardly grounds for disbanding the team. More critical was a $4,000 debt, which the club tried to retire by playing Sunday games, a move that didn't seem to help its financial situation but apparently so outraged other League clubs that Hulbert was convinced St. Louis was "dead past resurrection" by the season's close.[93]

It must not have been easy for Hulbert to impose the ultimate penalty on a club whose officers had been his close confidants in creating the National League, but it was a move that probably avoided any further public embarrassment for the League. Well before the League's annual meeting in 1877 Hulbert had been urging St. Louis to voluntarily give up its membership, advice its officers, conspicuously absent from the League meeting, seemed to have agreed to, making it possible for Hulbert to happily report "so we got rid of a *badly diseased* member."[94]

It should by no means be assumed the forceful and decisive moves the National League took in the wake of the Louisville scandal ended corruption within its ranks. Barely a year after the scandal broke the *Cincinnati Enquirer* was sounding another alarm that "the national game is engaged in a death contest this year with gambling in the form of combination pools."[95]

Once again rumor and innuendo had a number of National League players, like Indianapolis pitcher Ed "The Only" Nolan, throwing games, with even the old Red Stockings player, Cal McVey, coming under suspicion from his Cincinnati club for game tampering. Most of these charges, like those throughout baseball history, couldn't be formally substantiated, but the fact that Cincinnati pool operators refused to take bets on any games by the League's Indianapolis franchise certainly seemed to lend some credence to these suspicions.[96]

One notable phenomenon, the corrupt umpire, seems to have emerged only after the Louisville scandal, most likely because gamblers and pool sellers found it much more efficient to target a few underpaid and unappreciated officials than dozens of well paid ballplayers. League umpire Chapman was so incessantly hounded by gamblers and bookies he left the profession in 1880. League umpire Richard "Tricky Dick" Higham, on the other hand, seemed quite at home with them. Never far removed from controversy during his days as a pro player, and apparently even unmoved by Harry Wright's career advice "to do well by yourself," Higham was caught redhanded giving "pointers" to the gambling fraternity during the 1882 season. Though widely recognized as one of the National League's most competent umpires, Higham was summarily expelled by League officials, thus relegating him to baseball infamy as the only National League umpire, to this day, ever to be convicted of corruption.[97]

If the National League couldn't secure its integrity in practice, at least it could in image. This was, without doubt, the most enduring legacy of the Louisville scandal. As a consequence of its actions against internal corruption, the League assumed a role, however ineffective, as the moral vigilante over not only its players but every officer and official associated with the organization, with an expressed obligation to keep everyone connected with the League "in line," a posture that constituted a significant advance over the old National Association.

By doing this the National League was able to renew confidence in pro baseball, to an extent that the New York *World*, by 1878, could claim, despite considerable circumstantial evidence to the contrary, that "crookedness in the League arena has well nigh ceased." Spalding even flattered himself to proclaim the National League's tough stance against corruption actually gave outside organizers renewed confidence to form independent pro clubs, a "turning over a new leaf" outlook, that apparently so impressed *Wilkes,* the publication, in 1879, decided to lift its nearly decade old self-imposed ban on running pro baseball reports.[98]

It also turned out to be a highly resilient confidence, that would be able to deflect evidence of such potentially serious incidents as Cleveland catcher John Clapp's revelation of a bribery attempt in 1881, and the *Chicago Tribune*'s charges, in 1879, that Providence directors were betting on their own team. Hulbert himself, by now, was so confident in the League's strong image he could dismiss this latter complaint ("nothing in it," he claimed) as easily as he could O.P. Caylor's accusations, in 1881, that the League had covered up hard evidence of player corruption on the Buffalo team.[99]

The National League had, by now, reached such a point in its development that a wayward player or two could no longer seriously threaten its standing as "the 'squarest' sport in the country today," or raise any serious doubts the National League had ever done anything except "kept its rules straight and clean." Critics could still question the validity of these claims, but it could no longer deny the National League was the only baseball organization "which possesses the full power to ... enforce thoroughly honest service."[100]

It is with some sense of irony that the National League, during its early years, was able to secure such a sturdy public image at a time when it was struggling to establish any corresponding operational stability. The League's closed circuit format, which restricted championship competition to a small number of, presumably, solid, tested, stock clubs, was supposed to ensure greater reliability, stability and profitability among its membership. Yet all proved to be elusive during the National League's first two years.

With Boston the only club to complete its full schedule in 1876, the National League's inaugural year ended, from an operational basis, "unsatisfactorily." And if the failure and eventual expulsion of the Mutuals and Athletics, something that seemed so characteristic of the unstable old

National Association, is factored in, the *Clipper* seemed fully justified in claiming the National League "does not appear to have improved matters" in managing pro baseball.[101]

Financially as well it soon became clear there would be "no fortunes in the game this year," with only Chicago able to show a clear profit at the end of the 1876 season. Things didn't improve during the League's second year either. Expectations that most National League clubs, in 1877, would "grow rich this year" also ended in disappointment, with pennant winner Boston even showing a loss. Even Hulbert, who had to endure an almost complete reversal of fortune in both competitive results and financial returns for his own club that season, confided to Boston president N.T. Appolonio "there *are* doubts about the future. The business is not pleasant."[102]

Probably the National League's most visible shortcoming was its inability to secure a stable and secure membership, something it always asserted in justification for its closed circuit format. Over its first three years, in fact, the National League saw a greater changeover in member clubs than the old National Association experienced over the same period of its existence, with only Chicago and Boston, of the National League's charter members, still around by the end of the League's third season. It was, of course, to the National League's credit that only one of these clubs, Syracuse, failed during mid-season, while others had been expelled for violation of League policies and practices, sufficient grounds, it may have seemed, for the *Chicago Tribune* to assert, by the middle of the 1878 season, that the National League was still by far the most reliable baseball organization in the country. But the failure of three more National League clubs by the end of that season — Milwaukee, Indianapolis and Syracuse — seemed to flat out contradict the paper's assertion the League admits only "strong, honorable and deserving clubs."[103]

Just exactly why the National League admitted the clubs it did, and not others, is one of the more puzzling aspects of its operations during these early years. The statutory requirement that no National League club be domiciled in a city with a population less than 75,000 was frequently ignored (neither Hartford, Troy nor Worcester met the criterion). Nor did the League ever seem to show an eagerness, with the exception of Cincinnati, to re-establish a presence in those cities whose National League clubs had earlier failed, such as New York, Philadelphia or St. Louis, as if there was an implied judgment such cities couldn't support baseball the way the League wanted them to.

The criterion Hulbert seemed to use in judging the worthiness of non–National League clubs was their ability to draw on League grounds, certainly an important consideration for the League's top clubs such as Chicago and Boston. Given Hulbert's indomitable influence upon League deliberations as its president during these years, this seems to most effectively explain why such mid-sized cities as Indianapolis, Syracuse and Worcester were admitted, all of whom showed exceptionally successful records against National League competition when they were independent clubs, regardless of other considerations.[104]

From the vantage point of the League's most nationally focused clubs, Chicago and Boston, this seemed to be the most logical criterion. Wright always believed "It is impractical for a first-class club to earn its living and to travel thousands of miles to play games unless it has something to play for of more interest than a local or state championship."[105]

But this, however, didn't represent the competitive horizons for most of the country's other pro clubs, many of whom were skeptical of the benefits of belonging to the National League. The Lowells, one of the strongest non–National League clubs, were highly doubtful of Wright's assurance that playing mostly National League clubs "will prove the sole attraction" to their games, and thus declined to join the League despite Wright's efforts to exempt them from the 50 cent ticket price requirement. Buffalo also initially expressed reservations about joining the League, as did Cleveland, which didn't want its club "wasting its receipts in railroad fare and hotel bills and standing second or first in some championship."[106]

For many newly admitted National League clubs these concerns would prove to be painfully accurate. Most had only been strong local or regional clubs run by inexperienced yet overly optimistic officers who only had to deal with low budget salaries and operational costs. As a consequence most of these officials were simply not up to the increased demands of having to now operate a club on a fully national level.

From just a financial aspect, belonging to the National League entailed a considerable escalation in expenses and obligations, far more than most mid-sized city clubs could meet. Expenses for running a National League club in 1877 cost, on average, $1,600 a month, excluding salaries. And if any organization aspired to equal Chicago's competitive standards at this time, it would have to be willing to expend, as Hulbert's club did in 1877, $240 for every home game, $55 a day while on the road, not including salaries.[107]

Newly admitted National League clubs were also obliged to raise their ticket prices to 50 cents, had to cut back on their contacts with local rivals, and, to stay competitive, perfect the cut-throat practice of recruiting top ballplaying talent. In most instances newly admitted League clubs weren't able to effectively manage these requirements to their advantage. Most found themselves over matched in a competitive environment where they had to play top-notch opposition day in and day out, in which a lack of success quickly deflated local support and interest, both at home and on the road, and inevitably led to a progressively deteriorating revenue flow.

The consequences of such unwarranted local aspirations were perhaps best illustrated with the National League's Indianapolis club. This organization had been admitted to the League in 1878 largely on its stellar record in the League Alliance, the small satellite organization of independent pro clubs sponsored by the National League. Much of Indianapolis' pre–National League success was due to the exploits of its outstanding pitcher, Ed "The Only" Nolan, whose fire-balling pace was as superior to that of the average pro pitcher "as an old smooth-bore musket would compare with that of a shot from a Springfield rifle."[108]

Once in the National League, however, the Indianapolis club proved to be no more than an also-ran. Home attendance soon declined, putting such a squeeze on finances club officers, to "get out of the hole," decided to transfer the club to St. Louis midway through the season. The decision won the blessing of Hulbert and Wright but the club's three games in St. Louis against Boston proved to be no more remunerative, leaving the organization to complete its season as a "homeless club," playing most of its remaining games on the road. By now the club's financial situation was also in complete disarray, with players owed backpay, rumors of missing funds and other assorted monetary "funny business." Rumors even had it that Hulbert, to keep the club afloat, had guaranteed its player salaries, something that, if true, still couldn't save the club from insolvency and eventual withdrawal from the League at the end of 1878.[109]

How unreliable could be the judgment of both Chicago and Boston in estimating the viability of League membership was even more evident during the short and turbulent history of the League's 1878 Milwaukee franchise. Harry Wright was convinced this club would be a strong competitor, while the *Chicago Tribune* thought its manager, W. P. Rogers, was "a good businessman." But the club was never a contender and quickly fell into debt, a situation that reached crisis proportions when its players refused to play for a short period because of unpaid salaries. At home attendance fell off so sharply Providence preferred to forfeit a rained out game rather than stay over another day in the city. On the road, club managers left behind so many unpaid hotel bills the *Chicago Tribune* denounced the club as "a fraud." Faced with a League ultimatum to make good on its debts or face expulsion, the club preferred the latter.[110]

For those newly admitted clubs who were able to develop a fairly competitive standard of play, like Syracuse, National League regulations often undermined their efforts to maintain consistent local support.

As an "old established club" among the many strictly semi-pro clubs of upstate New York, and reputed to be one of the best paying non–National League cities, Syracuse gained admission to the National League in 1879 on the basis of its impressive record against League clubs, which included a 2–0 win over Chicago during that club's pennant winning season. Wright had sold its president, Robert Townsend, on the financial benefits of League membership, but these assurances proved to be illusionary, primarily because the club underestimated how deeply the League's 50 cent ticket requirement cut into its attendance base of "mechanics, bookkeepers and clerks." The club's July 4 game, traditionally the biggest drawing date of the baseball season, attracted a mere 300 spectators, and not many more must have been at its three games with Troy, since the visiting club's share of the total gate receipts for that series amounted to a paltry $89.65. Despite Syracuse's fairly competitive reputation the most glaring feature of its home games were "the empty benches which stare [club directors] in the face."[111]

Unable to stem the flow of red ink, the Syracuse president, with a good month left in the season, simply disbanded the club, got married, went off to California and left unfulfilled the *Clipper*'s assertion, made on the club's behalf a short time earlier, that "the disbandment of a league team was something entirely out of the question."[112]

Failure within the National League was by no means limited to clubs in mid-sized markets, as the Brooklyn Hartfords discovered. Club president Morgan Bulkeley had left Hartford at the end of 1876 in search of greener pastures in Brooklyn after the Mutuals were expelled, but the move hardly proved to be a financial bonanza. The club never seemed able to establish a loyal fan base, though a number of its players were from Brooklyn and, at one point, the team even adopted the old Atlantics uniform. Even the favorable financial concessions the League had extended the club (the Hartfords were only required to pay visiting National League teams 12½ cents rather than the customary 15 cents per ticket) couldn't compensate for a lack of fan support, as Boston itself discovered, this big-draw club earning a mere $454 from its four games in Brooklyn.[113]

To help right the ship the Hartford players had, themselves, agreed to voluntary pay cuts at the beginning of the season, but as early as July of 1877 Bulkeley was already strongly hinting to Hulbert he was "getting out of baseball." True to his word, the Hartford club president was a no-show at the League meeting that year and didn't seem to care the least that his National League franchise was consequently declared "vacated." So it came to pass that Bulkeley, the National League's first president, who stands enshrined in the Baseball Hall of Fame solely for that reason, simply decided to walk away from baseball without so much as an afterthought.[114]

If one seeks an explanation for the National League's early instability, and its apparent inability to assert some form of collective support among its member clubs, the answer is actually self-suggestive: the National League's overriding purpose, at least under Hulbert's tenure, wasn't to ensure club stability or profitability, but to maintain an indivisible achievement center.

It was far more important for the National League to ensure that it, and it alone, represented the highest expression of baseball excellence, not only as the sovereign overlord of the recognized national championship, but by representing everything about the game that should be publicly aspired to. Individual clubs that weren't able to meet the conditions necessary to uphold this responsibility were not only allowed to fail, it was generally believed to be better if they did. "The base ball business in America will never flourish," the *Chicago Tribune* claimed at the end of the National League's first season, "until the principle of the survival of the fittest is carried out."[115]

This is why Leiffer's claim that Hulbert most benefited organized baseball because he "shifted the focus ... from building great teams to composing sets of potential contenders" isn't entirely correct. Hulbert was primarily concerned with the League's collective status, and this only required that there be at least a few clubs, any clubs, on the basis of their competitive standing and moral image, that could maintain the League's achievement level. Proof of this can be found in Hulbert's correspondence itself, where one finds no expressions of remorse or regret over failed and expelled clubs but, instead, an almost biblical tone of just desserts. For every club that failed to make the National League grade a replacement could easily be found, which, for Hulbert could have been clubs in as various and far-flung locations as Pittsburgh, Philadelphia, Rochester or even London, Ontario.[116]

This, then, was the National League's overriding mission as Hulbert saw it, to which everything else, club stability, profitability, even moral principal, was expedient. And Hulbert would soon demonstrate he was willing and capable of using these expedients to their fullest extent for the preservation and prosperity of the National League.

6

William Hulbert and
Baseball as an Enterprise
of Cultural Distortion

With the National League all of baseball's formative characteristics that had appeared in antebellum New York reached their final stage of development. Baseball's origins in a single urban center had established an early and overwhelming social focus upon achievement. The rise of post–Civil War professionalism made the game's highest achievement level a transferable commodity accessible to any community. The National Association, with its championship format, had set conditions for accessing this achievement. The National League, by retaining the right to self-qualify all championship aspirants, completed this irresistible drift towards organizing "the best against the best" by finally eliminating all local access to the game's highest achievement level.

I've also tried to show that this course of development, no matter how irresistible, also ran counter to a deep social sense of geographic obligation, that the highest achievement level baseball represented could only be legitimate as the expression of local resources. Because baseball's rapid technical development in New York had established a premature achievement standard for the rest of the country, this sense of local obligation was never able to organize itself effectively since the free mobility of baseball talent could be easily utilized to reach baseball's highest competitive level without relying upon local resources. The National League, in establishing a closed circuit competition, may have organizationally suppressed this sense of obligation for local achievement access, but it couldn't eliminate it.

As baseball continued to expand and develop through the 1870s more and more clubs were organized, with increasingly higher talent levels and managerial expertise spread over a much broader and diverse geographic network. Identified more firmly with their geographic localities and the support of local or regional talent, these clubs began to exert persistent, if poorly organized, upward pressure to gain access to the achievement level represented by the National League, something observers anticipated would happen with the League's closed circuit format.[1]

By the late 1870s a curious state of cross purposes was developing in organized baseball. As more and more clubs, in diverse geographic areas, were slowly working to raise themselves up to baseball's highest achievement level, the National League, to maintain control of the standards and qualifications for baseball's highest achievement focus, found itself actually influencing, if not outright opposing, baseball as it was organizing outside its jurisdiction. The greatest danger to the system of baseball the National League represented wasn't member instability or unprofitabilty, but the possibility that the single, indivisible achievement center it represented would be dissolved.

And this could come about one of two ways. First, there was always the possibility National League clubs would be drawn down from the championship focus the National League represented (only the best playing against the best, on a national basis) to anchor a purely regional or sectional championship focus that drew its strength and appeal from an obligation to local or sectional, rather than national, rivalries.

Just about every National League club, during the League's early years, experienced, in varying degrees, some competitive drift away from national to local and regional competitive networks and rivalries. Boston, in 1876, arranged a series of games, above and beyond their regular National League games, with Hartford for the "New England Championship," something it also did with the strong Lowell club in 1877. Plans to actually form something of a "league within a league" among the top New England clubs in and out of the National League had advanced to such a stage, in 1879, that Harry Wright attended its planning meeting that year.[2]

Most of the International Association clubs, while playing for their own national championship, were also simultaneously competing for the New York State championship, with the stronger of these clubs frequently trying to assert their local standing by challenging the area's best National League club, as Syracuse did in 1876, challenging the Mutuals for the New York state championship, a title the New York Metropolitans, a non–National League club, also challenged the National League's Troy club for in 1880. Even Chicago, the very symbol and strength of nationalism in baseball competition, found the public took unusually strong interest in its sectional rivalry with St. Louis, the *Clipper* going so far as to claim winning this series was far more important to Chicago than even winning the pennant.[3]

Above and beyond the possibility National League clubs would limit their achievement focus to local or regional championships, was the real and persistent possibility they would divide along the lines mapped out by the natural and long standing rivalry between East and West. When the National League was first organized the *Clipper* actually interpreted this as a merger of "the two great sections" of the country into a single, unified, baseball competition, yet without obliterating their sectional identities, the rivalry between which the *Chicago Times* always claimed "superseded" the National League championship itself.[4]

Throughout the National League's early years the press could never completely overcome their force of habit in viewing the League, above all else, as an ongoing rivalry between eastern and western baseball. Papers in both sections always tabulated League results on the basis of east versus west, something that always fueled speculation a time might come when it would be better to determine a national championship by having the best teams from the two sections play a decisive series rather than have them play together in a unified competition.[5]

The second threat to the National League, and one that was far more realistic, was the establishment of alternative achievement centers among the better non–League pro clubs, which could challenge the National League's claims it represented the best in baseball and was the only competition worthy of public following and support.

The International Association, by its second year, in 1878, was certainly presenting the National League with a very troublesome, if not outright threatening, challenge to this claim as the top baseball organization. With the International Association numbering 26 of the strongest non–League clubs among its membership that year (though only 13 entered its championship competition that season), some observers believed the International championship could very well "assume an importance fully equal to that of the League."[6]

Man for man the International clubs weren't nearly as strong as their National League counterparts, but with their talent pool strengthened by players who would "drift out" of the National League from either club failures or limited playing opportunities, the International Association had the makings of a formidable competitive organization. Its better clubs could show impressive results against the National League, such as the Utica club, which beat three League teams in 1878, proof to some that "the international clubs have batted and fielded better than the League teams." In New Bedford's win over Providence, the *Clipper* as well found a "conclusive argument the international clubs can play as good a game as the League nines."[7]

Faced with these two potential threats to the National League's status as baseball's single focus of achievement, Hulbert put the League on a direction that would profoundly change the course of organized baseball. First, he realized the League would have to adopt a stance of active opposition to any organizational trends or developments in baseball that looked as if they could, in any way, lead to a competing achievement center. Unlike the old National Association, whose open championship actually encouraged and challenged outside clubs to work up to the championship level it represented, the National League, with its closed circuit, found itself working to prevent clubs from achieving a status comparable to League clubs.

Second, to counter any possible drift by National League clubs to regional or sectional ties, Hulbert had to continually impress upon both League and potential League clubs the value of belonging to the National League. To accomplish this Hulbert had to work to bring the League's membership into closer interdependence by enforcing greater uniformity of practices and objectives, even if this meant member clubs had to relinquish some of their autonomy or responsiveness to local markets.

Whether the International Association was an organization that would ever be "on equal footing" with the National League, as its proponents claimed, is unclear. The organization was regional in scope (mostly limited to clubs in New England and upstate New York) and most of its success against League teams were in less than meaningful pre or postseason exhibition games. Nonetheless, Hulbert felt the International Association posed enough danger to the National League to initiate a policy of active opposition to it from 1878 to 1880. Working within the constraints of the League's professed purpose of "elevating" baseball, and the still important revenue considerations of playing non–League clubs, Hulbert didn't adopt a policy of outright hostility towards the International Association clubs so much as a subtle, yet premeditated, effort to destabilize them and eventually subordinate them to the League's influence.[8]

The National League had long been "picking up country half dollars" playing exhibition games against non–League clubs, a revenue source that was quite substantial for a number of National League clubs. Some, like Louisville, earned more than half their gross annual receipts from non–League games, with even League champion Boston taking in one third of its total road receipts, during its championship year of 1877, from non–League games.[9]

It was clearly to the National League's interest to disarm or neutralize the International Association's competitive strength yet retain its presence as a revenue source. Such a relationship of non-threatening subordination would also benefit the League by reducing the International Association to the status of a largely developmental competition limited to building up and training raw, untested, talent that could then be, as Hulbert saw it, "bought up cheap" by National League clubs.[10]

Officially, the National League's policy towards the International Association was always one of peaceful co-existence. In his public pronouncements Hulbert always insisted every unsuccessful non–League organization failed because it simply "ruined itself" from mismanagement or poor competitive practices. It was the line Harry Wright also espoused, when he, in 1878, reassured Syracuse president Robert Townsend that, as regards to the International Association, "no written or spoken thing has been put forth by a member of the League in which a motive for oppression can be traced."[11]

There is little doubt the International Association was hurt by some of its own narrow-sighted policies. The organization permitted exhibition games between member clubs during the regular season, something that certainly must have eroding public confidence in its caliber of play. The Association's policy of splitting gate receipts 50/50 between home and visiting teams was, in effect, also a subsidy for its weaker clubs, many of whom were financially "exhausted by one trip around the circle and a couple of rainy days."[12]

Even more irresponsible was the Association's requirement that all clubs guarantee visiting teams at least $75, an arrangement that allowed some visiting teams to frequently make more than their host clubs, especially in the Association's poorer drawing communities. It wasn't long before a number of International Association clubs realized it was actually far more lucrative to play away from home, while still others saw an opportunity to outright "swindle" their colleagues by playing as many road games as possible and then disbanding to avoid having to pay any guarantees during their home games. Pittsburgh and Binghamton pulled this against a number of the Association's New England clubs, "leaving the New England clubs to whistle for that $150 guarantee" they felt they were entitled to. The policy seems to have specifically brought down the Association's Live Oak club, of Lynn, Massachusetts, and was so disliked by the New Bedford manager, Frank Brancroft, that he initially refused to allow his club to join the International Association.[13]

It was the first of many savvy moves Bancroft would make on his way to earning a reputation as the "great American manager" during this highly opportunistic era of organized baseball. As the game's first hard and true "bottom line man," Bancroft demonstrated exceptional fiscal savvy in operational matters as well as a relentless flair for promotional original-ity. He continually promised "big money" to all clubs that would come to New Bedford, proclaiming, on the club letterhead, that this was the "best paying" baseball city in New England. To make sure his club lived up to this claim, he minimized hotel expenses by having his team travel in sleep-ing cars, once defaulted on a guarantee he owed Harry Wright and even managed to talk Hulbert out of imposing a ban on his club for playing a team that employed an expelled National League player. There was little doubt Bancroft had a far broader and more opportunistic baseball out-look than Hulbert, as evidenced by his successful baseball excursion to Cuba in 1878, the first of its kind, and even bolder, though unfulfilled, plan to take a baseball team to Australia.[14]

But even with the International Association's organizational weak-nesses well before its eyes, the National League wasn't about to assume a stance of non-intervention towards its competitor, notwithstanding any public declarations to the contrary. Almost as soon as plans for the Inter-national Association had begun to take shape Hulbert was confiding to Campbell Bishop "we ought to frustrate the International scheme and get control of all professional ball playing."[15]

The plan that Hulbert developed to bring down the International Association was a strange, ongoing, almost trial and error combination of feigned cooperation, individual enticement, and outright antagonism, a battle plan that was sometimes thinly veiled as official League policy while, at other times, was executed in secrecy and intrigue.

The easiest way to sidetrack the International Association was to dis-engage its strongest clubs from the organization for a, preferably, subor-dinate relationship within the National League. This was, in fact, the purpose of the League Alliance, a sort of mutual protection agreement the National League offered non–League clubs, guaranteeing their contracts and offering priority rights when playing National League teams, though not allowing them to play for the League championship. Hulbert hoped the Alliance would "draw the strong from the International movement" but it seemed to be popular with just a few western clubs such as Indi-anapolis, Milwaukee and Pittsburgh, only the Syracuse Stars joining from the east. The championship tournament the Alliance sponsored in 1877 was also no credit to itself, with its participants, Syracuse, Indianapolis, and the Alleghenies of Pittsburgh all conspiring to play a series of blatantly cor-rupt games, first in Pittsburgh and then again in Chicago.[16]

With the League Alliance holding little attraction for International Association clubs, Hulbert, just before the 1878 season, took a more direct approach in fomenting dissension among its membership by extending to six of its strongest clubs, Buffalo, Syracuse, Rochester, London, Lowell and Springfield, preferential treatment in their games with the National League. Under this agreement, known as the "Buffalo Compact" from the city where it was signed, the National League not only permitted these International Association clubs to charge 25 cents for home games against the National League rather than the mandatory 50 cent fee the League required from other non–League clubs, but also extended to the signatories priority rights for games with National League teams after September. The arrangement didn't, as the *Sunday Mercury* prophesied, lead to the immediate downfall of the International Association but it was successful in orientating its strongest clubs to the National League's sphere of influence, two of which, Buffalo and Syracuse, eventually joining the League at the end of that season.[17]

For those International Association clubs recalcitrant enough to resist subordination through either the League Alliance or the Buffalo Compact, the National League implemented a number of counter measures—some of questionable morality—to hinder, injure or outright disrupt their normal day-to-day operations. Beginning in 1878 the National League required a $100 guarantee from all Association clubs wishing to play League teams. This financial requirement was actually not as onerous as the ones Harry Wright had demanded for games with his Boston club during their National Association days, but the National League requirement applied to all its clubs, strong or weak, in an unconditional manner, an arrangement that put increased financial strain on the weaker International Association clubs.[18]

To further deny International Association clubs the financial and competitive benefits of contact with the National League, Hulbert, that same year, persuaded the other League clubs to adopt a controversial non-intercourse policy, which extended the National League's prohibition against playing outside clubs on League grounds during the regular season to pre and post season games as well. The policy was harshly criticized from all quarters, but Harry Wright justified it on the grounds it would make games between League clubs "of equal interest." However it was explained to the sporting public, the action, coupled with Hulbert's decision to expand the National League's schedule from 60 to 84 games in 1879 (which, he claimed, would make home games for all League clubs "more remunerative"), drastically curtailing competitive contacts between the two leagues, a development far more injurious to the International Association in terms of both financial viability and competitive respectability.[19]

In its dealing with individual International Association clubs, something that didn't seem to come under as much public scrutiny as its policy

positions, the National League was far more negligent of ethical considerations. Though the League, starting in 1877, honored, as a matter of
principle, non–League contracts after March 15, in practice it never hes-
itated to use whatever means it could to hire away promising players from
International Association clubs while preventing League players from
jumping to its competitor. Hulbert's advice to Cleveland president J.F.
Evans, who wanted to sign away a contracted International Association
player, revealed the League's turn-a-blind-eye stance in this issue, the
Chicago president noting such a move "would prove to be bad, but you
must be your own judge on the matter." The International Association
was certainly not amiss to the more sinister side of Hulbert's motives here,
with their secretary, J. A. Williams, releasing to the *Clipper* a telegram of
Hulbert's in which the League president openly declared "get all the men
you can of the Association, and break up ... the concern, if you can."[20]

It was advice National League clubs began to follow with greater fre-
quency and boldness during the late 1870s. Milwaukee was forced to back
down in its attempt to lure away George Bradley from New Bedford, but
Providence was successful in stealing away Dan O'Leary from the Association's Manchester, New Hampshire, club. By an outright "act of piracy"
Boston, in 1877, signed away two contracted players from the Lowells, but
Harry Wright's club even went beyond this in its attempts to get the
National's best players in 1880, persuading Hulbert to expel the strong
Washington, D.C., club from the League Alliance on the pretext of an
unpaid guarantee to Cleveland. At their Rochester meeting earlier that
year the National League clubs had reportedly even divvied up the Nation-
als' players among themselves in anticipation of this move.[21]

There didn't seem to be much the International Association could do
to protect itself from the League's "oppression," nor could it expect, by
this point, that public opinion would effectively deter the League from its
practices. In his attempt to sign away a player from the Albany club, the
president of the League's Troy franchise, in 1880, had no qualms in publicly admitting he "would do things in base ball that he would not do in
any other business."[22]

The International Association did try to present a unified opposition
to the League's incursions during the highly publicized Alex McKinnon
affair in 1879, but the League was even able to turn this to its advantage.
The National League had expelled McKinnon for jumping from Troy to
the International Association's Rochester club, a move that prevented
League clubs from not only playing Rochester but every other International Association club that had ever played Rochester. Despite the lost
financial opportunities this ban imposed upon them, the International

Association clubs firmly stood behind Rochester until it was discovered that Hulbert, through a secret arrangement with Rochester president Asa Soule, had allowed the Rochesters to reorganize and void the League's ban, a revelation that left a deep feeling of betrayal among other International Association clubs.[23]

In time, the National League's persistent and relentless attempts to thwart the International Association at every twist and turn paid off. By skimming off the Association's best talent, and restricting their competitive opportunities, the National League was able to firmly solidify its position of competitive superiority. In 1878 League clubs lost only 34 times to non–League teams, a number that fell to 20 the following year. Even with renewed competitive contacts that season, the National League lost only 31 games to outside clubs in 1880, strong evidence that the International Association clubs, by this time, "have lost valuable grounds in the race for public confidence and patronage with the League."[24]

Unable to secure a competitive standing comparable to the League, and highly vulnerable to its constrictive financial policies, most International Association clubs couldn't avoid insolvency. Throughout 1878 the Association experienced a "spontaneous combustion" of failure and disbandment within its ranks. The Tecumsehs, the International Association's champions in 1877, folded that August, as did the Hornells, followed closely by Binghamton, Manchester and Lowell. If Hartfords hadn't stepped forward to replace New Bedford and Worcester to replace the Live Oaks of Lynn during mid-season, the Association would probably not have survived to the end of the season.[25]

A number of anti–National League observers, most notably the *Clipper*, still held out hope the International Association (renamed, in 1879, the National Association after its sole international representative, the Tecumsehs, disbanded) could still become a viable organization, even going so far as to assure the public the National Association, with its more patron-friendly 25 cent ticket prices, was "making the money this year."[26]

Even if the nine clubs that represented the National Association in 1879 had put themselves on a more financially secure footing, they were still unable to do much about the National League's continued attempts to destabilize them. With its nearby rivals Buffalo, Syracuse and Troy (all of whom had used the International Association, it was charged, just as a "stepping stone" to join the League) now all in the National League, Utica found itself cut off from its traditional competitive contacts and was soon forced to disband. Springfield couldn't survive without games with the National League in September while Manchester, which had reorganized that season, saw its best players move on to the National League.[27]

By the end of 1879 even the National Association's "survivors" that came together in New York to plan next year's schedule must have realized that, by now, "the League is still and always will be on top." Over the winter, sporting publications reported a virtual "stampede" of National Association clubs clamoring to get into the National League. Some, like Worcester and Troy, were successful, others, like Springfield, were not, all leaving the National Association to start its 1880 season with no more than three members, Albany, the Nationals of Washington, D.C., and Baltimore. Even by trying to work through their schedule on "a go-as-you please style" that year it was soon apparent these remaining clubs, by mid-summer, were all "having a hard time this season." Baltimore was soon forced into insolvency while the Albany club officers were eventually forced to admit "unless, and until, Albany can get into the League they had better leave base ball severely alone."[28]

Only the Nationals, perhaps embittered by the League's rejection of their application early in 1880, continued to hold out. The club was a strong one, having beaten the League champion Chicago team six out of eleven times in 1880. But the club was so far off the major baseball travel routes it was forced to play most of its home games in Springfield and some even at Coney Island, where it hoped to "intercept" League clubs as they passed through the eastern corridor. "Adrift like a base ball comet" and with the National League plotting to get its players, the Nationals, by July, saw no other alternative than to join the League Alliance, finally ensuring that the National Association was "now nothing more than a myth."[29]

The National League owed much of its success against the International/National Association to a growing appreciation of the importance of collective, unified, action. Individual clubs were beginning to realize objectives came easier for those willing to concede a measure of autonomy for the "mutual interests" of the League as a whole.[30]

This must not have been easy given the intense competitive rivalry that existed among individual League clubs, and the general impression any drift towards a closer, more interdependent, arrangement among these clubs only worked to the personal benefit of Hulbert and his Chicago organization.

In some matters, like operational efficiency, it was fairly easy to establish uniform consent. Bargaining as a single commercial unit, the League was able to negotiate favorable railroad rates in 1879 and hotel rates a year later. League clubs agreed on a uniform per diem meal and board deduction for all its players in 1877 and, in 1880, even agreed to the short-lived experiment of adopting a single, League-wide, style of uniform. Turnstiles, mandated for all League grounds in 1877, ensured fair dealing between members over ticket receipts, while a no rain checks policy, adopted in 1879, forbade any ticket refunds for games in which more than an inning had been completed. The latter policy certainly must have been lucrative for League clubs but it also proved to be as unpopular with patrons as the League's stodgy ban, in 1881, on club nicknames.[31]

Mutual consent also smoothed over one of the more contentious issues among League members, umpire appointment and qualification. Since the days of the old National Association, clubs had reserved the right to nominate their own umpires, an arrangement that encouraged a less than impartial relationship between umpires and players, especially for those umpires who routinely socialized and traveled with teams, like Dicky Pearce, who would occasionally even practice with players from his nominating club.[32]

Quality was also an issue. With the typical umpire earning a meager $5 per game, some observers were concerned the profession was attracting only "the bum category," biased, negligent, poorly trained individuals like the ex–Troy player Phil Powers, who would show up to umpire games "in his shirt sleeves, usually with a dirty shirt at that, with seedy 'hand-me-downs.'"[33]

Fearful "the days of base ball are numbered unless the present system of umpiring is done away with" the League transferred the nominating process from individual clubs to the central office at the end of 1880 and, at the League's annual meeting in 1882, further dignified and elevated the profession by hiring four full-time umpires at the attractive salary of $1,000 per year.[34]

League clubs were also, by now, beginning to recognize that a positive public image sometimes necessitated a sacrifice in economic autonomy. The League's 50 cent ticket price had established this precedent years earlier, on the claim that baseball games as played by the National League "were better, had better surroundings and were conducted in a way to give more general satisfaction to the public." Even Henry Chadwick, a long time critic of the 50 cent policy had, by 1881, come around to believe any reduction in the price of pro games would "lower the character of attendance."[35]

The policy, however, still had its critics, even within League ranks, especially from the newer National League clubs, such as Buffalo, Syracuse and Worcester, all of whom had built their spectator base upon the more popular 25 cent ticket price. Buffalo tried to get the policy revoked at the 1879 National League meeting while Worcester passed up on its initial opportunity to join the League that year because of the requirement. Even the *Cincinnati Enquirer*, typically a hard liner on this matter, came to feel, in the face of an ever widening popular interest in pro baseball, that the 50 cent rule had become little more than "a managers mutual protection association."[36]

Once again, however, Hulbert, staunchly declaring that "once let the price of admission be lowered and the respectability of game is gone," took steps to prevent any drift away from League policy. While apparently showing some sensitivity to individual market conditions (he considered allowing Worcester into the League at a special 35 cent ticket rate, and had authorized, a few years earlier, Cincinnati's request to charge 25 cents for children), Hulbert was unwavering in his belief that baseball's image was so closely tied to high ticket prices the League simply "cannot afford to discount it." It was on this justification that he made sure 50 cent ticket prices, which had hereto only been an unofficial requirement among League clubs, became part of the National League constitution at the League's meeting in 1879.[37]

Hulbert also took upon himself, almost as a personal mission, defense of the League's good name against the more powerful financial temptations of Sunday games and on-premise liquor sales. A fair number of League clubs, among them St. Louis, Troy, Syracuse and even, at one time, Chicago itself, had, at one time or another, tapped into these revenue sources despite the League's standing impression that "Base-ball ... is supported by a class of people by whom these practices [beer sales, Sunday games] are regarded as an abomination." By this time most League clubs, however, were willing to comply with the National League's stance against these practices and readily passed Hulbert's insistence that liquor sales and Sunday games be constitutionally prohibited at the League's 1880 meeting.[38]

There was only one dissenting voice to all this: Cincinnati, an opponent who would prove to be particularly troublesome for Hulbert. Domiciled in a city with a strong tradition of the continental Sunday, and whose president, Justin Thorner, was a local brewery owner, the Cincinnati club had, by 1880, become heavily dependent upon the revenues generated from on-premise beer sales and rental of its grounds to local amateur clubs for their Sunday games. With the club going through severe organizational and financial difficulties over the 1879 season, which eventually had it "roaming somewhere around in the Eastern states like an animal without a keeper," Cincinnati officers were understandably opposed to Hulbert's proposed prohibition on Sunday games and beer sales, whose adoption would have reduced club revenues by nearly $3,000.[39]

Despite intense backroom negotiations, and considerable arm-twisting by Hulbert himself, the Cincinnati directors refused to back down from their demand "no beer, no ball," leaving the other League clubs little choice than to officially expel the club, a move that was upheld at the League's 1880 annual meeting. The whole affair represented the League's most serious crisis since the Louisville scandal, not the least because, for the first time, someone had actively resisted the League's claim it could pre-empt a club's autonomy over its local market. It must have been with a sense of relief that Hulbert, once the expulsion had been finalized, was able to telegraph Spalding "the delegate we feared the most won't swallow the whole hog."[40]

Hulbert also had to exert considerable personal influence and pressure to align member clubs behind his plans to extend direct League authority over its entire pool of players, a self professed proclamation that "its players are to be as much a matter of League concern as the enforcement of the obligations assumed by clubs and players."[41]

Initially this amounted to little more than attempts to restrict and curtail the growing economic freedom and influence among the game's top players, which the League tried to portray as excessive and financially unjustified. Capitalizing on the growing popular perception that most pro baseballers, well paid for only seven months of stressless work, had now become "pampered children of luxury," who, in the course of their playing, "take in the beautiful country east and west in pleasant pilgrimages, to live on the fat of the land and to have a jolly high monkey-monk of a time generally."[42]

Much of this was rhetorical, but over the years a number of pro players had tried to leverage their market value in such an abusive way as to incite official action, among them John Clapp who, in 1876, had put himself "on the auction block" trying to optimize his salary offers by playing clubs off against each other. The O'Rourke brothers of Boston used a similar tactic to win exemptions from their per diem traveling and uniform deductions, while the notorious James Devlin canvassed so many clubs fishing for offers he was nicknamed "telegram" Devlin. These were all incidents that made the fraternity vulnerable to the growing impression pro players were becoming "little better than pensioners on the stock holders bounty."[43]

Over the years club owners had resorted to a variety of maneuvers, some rather unscrupulous, to get players "down off their high horses." Chicago attempted, in 1871, to pressure Ned Cuthbert into signing by withholding his backpay, while Boston, in 1882, tried to get Tom Deasley to sign by intimidating his wife.[44]

It wasn't until Hulbert — going on the no-nonsense managerial principle that "the belief in phenoms has pretty much passed away, and, instead, there is faith in hard work, and plenty of it" — began to assert his authority as League president that the National League undertook a systematic and unified effort to control their labor supply. After 1878 League clubs were no longer permitted to extend winter advances to their players, a policy Chicago had been strictly enforcing over the previous two seasons. As of that year salaried players were also forbidden to represent their clubs at League meetings, and, beginning in 1880, all players were required to sign uniform League-wide contracts, documents which also allowed League clubs to unilaterally release a player on a mere 20 days notice.[45]

Firmly set in his belief that "what is good for the League is good for ball-players," Hulbert also pushed through his most controversial player control policy, the reserve clause, at the League's 1879 meeting. This provision, known at that time as "the five man rule," permitted each National League club to designate five players who could not be signed by any other League club, in effect, establishing a sort of "back door" residency requirement that indefinitely bound these five players to their nominating club.[46]

Being, initially, a provisional agreement among League clubs, not a constitutional requirement, the reserve clause didn't arouse much controversy until it came up for renewal at the 1880 League meeting in Rochester. Cincinnati and Buffalo strongly opposed its renewal while Boston was on the fence, a predicament that seemed to make it impossible to garner the unanimous vote necessary for its renewal. But through some deft back room maneuvering in which Boston was promised Charles Snyder for its support, Buffalo John Clapp for its backing, and with Cincinnati expelled before the matter was put to a vote, Hulbert was eventually able to maneuver the provision through for renewal.[47]

Well aware that the moral deficiencies from not only the old National Association but also his own League's Louisville scandal were still fresh in the public's mind, Hulbert felt the National League finally had to do more than simply regulate players, it also had to enforce a code of "moral standards" over everything they did, on and off the field. While the old National Association had never presumed to impose any code of personal behavior upon its players, the National League now squarely demanded that its members become "exemplars of the game," not just workers performing their job well, but "princes of the game and honorable men in the full sense of the word."[48]

In itself this would have been a commendable expectation if League officers believed their players were fully amenable to moral self responsibility. But given management's almost uniform opinion, during this period, that the typical pro baseballer was "merely a grown boy" who "has no more sense than an army mule" and, consequently, had to be coerced and intimidated into acceptable behavior, these expectations soon aroused intense labor/management antagonism.[49]

The Providence directors certainly didn't disguise their contempt for the pro players on their team, who, they believed, "have been treated like gentlemen, as though their feelings must not be hurt, instead of being used like men hired to play ball." But these were rather generous sentiments compared to Hulbert's opinion of the fraternity. Whether he was demeaning the less objectionable players with such caustic nicknames as "Simpleton-Kelly" and "Sinful-Nolan," or openly condemning the most offensive as a "superhuman brat," there is little doubt Hulbert, at least on the basis of his correspondence, held a uniformly low opinion of those who represented the national game, unabashedly declaring to Arthur Soden, "the players as a class are worthless scalawags."[50]

To a certain extent the National League may have simply been trying to avoid what it saw transpire within its rival the International Association where a loose, undisciplined and largely unregulated attitude towards discipline had incited many of the Association's players to hold their managers in "utter contempt." But the objectionable behavior of numerous players within the National League itself, during these years, also didn't do anything to redeem the fraternity's poor public reputation.[51]

Generally speaking, concern over player misbehavior, by this time, had progressed beyond the traditional abuses of self-interest as commonly practiced by ballplayers (like Ed "The Only" Nolan's feigned injuries to get his release from an undesirable club) to the more comprehensive matter of character deficiencies, primarily drunkenness, the scourge of the 19th century ballplaying fraternity. The *Chicago Tribune* might have been able to find humor in a social issue all too well known to the general public in mockingly declaring "whisky — bad whisky, indeed very bad whisky — was not entirely a stranger to Arthur [Allison, of Cincinnati Reds' fame]. Had he taken good Bourbon instead of Cincinnati kill-me-quick, no one in Kentucky would have been angry with him." But observers of that time could hardly laugh away its effects on ball players like Mike Burke who, in 1878, once came to the ballfield so roaring drunk he assaulted his captain.[52]

At a time in American history when a developed sense of social welfare was still well in the future, it's not surprising such expressions of personal irresponsibility could hardly expect any public sympathy even in their most regrettable forms. So we can only assume the *Cincinnati Enquirer*, on learning that the unemployed, alcoholic, former Springfield pro ballplayer William Root had hung himself while in jail, was fully reflecting public sentiment in its pitiless, almost cold-blooded, declaration, "We commend Mr. Root's example."[53]

During the National League's first few years of existence the matter of player discipline had been largely left to individual clubs, whose policies differed widely in regard to both the identification and punishment of offenses. Many clubs only recognized breach of contract as a punishable offense, but Chicago would dock its players a percentage of their salaries for every game they missed even from illness or injury. In their attempt to head off trouble before it began, some officers, like Hulbert, had Pinkerton detectives watch over suspected players, while others, like the Indianapolis directors, had no qualms about opening their player's mail and telegrams.[54]

Set in his belief that the time had now come for "strict accountability" in player actions and behavior, Hulbert unveiled, at the League's 1880 Rochester meeting, a specific code of player conduct that was as sweeping in its demands as it was harsh in its penalties. In addition to the more obvious offenses as breach of contract, players could now be expelled on the more subjective offenses of "dissipation and general insubordination," as well as simple "indifference" in their play and conduct. Central to this new code was its strict and unqualified pronouncement that drunkenness was now "a positive disqualification in a ball player."[55]

In "applying the knife" to misconduct Hulbert took the further step, a year later, of ensuring uniform enforcement of the League's disciplinary code by pushing through an official blacklist that forbade any National League club from hiring players expelled from another League club. In practice the blacklist wasn't as effective a deterrent to player misconduct as anticipated, but Hulbert seemed satisfied that its very adoption had gone a long way to "publicly throw overboard" what he saw as "the worthless ungrateful low lived whelps" within the League's player ranks.[56]

Hulbert's unilateral attempt to legislate morality upon League players didn't transpire without some dissenting voices, both within and without his organization. From the earliest days of professionalism club management could hardly avoid accusations of hypocrisy in their self-appointed role as both moral judge and jury. William Craver, expelled from Chicago in 1871 for not coming up to the club's behavior expectations, sarcastically suggested that club directors "talk less about conduct becoming gentlemen and put in a little more practice in that direction." The Buffalo press may have followed the National League line when its club was in the fold, but in earlier years it could caustically proclaim, on the League's attempt to expel players to whom it owed backpay, "and this is the immaculate League."[57]

Some observers were sympathetic to the player's plight (among them the *Boston Herald*, which declared "no player with any self-respect would consent to be so completely under the subjugation of the manager") while still others openly advocated active resistance, the *Cincinnati Enquirer* declaring any players who didn't oppose the League's reserve clause "deserve to be slaves with the courage of a dog." For the most part, however, players had little recourse to the League's oppressive policies. After the failure of the National Association in 1880 the National League effectively became the only viable employment market for professional ballplayers, a situation that allowed it to proceed "on its way rejoicing, with an overbearing independence."[58]

There had been talk of a Player Protection movement as early as 1876 and even threats to form an independent player league in 1880 if the reserve clause wasn't revoked. But there was little hope any of these plans could have succeeded without public sympathy, which, by this time, was squarely on the side of League management.[59]

Even Henry Chadwick, the League's most enduring critic, had become convinced, by 1881, the National League was now "the only organization crooked drunks or unreliable professionals fear." It was probably the most revealing indication the sporting public had, by now, come to accept the fact that the League's forceful and visible stance against all forms of corruption and player immorality "has condoned all their faults of legislative work."[60]

To secure its status as the country's representative baseball organization the National League had to not only keep its own member clubs in line and frustrate outside leagues, it also had to restrict its player's economic freedom, accomplishments that would hardly have been possible without the drive and tenacity of its president, William Hulbert, who continued to successfully leverage the economic and competitive strength of his Chicago club in the cause of his personal agenda.

Efficiently run by a mere thirty stockholders, who, in 1876 had secretly, if not illegally, rechartered the club for "compactness of interest," and prospering under a sweetheart lease arrangement with the city of Chicago, that reduced its yearly rent, on a million dollar piece of property, from $3,500 to $1,000, Chicago continued to be the National League's economic engine.[61]

Year in and year out the club attracted more spectators than any other National League club, a record 117,000 in 1882, proof positive, according to the *Chicago Tribune*, that "no city in America except Chicago ... can turn out such crowds."[62]

The rest of the League clubs were hardly in a position to resent this, with the Chicago fans, from the very first days of the National League, virtually bankrolling the rest of the League. Even with receipts from only a third of the Chicago gate (the League allowance for visiting clubs), Boston cleared $1,500 from its windy city games in 1880, Providence $1,800 from its first three Chicago games that same year, while Hartford cleared an impressive $4,000 on its Chicago stops in 1876. In one astonishing game, against Troy on July 4, 1882, Chicago alone took in more than all the other League clubs did in their games that day combined, giving the *Chicago Tribune* plenty of reasons to gloat "What would the rest of the League do without Chicago to help pay salaries and expenses?"[63]

Hulbert certainly had the resources to expect the best from his club, but he never seemed to take anything for granted. More than any other National League club of this period the White Stockings embodied the character of its taskmaster, a team run on the "Chicago plan," which could be effectively described as a culture of unquestioned obedience, intolerance of failure and an absolute expectation that the team perform "as one body. Its scores know no individuals." As someone who never "cared a snap" whether his players got along personally so long as they exerted maximum effort, Hulbert wasn't above ridiculing or intimidating anyone who came up short of these expectations, as he did with Paul Hines, threatening to send the underachieving outfielder home to his father "with half your salary" if his performance didn't improve.[64]

While putting forth his team as a model of "discipline and management" Hulbert also expected his players to extend their aggression to the very limits of competitive propriety. "Play the game with desperation" Hulbert advised Lew Brown, "knock your opponents off bases. Run, Run, Run ... kick for points but remember always that nothing wanton is to be done." Once known only for the ramrod "go for *everything*" type of ballplay he advocated during the National Association days, Hulbert, in his mature years in the National League, championed a more poised, collected force of effort "a nine that don't [sic] make e.a.c.p. [errors at critical points] and who can bat well enough to force the other fellows to make e.a.c.p-s."[65]

In the matter of playing innovations Chicago was also a trend setter, with its captain, Cap Anson, coming up with new tactical devices every season, among them the idea of rotating pitchers, which the White Stockings first introduced into League play during 1880. Even those thoroughly disapproving of the way Hulbert "runs the machine at full speed" had to concede "they [the White Stockings] can show a crowd more points in one game of ball than any other club in the country can during the season."[66]

If judged solely on the basis of end results Chicago was virtually above criticism altogether. Its 1880 team won 23 games in a row while running away with the pennant that year, a collection of players so strong some felt the team could have beaten a picked nine from all the other National League clubs that season. It was the first of three straight pennants Chicago would win between 1880 and 1882, establishing a baseball dynasty second only to Boston in its duration and one that was no less respected throughout the baseball fraternity (every pro ballplayer, it was claimed, wanted to play for Chicago). Whatever resentment critics or competitors may have felt towards Hulbert's team, there was no questioning the fact that the sporting public as a whole "never fails to be excited by the kind of ball play the White Stockings are doing."[67]

The players may have made Chicago a winner on the field but it was Hulbert who was "entitled to *all* the credit" for building his organization and its civic identity into "the representative base ball city of the country." It was this culture of success and anticipation of only success that, year after year, reinforced Hulbert's confidence and certainty that he had it right with the baseball business. "I know the value of this enterprise," he confided to Nick Young at the end of the 1880 season, "I could get a living for a ball team on a barren rock when another would fail in a city of 1,000,000 people."[68]

Chicago's competitive and economic dominance of the National League provided Hulbert with a powerful weapon to influence and direct the League's policies, something he used frequently, effectively, and controversially during his tenure as League president, a position he had assumed at the end of the League's first season.

It would be a great mistake to assume that Hulbert, as the duly elected League president, was under any mandate to pursue his policies with impartiality or any concern for the mutual well-being of all National League clubs as a whole. At almost every twist and turn, at almost every policy juncture, Hulbert seemed to be motivated by a single overriding directive: "what is good for base ball in Chicago is good for the league as a whole."[69]

In effect, Hulbert was simply integrating the League's policy objectives with Chicago's perceived historical destiny in American baseball. Chicago needed strong, viable opponents, especially out east, and, to this end, Hulbert did usually work for the mutual benefit and interests of member clubs. But Chicago's existence as a baseball competitor also demanded that it alone dominate this, or any other, league arrangement, and to this end Hulbert worked vigorously and relentlessly in asserting the interests of his club by using virtually any means to ensure all League decisions resulted in, as one critic put it, "turkey for himself and buzzard for the other [National League] clubs."[70]

It was clear neither Hulbert nor his successors at Chicago felt constrained by either official constitutional requirements or the niceties of accepted business practices in working for Chicago's interests. To reduce expenses Hulbert changed, without authorization, Chicago's schedule with Milwaukee in 1878, and persuaded Indianapolis to also transfer one of its home games to Chicago that same year. At a critical juncture in the 1882 pennant race Chicago also persuaded Buffalo to transfer three of its home games to Chicago in exchange for an extra generous cut of gate receipts. That same year Chicago virtually forced Cleveland to also switch one of its home games to Chicago, typical Hulbert-like behavior according to the *Cleveland Plain Dealer*, which charged "the Chicago club management, when not busy with trying to boss every other club in the League, is endeavoring to cheat all the rest in some way."[71]

Hulbert showed himself to be no less unscrupulous in the brutal competition for top player talent. Chicago's reputation for virtually stealing away contracted players from non–League clubs was known far and wide ("every country club has one good bat," the *Chicago Tribune* boasted, "which he [Anson, the Chicago captain] invariably confiscates for the King's service"). But the club also had no qualms about trying to obtain talented players from other League clubs any way it could. In direct violation of League rules, Hulbert tried to swap players to get Milwaukee's stand-out catcher Charlie Bennett and, in 1879, double-crossed the Troy managers by signing Fred Goldsmith, a move that seemed to virtually confirm the general impression that "He [Hulbert] can steal players and it's all right."[72]

And if anyone believed a respect for the dignity of his office would possibly deter Hulbert from some of these practices, they were quite mistaken. As League president Hulbert often had access to inside information on the status of member clubs ("I have an intimate knowledge of the internal conditions as to the finances of many clubs" he boasted to one correspondent), information that he didn't hesitate to use to his advantage in securing top players from League clubs that were about to fail. Acting on the knowledge that Indianapolis was about to disband at the end of 1878, Hulbert sent Spalding into the city "in a mysterious manner" to secretly sign away its best players before any other League club even knew Indianapolis was in financial trouble.[73]

Hulbert repeated this same strategy with Syracuse, secretly signing away one of its star players before any other League club was aware Syracuse had disbanded, a move he justified on the grounds all players from disbanded clubs were "public property" and consequently available on a strictly first-come-first-served basis. It was even rumored Hulbert had agents strategically stationed in all National League cities who could quickly move in, on a telegram's notice, and sign unreserved players as soon as they were known at the League's annual meeting.[74]

One National League club in particular, Cincinnati, Hulbert seemed to look on as virtually his own personal fiefdom, exploiting a strange relationship of unilateral trust, dependence and an unrealistic sense of self-importance. From the time Cincinnati first returned to professional baseball in 1876 Hulbert always seemed to be something of a shadow director for the club, an ominous relation given the fact that Cincinnati's own management was either incapable or unwilling to assert its own responsibilities. In exchange for arranging Cincinnati's schedule and representing it at League meetings, Hulbert seemed to have obligated Cincinnati president Sid Keck, a meat packer with limited abilities as a baseball manager, to unquestioned allegiance to Chicago policies, which he showed by backing, in 1877, Hulbert's proposed schedule as well as his move to adopt a more lively League ball (which would help Chicago's heavy hitters).[75]

If Cincinnati officers believed such a supportive relationship with Hulbert had safeguarded them from his self-interested scheming they were rudely awakened soon after the 1877 season began. This Cincinnati team, like the inept, incompetent one of a year earlier, was soon "found sucking the hind teat" with an equally deteriorating financial situation that was compounded by the severe downturn Keck's own business was going through at that time. Hulbert was not only well aware of Keck's personal problems, he was one of the few who knew Cincinnati hadn't paid its $100 League dues, inside information he hid from other League clubs by asking National League secretary Nick Young to "overlook for a time the default of the Cincinnati Club" and not notify anyone of its true status.[76]

Well aware that Cincinnati was, technically, not a member of the League, Hulbert quickly moved to exploit the situation. He secretly sent Lewis Meacham into Cincinnati in early June and had the reporter sign away two of the club's best players, Joe Hallinan and Charley Jones, by convincing them Cincinnati was on the verge of disbanding. The entire incident caused an outrage in baseball circles, especially among Cincinnati's new directors, who had replaced Keck and come up with sufficient funding to keep the club in the League. After a stormy meeting with Cincinnati officers, Hulbert, while still claiming full legal justification for his raid, eventually agreed to return Jones, though not until he'd played for Chicago in two critical games against St. Louis. The entire incident was a classic example of Hulbert's ability to exploit member clubs to Chicago's advantage without going so far as to destroy their viability as stable competitors. As the *St. Louis Globe* clearly recognized, it was a situation where Chicago "wants Jones and also wants the Cincinnati Club to exist."[77]

In this instance and others Hulbert's schemes were indirectly encouraged by Cincinnati's unrealistic opinion of its self-importance to the

League. By the end of the 1879 season, with its new, and equally incapable, president J.M. Neff "disgusted with base ball," Cincinnati was again in serious financial difficulties and in danger of dropping out of the National League. The *Cincinnati Enquirer*, however, was so self-deluded about the club's importance to the League it claimed "he'll [Hulbert] cry for it as a baby cries for its tin whistle" if Cincinnati were allowed to fail. At one time this may have been true, but in this instance it virtually conceded to Hulbert a right to plunder the club once again. Acting as Neff's representative at the League meeting that year, Hulbert quickly moved to sign away its up-and-coming star Mike Kelly, a move that, once known, led to Neff's wholesale condemnation as "a cat's paw of Hulbert."[78]

When he wasn't directly exploiting other League clubs for his benefit, Hulbert was strong-arming them to stay on the straight and narrow with League policies, even when this was beginning to reach a point of demanding considerable financial self-sacrifice.

Bristling under Hulbert's persistent and uncompromising demand it charge 50 cents for tickets, a policy that would eventually lead to the club's downfall, Syracuse knew first hand that "no one is more responsible for the arrogant position which the League assumes ... than President Hulbert." Directors of the Troy club were also incensed at Hulbert's demand that they desist from all competitive contacts with their nearby rival Albany to satisfy the League's policy prohibiting member clubs from playing any regular season games against anyone within five miles of their home grounds. The dispute was eventually resolved in Troy's favor but the local press was so infuriated with Hulbert it wistfully demanded "will someone kindly choke the fellow."[79]

By far the most controversial of Hulbert's directives was his non-intercourse decree, pushed through at the 1877 League meeting, that forbade any National League club from playing outside teams on League grounds, even before the regular National League season had begun or after it had finished. Adopted on the rather vague justification that this would make games among league clubs "of equal interest," the policy was, in reality, a thinly veiled attempt to deny the International Association most of the competitive and financial benefits it could gain from its contacts with the League.[80]

It appears Hulbert was only able to slip the policy through because the new League clubs admitted that year (Hartford, St. Louis, and Louisville had dropped out while Hulbert himself represented Cincinnati) didn't appear ready to challenge the constitutionality of the move, more proof, according to the *Sunday Mercury*, that "whenever the Chicago Club has an object to accomplish it is always attained while the [National League] constitution is thrown to the four winds."[81]

Only as the 1878 season was about to begin did the rest of the League clubs begin to realize the bad predicament they had got themselves into. Providence manager Ben Douglas, realizing his team would have to head west without the financial assistance of stop-over games against non–League teams, complained to Harry Wright "it's a long jump from Prov[idence] to Chicago without getting one cent." Even the League's western clubs, reportedly strong supporters of the policy, began to waver once they realized its full financial ramifications. Cincinnati president J.M. Neff, for one, objected that his club "will lose considerable money this season" because it won't be able to host pre-season games.[82]

Harry Wright seems to have been in favor of the policy, but his sentiment didn't seem to be shared by all the Boston club directors or the eastern press, the *Boston Globe* declaring Hulbert's competitive restrictions had made the National League entirely "too exclusive for the average Yankee." Boston and Providence were actually able to get around the prohibition during pre-season by hosting Harvard and Yale under the guise of "picked nines," but discontent towards the policy had, by midseason, become so widespread it began to loom as a very real danger to League unity.[83]

Fueled by the growing belief that profitability would only be possible if the National League were divided into separate east-west circuits, the eastern press began to openly advocate, following the *Boston Herald*, that "the sooner it is done [breakup of the National League] the better" it would be for pro baseball. It was a disturbing sentiment even for the *Clipper*, which knew the dissolution of the League's bedrock Chicago/Boston axis would virtually ensure the organization would degenerate into little more than a "sectional organization."[84]

With dissatisfaction over his non-intercourse policy growing so intense that the very breakup of the National League "was seriously discussed" at the League's annual meeting in 1878, even Hulbert himself couldn't prevent member clubs from overruling his policy at that meeting, the first, and only, major policy setback Hulbert would experience during his tenure as League president.[85]

Given such an atmosphere of resentment and animosity towards Chicago's domineering authority over the League, it shouldn't be surprising that dissatisfied observers welcomed and celebrated every indication of that club's weakness or decline. Chicago's competitive failings in 1877 gave the Philadelphia *Sunday Republic*, perhaps still smarting from the League's high-handed treatment of its Athletics, a chance to declare "where, oh where is the high-handed Hubrart [sic] ... perhaps when he gets his wires all pulled he will be able to astonish somebody." Another casualty of League policies, Syracuse, lashed out at Chicago's failed pennant hopes in 1879, sarcastically exclaiming "Dr. Schliemann is digging in the ruins of Troy and the *Chicago Times* thinks that perhaps he will be able to find the remains of its baseball club."[86]

Not to be outdone in expressing anti–Chicago sentiment, the Cincinnati press, that same year, analogized the White Stockings' misfortunes to Chicago's own presumptions of grandeur. "Chicago is a great city," the *Cincinnati Enquirer* sneered, "It has an extended lake front and exposed rear ... the city has a daily journal that on one occasion published with each number ninety-six pages, all but four of which were filled with delinquent tax lists."[87]

Towards Hulbert himself the baseball fraternity, even within League ranks, couldn't avoid a posture of contemptuous deference. Though known to his admirers, even by this time, as the "father of the League," Hulbert was, to Troy, "the great 'I Am' of the League," to St. Louis, the "base ball pope," whose comprehensive, yet self-effacing, tyranny over the League the *St. Louis Globe-Democrat* could hardly tolerate. "The Boss [Hulbert] says 'my club will win the championship,'" the paper reported, with the jabbing reply, "Which does he mean? He owns eight."[88]

But perhaps the strongest testimony to the effectiveness of Hulbert's style and personality can be seen in the fact no one ever seriously challenged his leadership. Year after year even through frequently "stormy and inharmonious" League meetings Hulbert was re-elected president, a half-hearted opposition, in 1879, by Providence president Henry Root, a "mean, narrow-minded, revengeful man," being easily and decisively turned back.[89]

Only a resolute, unanimous insistence by the other League clubs, in fact, prevented Hulbert from voluntarily stepping down from the presidency in 1880, by which time, however, he seems to have become quite accommodating to, and unaffected by, the administrative shortcomings and ineptitude of his colleagues. "Your business must continue to be entrusted to a lot of brainless jackasses," he confided to the president of the Cincinnati club, "but after all, there is excitement."[90]

By the fourth year of his tenure as president Hulbert had gone a long way in solidifying, with his contradictory management style, the National League's "remarkable instinct for self-preservation," a style that, on the one hand, publicly professed only highly principled conduct while, on the other, was willing to unscrupulously disregard all proprieties for self-serving ends.[91]

So Hulbert could calmly and firmly assure his League colleagues "all my doings are above board" with his treatment of Cincinnati in 1877, at the very time the *Cincinnati Enquirer* was screaming his theft of Jones and Hallinan "should damn the institution [National League] for all its rottenness and deceitfulness past all redemption." And when Boston borrowed George Wright from Providence for a single game against Chicago in 1880, a move on firmer legal footing than Chicago's short term use of Hallinan and Jones against St. Louis in 1877, Hulbert had the temerity to condemn the action, which he claimed "broke faith not only with Chicago, but all clubs in the league" and was totally "devoid of the qualities of true sportsmen."[92]

Likewise, the man who at one point thought the very term baseball was "too common" a designation for such a great and elevated American sport allowed his club to offend the national conscience by playing a League game on the day of president Garfield's funeral, something that so outraged even the *Chicago Tribune* the paper vowed it would no longer "recognize the club as a Chicago institution" and refused to run any baseball reports for the next eight months.[93]

If the National League seemed to be an inherently contradictory institution this was as much a result of its conditions for survival as it was Hulbert's organizational zeal and vision. To maintain the integrity of its closed circuit format, the National League was virtually obligated to maintain a distortion in the American sporting culture, devoting all its resources to actively ensuring that "no first class club shall live outside the League and only eight shall live in the League."[94]

Unsustainable, if not socially unacceptable, as such an arrangement for pro baseball may have seemed to observers, both in and outside the League, Hulbert had made it a workable reality. The National League, under his tenure, had suppressed all alternative achievement centers (competing leagues), imposed a moral discrimination upon the game's patronage, restricted the free movement of ballplaying talent as well as the market responsiveness of member clubs, all accomplished in the name of "elevating" baseball.

To such long time baseball observers as the *Clipper* the entire way America's national game had developed into an institution, at its highest level of representation, committed to using whatever means were necessary to ensure a restricted self perpetuation, certainly seemed contrived and unnatural. At least it could find no other way to explain the development than to declare "It is concluded on all hands that the base ball business has not yet followed as closely the laws governing the other pursuits of man as it should."[95]

7

The American Association and the Polarization of Achievement

As the 1881 season began, the National League, for the first time in its history, was enjoying a period of relative prosperity, dominance and stability. Under Hulbert's leadership the League had successfully turned back all challenges, both within and without, to its status as the premier baseball organization in America. With the demise of the National Association at the end of the previous season "the weeds of the business have been pretty well killed off," leaving the National League, as its long time critic the *Clipper* even had to concede, as the sole professional organization in baseball.[1]

Operationally as well, the National League had developed into a more mature, well-coordinated and stable organization. Now in its second year without a failed franchise, the League was running fairly smoothly and efficiently, able to complete, with the exception of only two rainouts, every one of its scheduled games that year. A maturing sense of mutual obligation and cooperation had so smoothed the differences between most member clubs that the League's annual meeting that year, for the first time, "passed without President Hulbert once bringing his fist down on the table till things jiggled," probably the most incontestable evidence that "the League was never as strong as now."[2]

With no competition from outside leagues, and its labor costs under control, the National League was also able to improve its financial picture. Chicago, as usual, continued to be the organization's most profitable operation, but even the League's newcomer that season, Detroit, was able to generate such a handsome profit ($6,000) its shareholders demanded a dividend. More importantly, even those clubs that weren't as financially well off (such as Troy, which reportedly lost $11,000 over its first two years

127

in the National League) were convinced the value of their operations were appreciating, with prospects for actual long-term profitability so favorable the *Chicago Tribune* could claim "Every club values its League franchise, and will strain every nerve and submit to heavy financial loss rather than default on its duty towards the League."[3]

But in a number of ways all this security was illusory. The League's status didn't represent a final resolution to the conflicts within baseball so much as their temporary suppression, a situation which, to maintain, forced the League to overextend itself to the point of vulnerability. The most glaring example of this was in the League's support of franchises in two small, financially unsustainable, communities, Troy and Worcester, both having been admitted into the National League to either undermine outside organizations or preempt their formation.

Troy, for instance, had not only proved to be a fairly strong and prosperous independent club (it reportedly took in $13,000 in 1878) it could have, in conjunction with nearby Albany, possibly anchored a strong competing eastern league, especially with its intentions to enter the National Association in 1879. But even then some League clubs weren't fully convinced Troy should be admitted (even Hulbert felt the club could become a "bad egg"), an objection that was only overcome after considerable back room bargaining among the more supportive League clubs.[4]

Hulbert's strategy of preempting the formation of competing leagues by absorbing their potentially strongest members most likely also accounts for Worcester's admission. The club, as a member of the National Association, had been "a terror to National League clubs," winning games from six of them in 1879, including an impressive 11–0 win over Chicago itself, always a strong recommendation, in Hulbert's eyes, for any non–League club. The fact that Worcester, at this time, was capably managed by Frank Bancroft, and strongly endorsed by Boston, also helped its cause, especially since Hulbert, in 1880, needed one additional team to complete the League's eight team circuit.[5]

Even to outside observers the admission of Troy and Worcester, from such transparently ulterior motives, had made the League, now sidetracked, as a result of its policies, into supporting two subsidized members, a "show association" if not an outright "retreat for indigent clubs." And here, for some unaccountable reason, Hulbert seems to have suspended his otherwise ruthless expediency in League decisions. The Chicago president firmly committed himself to the League's two small market members, declaring he would "never consent that any existing [National League] member should be crowded out" even when other interests indicated the League would have been much better served if he'd abandon his personal grudge against establishing clubs in Philadelphia and St. Louis or admit the New York Metropolitans, the country's strongest independent club.[6]

In his unwavering stance on the League's 50 cent ticket policy, Hulbert was also, by now, running into resistance from both changing times and popular sentiment. Ignoring the obvious fact that the number of scheduled games played by the typical pro club had dramatically increased from a mere 30 in 1871 to 84 by 1881, the National League stubbornly maintained a "special event" mentality towards its product, believing League games were somehow still rare, highly valued, commodities discriminating patrons were willing to pay dearly to enjoy.

Never at ease with, and frequently resentful of, the National League's 50 cent policy for restricting their responsiveness to local markets, some member clubs were, by now, taking active steps to circumvent the letter, if not the spirit, of the law, among them Cleveland, whose own president contradicted the *Chicago Tribune*'s claim the club wasn't being financially injured by the 50 cent rule. Cincinnati, hoping to boost sagging attendance at the end of 1878, reduced ticket prices to 30 cents, while Troy, a year later, began to issue three game coupons for a dollar. Beginning in 1882 Boston adopted a 25 cent admission fee for all its games in April and October and, from 1880 on, anyone who attended a Providence game after the fourth inning could get in for a dime.[7] With the official National League policy only stipulating 50 cent tickets be charged for adult males, Buffalo, one of the League's most persistent critics of the 50 cent rule, began, in 1882, to admit ladies for a quarter, children for a dime, a policy flexibility Bancroft had talked Hulbert into allowing for Worcester in 1880.[8]

Just how much financial opportunism the National League was denying itself with its 50 cent policy became fully evident from the success of the New York Metropolitans, an independent club organized by former New Bedford manager James Mutrie, over the summer of 1880, with a mere $400 borrowed from businessman John Day. With New York baseball now presumably cleansed "of the old air of crookedness" that had surrounded the Mutuals, the Mets immediately and overwhelmingly became "a regular base ball bonanza." The Mets took in more than $30,000 during its first full season in 1881, far more than most National League clubs, and more than enough to give the club enough financial leverage to even refuse the standard $100 guarantee the League required for games with outside clubs. It certainly must have come as something of an embarrassment to the National League that an independent club had become "the base ball financial success of the season," especially since a former National League player himself, Bob Ferguson, had always insisted "a fortune [is] at the command" of anyone willing to put together a pro club in New York.[9]

More significantly, the Mets had built their success on two practices the League had long considered impractical. Acceding to the long-standing belief that fifty cent baseball would never be accepted by the New York sporting public, the Mets set their ticket prices at 25 cents, a move that immediately made the Mets one of the country's top drawing ballclubs, with an average attendance over 2,500 in 1882.[10]

Most surprising of all, the Mets were able to prosper financially as an almost exclusively home-based club, playing only local clubs or League teams that passed through New York. Though the Mets were receiving invitations to play over 200 games by the start of their second season, they never traveled any further than Boston for any game that year, an arrangement that squarely flew in the face of the *Chicago Tribune*'s long standing contention that no pro club could make money without traveling.[11]

The Mets, however, were only a single independent club. A far more serious threat to the League was the ever present possibility that its closed circuit format would incite the formation of competing achievement centers, the conditions for which continued to persist well after the demise of the National Association. Mike Scanlan, the former Washington, D.C., Nationals manager, no doubt embittered over the way the League treated his club, was calling for the formation of a new league at the end of the 1880 season, about the same time other rumors had the Mets spearheading the formation of a new eastern league.[12]

The loudest voice of discontent, however, didn't originate outside of but within the League, through the ongoing protests of the *Cincinnati Enquirer* baseball editor Oliver P. Caylor. Sympathetic with the National League's mission in general, but not Hulbert's policies in particular, Caylor grew increasingly critical of the League's hypocritical actions (the "Great Moral Show" as he dubbed it) as well as its increasing restrictions over club autonomy and player independence. Caylor was particularly critical of the League's reserve clause, on which he was relentlessly "making war" over the 1880 season, to the point of warning the League its renewal would lead to the formation of a break-away league.[13]

As it turned out, Caylor found himself in a position to actively oppose the National League with the expulsion of his Cincinnati club at the end of 1880. Cincinnati was certainly not the first expelled League club to become a focal point of League resistance. The old Philadelphia Athletics, which had been haunted "like a ghostly tormentor" for their misguided decision to even join the National League, had tried to rally opposition to the League when it was expelled in 1876. But Caylor, through the pages of his paper, was able to exert far more effective influence in solidifying this fragmented discontent with the League and, as a consequence, managed to set himself apart, of all League critics, as the "only one they [National League] are afraid of."[14]

Within a month of his club's expulsion Cincinnati president L. A. Harris was already floating the idea of forming a competing league. Nothing came of this, nor did anything materialize from a New York meeting planned for this purpose in November, 1880, developments that seemed to fully support the *Chicago Tribune's* prediction any organization created to oppose the National League "will be a corpse long before the close of 1881." Things, however, began to take more definite shape during an "informal" meeting among three club representatives at Pittsburgh in October, 1881, plans that finally led to the formation of a full-fledged league, the American Association, at a follow up meeting among six baseball delegates in Cincinnati later that month.[15]

Founded on the principle of "liberty for all," the new league reverted to a strictly "home rule policy" that permitted each of its six member clubs in Cincinnati, Pittsburgh, Louisville, St. Louis, Philadelphia and Baltimore, to "reap the benefits of its own patronage" through greater autonomy and responsiveness towards their local markets. Individual clubs were free to set their own ticket prices and were delegated the right to authorize Sunday games and on-premise liquor sales, an option all the Association's clubs utilized except Louisville and Philadelphia.[16]

The American Association's strength, however, lay in its similarities to, not differences from, the National League. Going out of its way to reassure the public that this new league was "in no way connected with, or a successor to, the defunct International Association," the American Association retained the basic organizational structure that had proved successful with the National League; a closed circuit competition that reflected a truly national, rather than regional, competitive structure. In contracts, umpiring arrangements, scheduling and other operational matters, the American Association, in fact, was pretty much a straight-out reflection of the National League, only one without "all arrogant and tyrannical features" of the senior circuit.[17]

Initially the National League seemed to take a watchful, even conciliatory, interest in this new league. Hard-liners like Detroit may have felt the League should simply ignore its competitor "as are the gangs of barefooted boys who play ball on the common." But the *Chicago Tribune* didn't see why "both bodies could exist harmoniously," while the cross town *Chicago Times*, in a rare display of editorial independence, believed an expanded landscape of sixteen pro clubs would actually help make baseball "more truly national."[18]

Of course, the only opinion that could materially affect inter-league relations was Hulbert's, and as the two leagues moved closer to the 1882 season it became evident the National League president didn't at all share such conciliatory sentiments. In a series of lengthy letters to American Association president H. D. McKnight, Hulbert made it clear the "Cincinnati plan" of Sunday games, cheap admission fees, and on-premise liquor sales could never succeed in baseball. "You cannot afford to bid for the patronage of the degraded" he proclaimed, adding that any and all attempts to justify these policies on the basis of financial expediency or club autonomy were simply the "rankest fallacies." [19]

The American Association, however, was neither intimidated nor deterred by Hulbert's criticism (McKnight was particularly incensed with Hulbert's arrogant and unjustified rationale for expelling Boston's Charley Jones, something Caylor found so outrageous he wanted the American Association to review all League expulsions). As a consequence, the League next tried to isolate Association members by pressuring them into joining the League Alliance, something that would have effectively subordinated them to the status of a "training school for the League."[20]

Having successfully prevented the Mets from joining the American Association by way of some favorable guarantee arrangements, Hulbert attempted to preempt the new league by setting up a League Alliance club in New York and, to directly compete with the American Association club in Philadelphia, granted a League Alliance franchise to that city. Protected by the League's new policy of permitting only one League Alliance club per city, and favored by an exemption from the League's 50 cent ticket policy, these National League satellite clubs in New York and Philadelphia started with considerable financial advantages which, Hulbert even hinted, could be further increased if some regular League teams would lose to them.[21]

A glaring disparity in competitive results between the two leagues must have also raised some concern about the American Association's viability. Association teams lost every one of their pre-season games against League clubs at the start of the 1882 season, results so discouraging the *Pittsburg Dispatch* thought it had been a mistake to even play National League clubs, which simply allowed them to undeservedly profit off the American Association. It all tended to confirm Hulbert's contention there was only enough top playing talent for eight pro teams, not twelve, as the *St. Louis Democrat* always insisted.[22]

Competitive contacts between the two leagues, however, weren't to continue much longer. Even before the 1882 season had begun, relations between the two bodies had been strained ever since Troy had enticed Billy Holbert to break his contract with Pittsburgh, and Boston had lured Sam

Wise away from Cincinnati. One is left with the impression the National League was specifically looking for an opportunity to break off relations with the American Association, which finally came about in May, when the Athletics officially expelled John Troy for breaking his contract and jumping to Detroit. The expulsion not only immediately halted all competitive contacts between the two leagues, it effectively meant "war is at last opened" between the two organizations in all baseball matters.[23]

If Hulbert himself had been confident he could "so squelch the American Association that it will prevent any similar enterprise arising in the future" by competitively isolating it, a policy that had proved effective against the International Association, the League's faith in this course began to be considerably shaken as the 1882 season progressed.[24]

From the very beginning the American Association not only proved to be financially self-sustaining, it was attracting more fans to its games than the National League was. The Athletics had already sold 84,000 tickets by June, a figure that seems to confirm the claim American Association clubs were, by mid-season, outdrawing all League clubs except Chicago. More than 20,000 fans turned out for a single Saturday game between St. Louis and Cincinnati, another 3,400 for a late season game in Cincinnati, even though the home club had long since clinched the pennant.[25]

Sunday games proved to be especially popular. On average, St. Louis drew nearly 10,000 fans to its Sunday games, not surprising since the club, a year earlier, had been attracting over 5,000 fans to its Sunday games against such second-class teams as Dubuque and the Cincinnati Buckeyes. Sunday games were also popular in Cincinnati, and even ultra-conservative Louisville, the latter drawing a "crushing audience" to one of its Sunday games.[26]

Well aware that every person in the stands was a potential consumer, those American Association clubs that permitted on-premise liquor sales reaped additional financial returns. Just how much this revenue source generated is unclear, but if some 70 "waiters" did, in fact, work the crowds selling beer at places like St. Louis, it's not improbable this income exceeded the $6,000 the Mets reportedly made from their on-premise liquor sales that year.[27]

Taken together, all these income sources— 25 cent tickets, Sunday games and liquor sales— provided most American Association clubs with an exceptionally strong cash flow. By mid-season Pittsburgh had reportedly already cleared $2,700 while the Athletics, by that same time, had grossed over $50,000. Cincinnati ended their first season so flush with cash the club was able to pay off its guarantor notes ahead of schedule.[28]

The economic benefits of the American Association policies were certainly not lost on the National League. Compared to the paltry $115 it took in from three 50 cent games at Worcester, Buffalo earned over $3,000 from the 25 cent games it played against the League's New York and Philadelphia satellite clubs. From just five games in Philadelphia at 25 cents Detroit earned more ($1,356 to $1,258) than it did from all the other 12 League games it played on its eastern tour. Faced with figures like this, in fact, Bancroft, Detroit's manager, for one, was not only openly conceding the American Association "has proved cheap admission fees pay," he even began to lobby for the right of each League club to individually set their own ticket prices.[29]

The collective success of its policies left little doubt the American Association, by mid-season, was "no longer an experiment," and certainly not the "abortion of the league" its detractors had earlier proclaimed. By season's end the American Association had become "an established fact" upon the baseball landscape, perhaps not strong and secure enough to become, as the *Clipper* anticipated, the country's top baseball organization, but certainly prosperous enough, as the *Chicago Times* feared, to be in a position to match the League, dollar for dollar, in the competition for the country's top ballplaying talent.[30]

The National League was clearly facing the most serious threat to its status since its first year of existence, a situation further complicated by Hulbert's death just as the 1882 season was beginning. In itself, this development wasn't unexpected. Hulbert had become so incapacitated from what appears to have been progressive heart failure (the first symptoms seem to have appeared as early as November of the previous year) he had relinquished his day-to-day responsibilities as League president to Boston president Arthur Soden in March.[31]

The fact that Hulbert's close associate at Chicago, A.G. Mills, had been designated the League's heir apparent as far back as December of 1881, seems to indicate the League wanted to continue on the path Hulbert had laid out for it, despite an apparent lack of unanimity on the matter. Those who felt Hulbert had always been the "backbone" of the National League saw his death as an "irreparable loss" that forebode troubled times for the League, "with a fair prospect of it [the National League] going to the dogs ere another season closes."[32]

For those, however, who'd been thwarted by the League's autocratic polices, such as Cleveland and Detroit, the feeling was "it is now about time, now that Hurlbut [sic] is dead, for the League to loose itself from Chicago's thralldom" if not outright "throw off the yoke of Chicago bossism" altogether. For the League delegates who came together for a special meeting in

Philadelphia that September, it must have been more than self-evident that "never was a strong and clear head needed so much as now" to renew and re-direct the National League on its course.[33]

The most important development that came out of that meeting was the decision to completely backtrack on Hulbert's unconditional support of the League's small market clubs, Troy and Worcester, a decision that was as evident in its benefits as it was messy in its execution. Dissatisfaction with Troy and Worcester, the "hangers on" of the League, as the *Clipper* now dubbed them, had been growing throughout the 1882 season, the Detroit *Free Press* out-and-out declaring the two organizations simply "have no business in the League."[34]

The deteriorating financial and competitive position of the two clubs certainly provided plenty of ammunition for their critics. Worcester had drawn no more than 700 spectators to its opener in 1881, while Troy, that same season, was having a hard time motivating their players since most were expecting their club to disband any day.[35]

By the beginning of the 1882 season even Harry Wright conceded games with these two National League clubs had now become "in the estimation of the public of secondary importance," and their on-field performance certainly didn't do anything to offset rumors this would be their last year in the League. Crippled by a 16 game losing steak, Troy was only able to attract an average home attendance of 630 that season. The situation for Worcester wasn't much better, the club playing so poorly that season a mere 20 spectators showed up for its final home game.[36]

Just how the National League was going to get rid of its two weakest sisters, however, presented something of a problem. With neither club, technically, in violation of any League rule, and neither willing to voluntarily "resign" from the League, the other National League clubs, who convened that September in Philadelphia specifically to resolve the matter, had to resort to "star chamber" tactics to achieve their ends.[37]

The Troy and Worcester delegates were led to believe the matter would be decided at a later date, and that the meeting was, therefore, adjoined. The Troy delegate, A. L. Hotchkin, however, rather than leaving town, returned to the League meeting room the next day and found, as he had suspected, that the other League delegates had reconvened to finalize the Troy/Worcester expulsion among themselves. Realizing the League's intent to exclude his club couldn't be avoided, Hotchkin accepted its decision and even agreed to dine with League delegates that evening.[38]

The League's unilateral decision to expel Troy and Worcester, however, had other, more disruptive, consequences. When the Worcester officers heard of the decision they threatened to immediately dissolve the club and leave its schedule uncompleted, a threat they never carried out, but one that forced Chicago, not wanting to be left with empty dates as had happened to it when Syracuse suddenly failed three years earlier, to make a special arrangement with Providence to play an extra series of games as a precaution.[39]

The Troy and Worcester expulsions, in both execution and consequence, were certainly no credit to the National League, but it had forced the organization to acknowledge the preeminent importance of market factors. And as far as public image was concerned, the League was able to resolve the matter in a way that upheld, at least technically, its long-standing boast "when a club gets into the league it neither dies nor resigns."[40]

With the Troy and Worcester expulsions the National League had eliminated the most serious internal liabilities of Hulbert's policies, leaving the League now free to also modify his policies against competing organizations. By the end of the 1882 season the League was not only beginning to realize the tactics it had used to bring down the International Association — competitive isolation, player raids — weren't succeeding with the American Association, it was also coming to the understanding that perhaps it would be financially inexpedient if they did. Most League clubs had earned good money from their pre-season games with American Association clubs, something their League Alliance members in New York and Philadelphia were even more dependent upon. The League's Philadelphia club drew far more fans to its pre-season games against the Athletics (10,000 for just two games, that brought over $4,000 into the club's coffers) than it did for any of its games against National League teams. It was all a sharp rebuff to the League's long-standing belief that no city could support more than one first-class club.[41]

With such lucrative returns at its fingertips the National League itself, in fact, began to make the first overtures of reconciliation towards the American Association, trying to persuade the Athletics to lift their expulsion of John Troy so that competitive contacts between the two leagues could be re-established.[42]

This the American Association wasn't willing to do, but its opportunistic Cincinnati franchise was able to get around this prohibition by releasing its players at the end of the American Association's regular season, reforming them as "private citizens," and then playing a number of post-season games against Cleveland and Chicago. Other American Association clubs were so upset with Cincinnati's ploy they threatened to expel the club, but they could hardly be serious about expelling their pennant winner, especially one that had revealed the financial benefits of renewed inter-league play (the Cincinnati games at Cleveland alone drew over 12,000 spectators).[43]

Recognizing the inexpediency of continued hostility, the two leagues began to send out feelers to each other over the winter, eventually resulting in a reconciliation meeting in New York in February, 1883. Coming to terms on the touchy matter of expelled players, and agreeing to honor each other's contracts, the two organizations were able to renew competitive contacts and conclude the history making meeting with the "best of harmony."[44]

The reconciliation between the National League and the American Association brought competitive stability to organized baseball, but it didn't bring unity. The two organizations remained competitively separate (Caylor's idea of arranging a combined schedule for the two leagues was rejected), maintained their own policies, and continued to claim each represented the highest expression of competitive baseball.[45]

As such, the National League/American Association accord represented a terminal stage in baseball's organizational development. No longer was there any danger that baseball's achievement center would be dissolved or drawn down into local or regional competitions. No longer was there any fear that moral opposition could seriously deter social acceptance of "the best against the best." These were the consequences of Hulbert's policies and practices, a baseball legacy that has endured to this day.

A broadening and intensifying pressure to access the achievement center represented by the National League continued to persist, but, in the future, this could only be expressed by replicating, as the American Association did, the closed circuit, large city attachment structure established by the National League. Even under Hulbert's leadership the National League couldn't prevent a bi-polarizaton of its achievement center, and its wary, begrudging relationship with the American Association precluded any possibility this could be undone. But the specific structure professional baseball would have to follow in the future was now established.

The National League/American Association accord hadn't immunized organized baseball from continued agitation to access its highest achievement level, it simply "lateralized" this agitation. New leagues would come and go, new battles for players and markets would continue to be fought over the next two decades within organized baseball. But all these attempts to access or assume baseball's highest achievement level could do no more than duplicate or follow the closely controlled, closed circuit structure that had been established by the National League. No longer could this achievement focus ever be accessed "from below," from a rising level of locally based achievement. It's a cultural dynamic that has characterized baseball to this day.

Epilogue

Who should be allowed to compete? What should they compete for? Who shall determine this? These, the most important questions a society must resolve for its sporting culture, America first faced with baseball.

I've tried to show that America's sporting public demanded an overwhelming achievement orientation for baseball, itself the result of the peculiar circumstances that affected the game during its development in New York City. This, in turn, set in motion a specific course of events that gave rise to professionalism, the establishment of a closed circuit competition and, eventually, a fragmentation of the game's competitive center.

By the early 1880s organized baseball had effectively reached a state of competitive maturity, but it was also a state that was inherently unstable. Unable to maintain an indivisible achievement center, organized baseball set itself upon a 20 year odyssey of watchfulness and defensiveness, during which the National League had to continually resist the formation of competing leagues while, at the same time, trying to incessantly control and subordinate the persistent social pressure to access the game's highest competitive level by means of an ever expanding and deepening array of agreements, compacts, syndicates, and club relocations that would eventually become the Byzantine network of organized baseball.

It could be said, as many scholars have claimed, that organized baseball, despite its tempestuous origins and turbulent development, had, with the "peace" between the National and American Leagues in 1903, managed to comprehensively succeed in this scheme. For the next 50 years organized baseball faced no serious threat to its competitive dominance. No new leagues emerged during that period and not a single one of its sixteen professional clubs failed over that time period.

But if we look at this in the perspective of baseball's earlier history it becomes more evident this was all accomplished at considerable social cost.

In the half century after 1903 the American sporting public did enjoy the benefit of consistently high quality baseball in a stable competitive structure. But with the American population doubling during that period, such a fixed and inflexible competitive organization effectively denied many talented, deserving, athletes, of all races, from ever playing at baseball's highest competitive level. This also meant many communities were denied the privilege of enjoying major league baseball though population shifts and trends clearly warranted this. To say American society was best served under a sporting arrangement whose highest achievement level, for more than half a century, was restricted to, and determined by, only 16 teams, is tantamount to claiming America's higher education needs would have been best served by limiting education opportunities to only 16 colleges and universities, no more, nor less; institutions which, over a 50 year period, refused to award no more degrees in 1950 than they had in 1903. Clearly, this would be an arrangement American society would have found unacceptable, if not outrageous. Yet organized baseball, through its peculiar historical development, had so inured the American sporting public to an overwhelmingly achievement focus that the game never, over this length of time, encountered any serious social objections.

It's been common for contemporary sports observers, bewildered and frustrated by the conflicts and controversies of modern baseball, to seek the source of guilt for this state of affairs, blaming, at various times, owners, players and the sporting public itself. Historically, a search for culpability is somewhat misplaced. Baseball developed the way it did strictly as a reflection of what American society judged to be the most desirable social values for its competitive structure. To criticize this historical development is, in effect, to express regret that baseball developed when it did where it did. Had baseball emerged 30 or 40 years earlier than it did, developing slowly and concurrently in scattered, competitively separate, areas of the United States (rather than in a single large city) while only gradually establishing a national competitive network, the game could, in theory, have evolved more like English cricket, firmly rooted in a competitive obligation to locality. Conversely, had baseball emerged several decades after the Civil War, within an environment where the sporting public was more mature in its competitive outlook and supportive of an amateur ethic, the game could have possibly followed the same route as football or basketball, attached to colleges or athletic clubs, a course that would have been more organizationally stable and socially responsive, though less competitively focused upon "the best against the best."

One of the most historically defining characteristics of American society has always been a deep, almost selfish, tradition of local self-determination.

In matters such as political empowerment, public education, and business initiation, to name just a few, America has always had a belief that communal services should, ultimately, be under the control of, and responsive to, locality, whatever drawbacks this may entail in the way of economic efficiency or social judgment. Yet, with baseball, America, from almost the very beginning of the game's history, was willing to abnegate this right for the unconditional freedom to accommodate the game's highest competitive level.

Notes

Prologue

1. Eric Leiffer, *Making the Majors: The Transformation of Team Sports in America* (Cambridge: Harvard University Press, 1995), x, 5.

2. Warren Goldstein, *Playing for Keeps: A History of Early Baseball* (Ithaca: Cornell University Press, 1989), 132.

3. John Shawcroft, *The Official History of Derbyshire County Cricket Club* (London: Stanley Paul, 1970), 9; Keith Sandiford, "Amateurs and Professionals in Victorian County Cricket," *Albion,* vol. 15 (1983), 34.

4. Keith Sandiford and Wray Vamplew, "The Peculiar Economics of English Cricket Before 1914," *British Journal of Sports History,* vol. 3 (3), 1986, 320.

5. Leiffer, *Making the Majors,* 98.

Chapter 1

1. *New York Tribune,* 5 Aug., 1869, 8; *World* (New York) 24 August, 1869, 5. As early as 1865 the Knickerbockers were playing a "throw back" game with their team from 1855; *World* (New York) 28 Sept., 1875, 5.

2. Benjamin Rader, *Baseball: A History of America's Game* (Urbana: University of Illinois Press, 1994), 5.

3. *Newark Daily Mercury,* 18 August, 1860, 3.

4. *Wilkes Spirit of the Times,* 20 July, 1861, 307; *New York Leader,* 5 Sept., 1857, 5; *Clipper,* 5 Oct., 1861, 197. Even the Excelsiors were reluctant "to turn out and exercise" during the club's early days; *Porters Spirit of the Times* 25 July, 1857, 324.

5. George Kirsch, *The Creation of American Team Sports: Baseball and Cricket, 1838-1872* (Urbana: University of Illinois Press, 1989), 55–56.

6. *New York Leader,* 29 Aug., 1857, 5; *Clipper,* 11 Sept., 1858, 162; *Sunday Mercury* (New York) 23 Oct., 1859, 5. The *New York Tribune* even claimed its home town type of baseball was "a bastard game, worthy only of boys of ten years of age." *Sunday Mercury* (New York) 23 Oct., 1859, 5.

7. *Racine Journal,* 14 Aug., 1867, 2.

8. *Porters,* 7 March, 1857, 5.

9. Charles Peverelly, *Book of American Pastimes* (New York: 1866), 347; *New York Herald,* 12 June, 1855, 8; 23 June, 1855, 1.

10. *Brooklyn Daily Eagle*, 4 Aug., 1855, 3; 8 Aug., 1855, 3; *New York Evening Express*, 22 Aug., 1855, 4; *Porters*, 18 Aug., 1855, 319; 22 Sept., 1855, 373; 8 Dec., 1855, 511.

11. *Brooklyn Daily Eagle*, 6 Aug., 1855, 2; *Newark Daily Mercury*, 1 June, 1860, 3; *Porters*, 14 November, 1857, 65; Harold Seymour, *Baseball: The Early Years* (New York: Oxford University Press, 1960), 20.

12. Goldstein, *Playing for Keeps*, 55; *Porters*, 20 Dec., 1856, 257; Peverelly, *Book of American Pastimes*, 353; *Porters*, 10 March, 1858, 37.

13. Tom Melville, *The Tented Field: A History of Cricket in America* (Bowling Green: Bowling Green State University Press, 1998), 38; *Porters*, 20 March, 1858, 65; *Clipper*, 2 May, 1857, 13; *Brooklyn Daily Times*, 15 Oct., 1855, 2.

14. *Porters*, 22 Sept., 1855, 511.

15. *Porters*, 7 March, 1857, 5; *Brooklyn Daily Times*, 16 Sept., 1857, 3; *Newark Daily Mercury*, 4 Aug., 1858, 2; *New York Ledger*, 30 April, 1859, 4. See also *New York Daily News*, 15 Sept., 1858, 5.

16. *New York Evening Express*, 11 Sept., 1858, 4; *Wilkes*, 11 March, 1865, 23; *Brooklyn Daily Eagle*, 25 June, 1858, 3.

17. *Porters*, 20 March, 1858, 37; 10 Jan., 1857, 309; *DeWitt's Base Ball Guide* (New York: DeWitts, 1869), 46.

18. *Porters*, 10 Jan., 1857, 309.

19. *Sunday Mercury* (New York), 22 May, 1859, 8; 28 Sept., 1862, 6; *New York Morning Express*, 26 May, 1860, 3; *New York Daily News*, 28 Sept., 1859, 8; 22 June, 1860, 8.

20. *New York Herald*, 22 Sept., 1855, 3; *Sunday Mercury* (New York), 25 Sept., 1859, 5; *New York Evening Express*, 1 Aug., 1859, 3.

21. Goldstein, *Playing for Keeps*, 53.

22. *DeWitt's Base Ball Guide*, 1869, 11; *New York Morning Express*, 1 Sept., 1858, 3; *Sunday Mercury* (New York), 29 May, 1859, 7; 7 Aug., 1864, 6; 14 Aug., 1859, 5; *Clipper*, 10 Nov., 1860, 234.

23. *Wilkes*, 1 Oct., 1864, 67; *New York Evening Express*, 3 Aug., 1859, 1.

24. *Wilkes*, 24 Dec., 1864, 260; *Clipper*, 15 April, 1865, 2; *Porters*, 20 Dec., 1856, 257; *New York Daily News*, 3 Aug., 1859, 1.

25. *Rockford Register*, 20 July, 1867, 3.

26. By 1860 *Porters* (24 March, 1860, 73) was complaining National Association delegates were being "selected with a view of their peculiar knowledge of parliamentary tactics and not as practical ball players," while *Wilkes* (22 Dec., 1866, 266) found the 1866 convention characterized by a "levity of manner and flippancy of speech."

27. Seymour, *Baseball: The Early Years*, 33; *New York Herald*, 22 July, 1858, 5; 29 June, 1855, 8; *Clipper*, 18 Feb., 1860, 349. The *Brooklyn Daily Eagle* (25 June, 1858, 3) didn't carry its first boxscore until June, 1858, about the same time the *New York Daily News* first began to cover baseball. While the employees of the *Clipper* had a company cricket team by 1860 they did not seem to have a baseball team. Even Henry Chadwick didn't play his first game of baseball until August of 1860; *New York Daily News*, 3 Oct., 1860, 8; 21 August, 1860, 1.

28. *New York Evening Express*, 29 June, 1855, 2; *New York Herald*, 16 June, 1855, 1; *Porters*, 9 June, 1855, 200.

29. *Daily Picayune* (New Orleans), 14 Aug., 1859, 4; *New York Evening Express*, 20 Aug., 1859, 4; *Cincinnati Enquirer*, 14 March, 1879, 8; *Brooklyn Daily Eagle*, 21 Sept., 1866, 3.

30. *Racine Journal*, 4 Aug., 1867, 2; *Janesville Gazette*, 30 July, 1866, 1; *Whitewater Register*, 27 July, 1866, 3; *New York Daily News*, 2 July, 1860, 1; 7 Aug., 1860, 7.

31. *Wilkes*, 5 May, 1860, 143; *Newark Daily Advertiser*, 12 Oct., 1865, 2; *Cincinnati Daily Times*, 26 Aug., 1868, 1; *Clipper*, 11 Aug., 1877, 157.

32. *Clipper*, 12 Aug., 1865, 138; 8 Sept., 1860, 164; quoted in Thomas Altherr, "'The Most Summery, Bold, Free & Spacious Game': Charles King Newcomb and Philadelphia Baseball, 1866–1871," *Pennsylvania History*, 52 (2), 1985, 80.

33. *Clipper*, 24 May, 1862, 42; 26 Sept., 1863, 190; 8 Sept., 1860, 164; *New York Evening Express*, 1 Aug., 1859, 3; *Brooklyn Daily Eagle*, 11 June, 1858, 3; *New York Leader*, 30 Oct., 1858, 5; *New York Herald*, 24 Aug., 1860, 5.

34. *Clipper*, 8 Nov., 1879, 258; *Boston Evening Transcript*, 22 July, 1875, 4.

35. *Bat and Ball* (Hartford), 1 May, 1867, 2; *Porters*, 20 June, 1857, 225; 22 May, 1858, 180.

36. *Clipper*, 15 July, 1865, 108; *New York Herald*, 8 July, 1865, 8; *New York Evening Express*, 27 July, 1865, 4; *New York Times*, 6 March, 1871, 6.

37. *National Chronicle*, 19 March, 1870, 85.

38. *New York Leader*, 24 July, 1858, 5; *New York Herald*, 9 Aug., 1867, 8; *World* (New York), 7 Aug., 1870, 1.

39. *Wilkes*, 3 July, 1869, 311; *St. Louis Republican*, 12 Aug., 1875, 8.

Chapter 2

1. *Clipper*, 24 May, 1862, 42; *Wilkes*, 26 Jan., 1861, 324; *Brooklyn Daily Eagle*, 4 May, 1866, 3; *Sunday Mercury* (New York), 26 Oct., 1862, 8; 21 June, 1863, 6; 18 March, 1860, 5.

2. *Wilkes*, 24 March, 1860, 37; 7 March, 1863, 11. There was still enough interest in the Massachusetts game to organize a league in 1866; *Wilkes*, 29 Sept., 1866, 68.

3. *Newark Daily Advertiser*, 7 Oct., 1865, 2; *Fitzgerald's City Item*, 5 Aug., 1865, 2; *American Chronicle of Sports and Pastimes*, 20 Feb., 1868, 57; *Boston Herald*, 31 Oct., 1865, 4.

4. *Brooklyn Daily Eagle*, 8 Sept., 1865, 2; *New York Herald*, 27 Aug., 1866, 2.

5. *Ball Players Chronicle*, 5 Sept., 1867, 5; *Clipper*, 10 June, 1865, 66; 17 June, 1865, 75.

6. *American Chronicle of Sports and Pastimes*, 4 June, 1868, 183; *New York Times*, 23 April, 1866, 8; *New York Tribune*, 25 Aug., 1868, 8; *Chicago Times*, 27 May, 1870, 5; *Sunday Mercury* (Philadelphia), 22 April, 1866, 3; *Brooklyn Daily Eagle*, 4 April, 1867, 2. This constant shifting of players probably accounts for the small number of matches between top clubs during the immediate post–Civil War years, clubs having "fought shy" of each other until their new players had completed their 30 day waiting period; *Brooklyn Daily Eagle*, 27 Aug., 1866, 2; *Newark Daily Advertiser*, 11 Aug., 1866, 2; *Clipper*, 27 July, 1867, 125.

7. *Wilkes*, 12 Sept., 1868, 55; *Clipper*, 27 July, 1867, 125.

8. *Brooklyn Daily Eagle*, 4 April, 1867, 2.

9. *Clipper*, 18 March, 1865, 386; *Brooklyn Daily Eagle*, 17 July, 1867, 2.

10. *Clipper*, 13 Oct., 1866, 210; 20 Oct., 1866, 219; 25 April, 1868, 18.

11. *Brooklyn Daily Eagle*, 4 April, 1867, 2; *Ball Players Chronicle*, 6 June, 1867, 2.

12. *Newark Daily Advertiser*, 19 Aug., 1865, 4.

13. *Ball Players Chronicle*, 1 Oct., 1868, 33; 5 March, 1868, 76.

14. *Sunday Mercury* (Philadelphia), 22 Sept., 1867, 3; *Wilkes*, 17 Oct., 1868, 138; *Cincinnati Daily Times*, 6 Sept., 1870, 1; *New York Tribune*, 30 May, 1867, 4.

15. *Clipper*, 5 Aug., 1865, 130; 16 Jan., 1869, 323; *Cincinnati Commercial*, 8 Feb., 1870, p. 8. It was claimed Tweed invested $5,000 in the Mutuals and underwrote the team's trip to New Orleans in 1869; *Cleveland Plain Dealer*, 20 July, 1871, 3; *National Chronicle*, 25 Dec., 1869, 322. Morrissey claimed his son, and not himself, was a member of the Haymakers, though he reportedly lost $10,000 betting on the club; *Cincinnati Daily Times*, 27 Aug., 1869, 2; *Troy Press*, 31 Aug., 1869, 3; *Cincinnati Daily Times*, 23 Aug., 1869, 2; *New York Tribune*, 23 Aug., 1869, 8.

16. *Sunday Mercury* (New York), 16 Oct., 1864, 7; *Clipper*, 16 Nov., 1861, 247; 26 March, 1859, 386; *Porters*, 26 March, 1859, 52.

17. *New York Daily News*, 12 Sept., 1859, 1.

18. *Brooklyn Eagle*, 27 Aug., 1877, 3; *DeWitt's Base Ball Guide*, 1869, 90; *New York Times*, 10 April, 1869, 11; *Wilkes*, 24 Oct., 1868, 148.

19. Goldstein, *Playing for Keeps*, 121, 127; Ronald Smith, *Sports and Freedom: The Rise of Big-Time College Athletics* (New York: Oxford, 1988), 172–3; *Cincinnati Commercial*, 22 Sept., 1879, 5; *Wilkes*, 23 Jan., 1869, 359.

20. *Clipper*, 15 Dec., 1866, 282; *American Chronicle of Sports and Pastimes*, 28 May, 1868, 172.

21. *Wilkes*, 1 Dec., 1866, 220; 19 Jan., 1867, 324. It must be remembered mid–19th century sports observers had an undeveloped understanding of natural talent, it being widely believed pros were better than amateurs simply because they had more opportunities to play and were better trained; *Cincinnati Daily Times*, 28 Nov., 1870, 1; *Spalding's Official Base Ball Guide* (Chicago: Spalding & Bros., 1881), 10.

22. *Sunday Mercury* (Philadelphia), 8 Nov., 1868, 4; *Bat and Ball*, 1 May, 1867, 1.

23. *Wilkes*, 24 July, 1869, 360.

24. *Wilkes*, 4 April, 1868, 99.

25. *Green Bay Advocate*, 30 Aug., 1866, 3; *Janesville Gazette*, 5 Sept., 1867, 1; *Wilkes*, 1 Dec., 1866, 220; *Whitewater Register*, 27 July, 1866, 3.

26. *Monroe Sentinel*, 15 May, 1867, 3.

27. *Elkhorn Independent*, 12 June, 1867, 3; *Whitewater Register*, 21 Sept., 1866, 3; S.W. Pope, *Patriotic Games* (New York: Oxford, 1997), 13; *Wilkes*, 8 Dec., 1860, 213.

28. *Clipper*, 24 June, 1865, 82; *Wilkes*, 6 July, 1867, 347; 27 July, 1867, 407. Even before the Civil War the New York Excelsiors, with their tours through upstate New York and the near South, had effectively established a "national" baseball standard for the rest of the country; *New York Daily News*, 25 Sept., 1860, 8.

29. *Rockford Register*, 3 Aug., 1867, 4.

30. *Chicago Republican*, 16 Aug., 1868, 4; *Chicago Tribune*, 1 Sept., 1869, 4.

31. *Wilkes*, 4 April, 1868, 99; *Chicago Tribune*, 16 July, 1871, 1; *World* (New York), 5 July, 1871, 5; *Wilkes*, 25 April, 1874, 244; *Clipper*, 11 April, 1868, 2. As late as 1880 it was claimed three quarters of all pro players came from the New York/Philadelphia metropolitan areas; *Buffalo Daily Courier*, 9 June, 1880, 2.

32. *American Chronicle of Sports and Pastimes*, 23 July, 1868, 262; *Cincinnati Daily Times*, 28 June, 1869, 2; *World* (New York), 21 Nov., 1870, 2; *Chicago Times*, 8 Aug., 1871, 5.

33. *Boston Evening Transcript*, 22 July, 1875, 4.

34. *National Chronicle*, 17 April, 1869, 59; *Sunday Mercury* (Philadelphia), 19 Nov., 1871, 3.

35. *Sunday Mercury* (Philadelphia), 11 April, 1875, 4; *Chicago Tribune*, 15 May, 1872, 6; *Chicago Times*, 3 Oct., 1874, 5.

36. *Rockford Register*, 7 May, 1870, 4; *Wilkes*, 7 Aug., 1869, 391.

37. Rowland Bowen, *Cricket: A History of Its Growth and Development Throughout the World* (London: Spottiswode, 1970), 50; Christopher Brookes, *English Cricket* (London: Weidenfeld, 1978), 120–122; F. S. Ashley-Cooper, *Nottinghamshire Cricket and Cricketers* (Nottingham: Saxton, 1923), 181; Derek Birley, *A Social History of English Cricket* (London: Aurum, 1999), 144–145, 181.

38. *National Chronicle*, 4 Dec., 1869, 297; *New York Herald*, 29 June, 1865, 8.

39. *Boston Post*, 17 May, 1867, 4; 5 Sept., 1867, 3; *Chicago Tribune*, 29 July, 1869, 4.

Chapter 3

1. Albert Spalding, *America's National Game* (Lincoln: University of Nebraska, 1992), 133; Goldstein, *Playing For Keeps*, 118.

2. The Mutuals and Atlantics were being referred to as "professional clubs" a good

year earlier than Cincinnati; *New England Base Ballist,* 22 Oct. 1868, 46; *Cincinnati Enquirer,* 20 Aug. 1875, 8; *Cincinnati Daily Gazette,* 7 July, 1866, 3; 26 May, 1865, 1.

3. *Cincinnati Commercial,* 2 March, 1879, 2. Scholars have traditionally relied upon Harry Ellard's *Baseball in Cincinnati: A History* (Cincinnati, 1907) for the early history of the Cincinnati club, but a far more valuable source is the series of articles the *Cincinnati Commercial* ran on this subject between March and April, 1879.

4. Seymour, *Baseball: The Early Years,* 59; *Cincinnati Enquirer,* 22 Aug. 1871, 8; 4 July, 1871, 4. Leiffer's interesting explanation, that Cincinnati failed because it couldn't "keep moving in search of new challenges," fits well with his assertion that pro clubs had to attach themselves to cities but, unfortunately, it's historically suspect. The Reds had achieved considerable "attachment" before 1869 and played roughly the same ratio of home/away games as other top pro clubs; Leiffer, *Making the Majors,* 38.

5. *Cincinnati Daily Times,* 23 Aug. 1867, 3; *Clipper,* 3 April, 1869, 411.

6. *Cincinnati Commercial,* 30 March, 1879, 1; *Cincinnati Daily Times,* 7 Oct. 1867, 3.

7. *Clipper,* 3 April, 1869, 411; *Cincinnati Commercial,* 30 March, 1879, 1; *Clipper,* 18 April, 1868, 11.

8. *Cincinnati Daily Times,* 3 Sept. 1868, 2; *Cincinnati Commercial,* 21 Aug. 1870, 5; *Clipper,* 27 March 1869, 403.

9. *New York Tribune,* 2 Oct. 1868, 5.

10. *Cincinnati Daily Times,* 25 Aug. 1868, 2; 10 July, 1868, 2.

11. *Cincinnati Daily Times,* 26 June, 1868, 1; *Cincinnati Commercial,* 30 March, 1879, 1; Greg Rhodes and John Erardi, *The First Boys of Summer: The 1869- 1870 Cincinnati Red Stockings* (Cincinnati: Road West, 1994), 11.

12. *Wilkes,* 3 April, 1869, 103; *Cincinnati Daily Times,* 3 Aug. 1870, 1; *Cincinnati Commercial,* 13 April, 1879, 12; William Davis, "The Origins of Baseball in Cincinnati" (MA Thesis, Ohio State University, 1948), 55; *Cincinnati Commercial* 13 April, 1879, 12.

13. *National Chronicle,* 15 May, 1869, 75; *New York Tribune,* 7 June, 1869, 2; *Wilkes,* 19 June, 1869, 278; Stephen Guschov, *The Red Stockings of Cincinnati: Base Ball's First All-Professional Team and Its Historic 1869 and 1870 Seasons* (Jefferson, N.C.: McFarland, 1998), 96.

14. *Turf, Field and Farm,* 2 July, 1869, 5; *Chicago Republican,* 23 Sept. 1870, 4; *Wilkes,* 12 Sept. 1868, 55; *National Chronicle,* 8 Jan. 1870, *Wilkes,* 26 Sept. 1868, 84.

15. *Wilkes,* 26 June, 1869, 291; *Cincinnati Chronicle,* 1 July, 1870, 5.

16. *Cincinnati Commercial,* 27 Nov. 1870, 8; *St. Louis Republican,* 1 June, 1875, 5.

17. *Clipper,* 1 Jan. 1870, 309; *Cincinnati Daily Times,* 6 July, 1869, 2; *Sunday Mercury* (Philadelphia), 2 Aug. 1868, 4; *Clipper,* 25 May, 1867, 52.

18. *Cincinnati Daily Times,* 28 June, 1869, 2; *Clipper,* 15 Jan. 1870, 325.

19. *New York Tribune,* 11 Aug. 1868, 8; *New England Base Ballist,* 9 Oct. 1868, 42.

20. *New York Tribune,* 13 July, 1869, 8; *World* (New York), 23 July, 1869, 8; *New York Tribune,* 17 July, 1869, 8; *World* (New York), 23 July, 1869, 8.

21. *Wilkes,* 24 July, 1869, 361; 23 Jan. 1869, 359.

22. *New York Times,* 19 June, 1870, 8; 23 Sept. 1870, 3; *New York Tribune,* 20 Sept. 1869, 8. By the end of 1870 Chicago's pro club was only playing "strictly first-class" teams; *Chicago Times,* 1 Oct. 1870, 3.

23. *Clipper,* 16 April, 1870, 13; 23 April, 1870, 21; *Chicago Tribune,* 16 Jan. 1870, 4; *Cincinnati Commercial,* 13 May, 1870, 5; *Turf, Field and Farm,* 23 Dec. 1870, 389; *Chicago Times,* 4 Oct. 1870, 2; *Clipper,* 10 July, 1869, 106.

24. *Turf, Field and Farm,* 29 July, 1870, 51; *Cincinnati Commercial,* 19 July, 1870, 5.

25. *Cincinnati Daily Times,* 5 July, 1869, 2; 11 Nov. 1869, 2; *Cincinnati Commercial* 8 Feb. 1870, 8.

26. *Cincinnati Enquirer,* 8 Dec. 1870, 8; *Cincinnati Daily Times,* 21 May, 1870, 1; *Chicago Tribune,* 17 Jan. 1871, 4.

27. *Cincinnati Commercial*, 16 Feb. 1870, 5; *Cincinnati Daily Times*, 8 Dec. 1870, 1; 10 Nov. 1870, 1. The Cincinnati club also supported a second nine and a junior team.

28. *Clipper*, 31 Oct. 1868, 234; *National Chronicle*, 5 March, 1870, 70.

29. *Cincinnati Commercial*, 13 April, 1879, 12; *World* (New York), 27 Nov. 1870, 7. The fact that Wright, in his correspondence, always addressed Champion as "Dear Sir" seems to indicate the two had a cordial, but not necessarily affectionate, relationship; Wright to Aaron Champion, March 10, 1871.

30. *Cincinnati Daily Times*, 8 Dec. 1870, 1; 28 Nov. 1871, 1; 27 May, 1869, 3; *Cincinnati Enquirer*, 8 Dec. 1870, 8.

31. *Cincinnati Enquirer*, 23 Nov. 1870, 8.

32. Sandiford, *Cricket and the Victorians,* 65-68; Brian Berachaw, *From the Stretford End: The Official History of the Lancashire County Cricket Club* (London: Partridge, 1990), 45; David Lemmon, *Official History of the Worcestershire County Cricket Club* (London: Helm, 1989), 51; Andrew Hignell, *History of the Glamorgan County Cricket Club* (London: Helm, 1988), 20.

33. *Clipper,* 20 Feb. 1869, 363; *Chicago Times,* 11 Aug. 1870, 4; *Clipper,* 21 Jan. 1871, 331; *Chicago Tribune*, 29 July, 1871, 4.

34. *Fort Wayne Daily Sentinel*, 29 March, 1871, 4; 27 July, 1871, 4; *Fort Wayne Daily Gazette*, 7 Sept. 1871, 4; 13 Sept. 1871, 4.

35. *Cleveland Plain Dealer,* 23 May, 1872, 3; 20 Aug. 1872, 3; quoted in the *Sunday Mercury* (Philadelphia), 14 July, 1872, 3.

Chapter 4

1. *Wilkes*, 31 Oct. 1868, 163.

2. *Cincinnati Daily Times*, 18 Aug. 1870, 1.

3. *World* (New York), 10 April, 1870, 7; 2 Oct. 1870, 2.

4. *Chicago Tribune*, 31 Aug. 1870, 4; *Cincinnati Daily Times*, 3 Nov. 1870, 1; *World* (New York), 13 Nov. 1870, 3; *Turf, Field and Farm*, 24 Dec. 1869, n.p.; *Clipper*, 4 Feb. 1871, 348.

5. *Clipper,* 4 Feb. 1871, 348; *Chicago Times,* 29 Jan. 1871, 7; *Clipper,* 4 Feb. 1871, 348.

6. *Clipper,* 7 Nov. 1868, 245; 10 Dec. 1870, 283; *New York Times,* 10 Nov. 1870, 3; *New England Base Ballist,* 10 Dec. 1868, 74; *Clipper,* 11 March, 1871, 387; *Chicago Tribune,* 24 March, 1871, 3.

7. Wright to Ben Douglas, April 26, 1872; *Clipper*, 25 March, 1871, 402.

8. *Proceedings of Convention of the National Association of Professional Base Ball Players* (Washington D.C. 1871), 6; *Chicago Tribune,* 3 March, 1871, 4; Wright to Hicks Hayhurst, Dec. 26, 1871.

9. *Chicago Tribune,* 16 June, 1871, 4; *Sunday Mercury* (Philadelphia), 21 Dec. 1873, 4; *World* (New York), 17 Oct. 1872, 8.

10. *Troy Daily Whig*, 28 Feb. 1871, 3; *Cleveland Plain Dealer*, 7 Nov. 1871, 3; *Boston Globe*, 17 July, 1873, 8; *Boston Daily Advertiser*, 21 Sept. 1872, 1; *Middletown Tribune*, 10 July, 1872.

11. *Clipper*, 16 March, 1872, 397; *Wilkes*, 8 March, 1873, 51.

12. *Boston Globe*, 3 March, 1874, 3; *Chicago Tribune,* 7 March, 1875, 5.

13. David Nemec, *The Beer and Whisky League* (New York: Lyons & Burford, 1994), 14; Ron McCulloch, *How Baseball Began* (Los Angeles: Warwick, 1995), 51; Thomas Gilbert, *Superstars and Monopoly Wars* (New York: Franklin Watts, 1995), 8.

14. *Cleveland Plain Dealer*, 30 April, 1872, 3; *Wilkes*, 27 April, 1872, 165. The *National Chronicle* (23 Oct. 1869, 226) had advocated an open pro competition in 1869.

15. *Baltimore American and Commercial Advertiser*, 28 May, 1872, 4; *World* (New York),

2 June, 1872, 1; *Sunday Mercury* (Philadelphia), 13 June, 1875, 3; *Chicago Tribune*, 30 May, 1875, 8; *Boston Globe*, 1 Nov. 1875, 3; *Baltimore Gazette*, 24 April, 1873, 4; *Clipper*, 11 Sept. 1875, 186; *St. Louis Republican*, 1 June, 1875, 2.

16. *New York Times*, 25 Aug. 1872, 8; *World* (New York), 8 Aug. 1871, 8; *Wilkes*, 22 Aug. 1874, 29; *Chicago Tribune*, 15 Aug. 1874, 12.

17. *New Haven Register*, 28 Sept. 1875, 4; *Courier Journal* (Louisville), 11 July, 1875, 8; *New Haven Register*, 25 Sept. 1875, 4; *World* (New York), 7 June, 1872, 8; 27 June, 1873, 5; *Philadelphia Times*, 14 June, 1875, 1; *Daily Gate City* (Keokuk), 11 June, 1875, 4.

18. *Philadelphia Times*, 27 May, 1875, 4; *Clipper*, 13 March, 1875, 397.

19. *Clipper*, 24 May, 1873, 58; *World* (New York), 30 Sept. 1873, 8; Wright to Norman Gassete, July 22, 1873.

20. David Voigt, *American Baseball, Volume 1: From Gentlemen's Sport to the Commissioner System* (College Station: Penn State University Press, 1983), 51.

21. Wright to J.N. Bartholomew, June 24, 1875.

22. *Clipper*, 28 Jan. 1871, 338; Wright to D.L. Reid, April 29, 1874; Wright to J. White, Dec. 27, 1872; *Boston Herald*, 5 Dec. 1871, 1; Wright to Sam Hensey, Aug. 18, 1879.

23. *New Haven Register*, 22 Nov. 1875, 4. *Forest and Stream* (16 Sept. 1875, 87) defined it as "thoroughly honest work, and strict attention to discipline and good training."

24. *Beadle's Dime Base-Ball Player* (New York: Beadle, 1875), 55; *Chicago Tribune*, 15 Jan. 1871, 4; Wright to W. Baker, March 16, 1878.

25. Wright to Henry Chadwick, Jan. 2, 1875.

26. *Chicago Tribune*, 10 Dec. 1876, 7; 8 Sept. 1875, 5; George Tuohey, *A History of the Boston Base Ball Club* (Boston: Quinn, 1897), 72, 202.

27. *Chicago Tribune*, 20 May, 1875, 6; *Clipper*, 7 Aug. 1875, 147.

28. *Wilkes*, 13 Sept. 114; *Chicago Times*, 27 Sept. 1874, 7; *Wilkes*, 13 Sept. 1873, 115; *World* (New York), 14 Oct. 1874, 10.

29. Nemec, *The Beer and Whisky League*, 14; Ted Vincent, *Mudville's Revenge* (New York: Seaview, 1981), 131; Seymour, *Baseball: The Early Years*, 60, 80.

30. *Wilkes*, 9 March, 1872, 53; *Chicago Tribune*, 18 Oct. 1876, 3; Wright to Henry Chadwick, Sept. 14, 1876; *Chicago Tribune*, 30 May, 1876, 6; *Troy Press*, 17 June, 1882, 3; *Argus* (Albany), 4 April, 1879, 5. Goldstein (*Playing For Keeps*, 135) is one of the few scholars whose recognized Ferguson's National Association presidency has "misled historians into overestimating the players influence."

31. *Clipper*, 7 Aug. 1875, 149.

32. *Sunday Mercury* (Philadelphia), 24 Sept. 1871, 4; *Clipper*, 23 March, 1872, 404.

33. *Wilkes*, 20 July, 1872, 357; *Chicago Tribune*, 9 Aug. 1874, 16; George Wright, *Record of the Boston Base Ball Club* (Boston: Rockwell & Churchill, 1874), 33; *DeWitt's Base Ball Guide*, 1874, 71; *DeWitt's Base Ball Guide*, 1872, 68.

34. *Boston Globe*, 23 Aug. 1875, 5; *World* (New York), 6 Aug. 1872, 5; 31 Aug. 1873, 8; *Baltimore Gazette*, 17 Sept. 1873, 8; *St. Louis Globe-Democrat*, 4 Sept. 1875, 5.

35. *World* (New York), 16 Aug. 1870, 8; 21 July, 1872, 5; *Wilkes*, 27 July, 1872, 375; *World* (New York), 14 Sept. 1873, 8.

36. *DeWitt's Base Ball Guide*, 1875, 50; Wright to James Ferguson, Jan. 5, 1874.

37. *Sunday Mercury* (New York), 15 July, 1860, 5; *Clipper*, 21 Dec. 1867, 291; *Boston Daily Journal*, 9 Nov. 1871, 4.

38. Gilbert, *Superstars and Monopoly Wars*, 12; Neil Stout, "1874 Baseball Tour Not Cricket to British," *Baseball Research Journal* (14), 1985, 85; *Forest and Stream*, 5 March, 1874, 62; *Boston Globe*, 7 Nov. 1874, 5; 13 Aug. 1874, 1.

39. *Rockford Register*, 11 Nov. 1871, 4.

40. Wright to Jason Hamill, May 16, 1872; *Wilkes*, 15 June, 1872, 279; *Clipper*, 19 Dec. 1874, 299; 13 July, 1875, 106. The *Clipper* (24 May, 1873, 58) had also felt "public interest in the game is not abating" in 1873.

41. *World* (New York), 15 May, 1873, 5; *Clipper*, 22 May, 1875, 61; 11 July, 1874, 115; 12 July, 1873, 115.

42. *Sunday Mercury* (Philadelphia), 19 Nov. 1871, 3; *Chicago Tribune*, 13 May, 1871, 4.

43. *World* (New York), 3 Nov. 1872, 2; *Chicago Tribune,* 3 Nov. 1873, 3.

44. *Clipper*, 21 June, 1873, 93; 8 Nov. 1873, 250; *Forest and Stream,* 11 Dec. 1873, 284; *Hartford Daily Times*, 15 Nov. 1875, 3.

45. Wright to Frank Clarke, April 17, 1874; Wright to T.J. Bryon, May 4, 1874; *Wilkes,* 3 Aug. 1872, 394; *Forest and Stream,* 4 Feb. 1875, 412; *New Haven Register*, 28 July, 1875, 4; *Clipper*, 18 Dec. 1875, 307; *Chicago Times*, 20 Jan. 1878, 4; Leiffer, *Making the Majors*, 59.

46. *Illinois State Journal*, 28 March, 1871, 2.

47. *New York Tribune*, 30 May, 1867, 4.

48. *Cincinnati Daily Times*, 6 Sept. 1870, 1; *New York Tribune*, 31 Aug. 1867, 1.

49. *Wilkes*, 16 Aug. 1873, 19; *Chicago Tribune*, 6 Aug. 1874, 8.

50. *Clipper,* 6 Nov. 1875, 250; 22 May, 1875, 58.

51. *New Haven Register*, 30 April, 1875, 4.

52. *World* (New York), 28 May, 1871, 1; *National Chronicle*, 4 Sept. 1869, 190; *Philadelphia Times*, 15 Oct. 1875, 4; *Forest and Stream*, 9 Dec. 1875, 278; *Chicago Tribune*, 13 Feb. 1876, 12.

53. *World* (New York), 28 May, 1871, 1.

54. *Clipper*, 27 Dec. 1873, 307; 6 Nov. 1875, 250; 12 Sept. 1874, 187; 29 May, 1875, 67; *Chicago Tribune*, 23 June, 1875, 5.

55. *Wilkes*, 4 Oct. 1873, 187; *Chicago Tribune*, 23 June, 1875, 5.

56. *Clipper*, 6 Dec. 1873, 282; *Beadle's Dime Base Ball Player*, 1875, 85; *Chicago Tribune*, 19 June, 1875, 5; *Clipper*, 6 Dec. 1873, 282.

57. *Boston Herald*, 5 June, 1881, 11.

58. *Clipper*, 24 Oct. 1868, 226; *Chicago Tribune*, 18 Feb. 1870, 4.

59. *New York Times*, 11 Sept. 1870, 4.

60. Charles Newcomb, *The Journals of Charles King Newcomb* (Providence: Brown University, 1946), 120.

61. *Wilkes*, 6 July, 1867, 347; Henry Chadwick, *The Game of Base Ball* (New York: Munroe, 1868), 81; *New York Tribune*, 12 Sept. 1868, 5.

62. *Sunday Mercury* (Philadelphia), 5 July, 1868, 3; *Wilkes,* 3 Aug. 1867, 427; *Cleveland Plain Dealer*, 11 Aug. 1871, 3.

63. *Troy Daily Whig*, 18 July, 1871, 3; *Chicago Times*, 28 June, 1870, 8.

64. *Baltimore American and Commercial Advertiser*, 18 June, 1872, 1; *St. Louis Republican*, 5 July, 1875, 8; *St. Louis Globe-Democrat*, 28 June, 1875, 8.

65. *DeWitt's Base Ball Guide*, 1869, 33.

66. *National Chronicle*, 9 April, 1870, 106; *Ohio State Journal*, 23 Sept. 1875, 4.

67. *St. Louis Globe-Democrat,* 1 Sept. 1875, 8; *Cincinnati Enquirer,* 20 July, 1879, 3; *Troy Press*, 17 June, 1881, 3; *Cincinnati Enquirer*, 9 Dec. 1881, 2. Even the moral strictures of the National League couldn't deter an outraged Providence batter, in 1882, from throwing his bat so hard it "would have killed" its intended target, the opposing pitcher; *Providence Daily Journal*, 24 Aug. 1882, 4.

68. *Sunday Mercury* (Philadelphia), 29 April, 1866, 4; *St. Louis Republican,* 27 Aug. 1876, 8; *St. Louis Globe-Democrat*, 27 May, 1882, 9.

69. *Chicago Tribune*, 22 Nov. 1874, 16; *Chicago Times*, 30 July, 1870, 5.

70. J. T. Crane, *Popular Amusements* (Cincinnati: Hitchcock & Walden, 1870), 81.

71. *Field and Stream*, 13 Oct. 1874, 335; *New York Times*, 8 March, 1872, 4.

72. *Chicago Tribune*, 28 June, 1871, 4; 18 May, 1871, 4; *World* (New York), 28 Aug. 1874, 2; 14 Aug. 1870, 5.

73. *Boston Post*, 27 Aug. 1867, 4; *National Chronicle*, 24 July, 1869, 144; *Harvard Advocate*, 24 June, 1870, 151.

74. *DeWitt's Base Ball Guide,* 1878, 38; Ric Sissons, *The Players: A Social History of the Professional Cricketer* (Sydney: Pluto, 1988), 74-75; Keith Sandiford, "Amateurs and Professionals in Victorian County Cricket," *Albion,* vol. 15 (1983), 32-51; Birely, *A Social History of English Cricket,* 133.

75. *Cincinnati Enquirer,* 29 Aug. 1875, 8.

76. *Sunday Mercury* (Philadelphia), 16 June, 1867, 4. *Forest and Stream* (26 March, 1874, 99) had found plenty of "genteel base ball rowdyism" among even the more reputable amateur clubs in New York.

77. *Chicago Tribune,* 18 June, 1882, 10.

78. *Chicago Tribune,* 20 Sept. 1874, 13; *American Chronicle of Sports and Pastimes,* 13 Feb. 1868, 50.

79. *Indianapolis Journal,* 25 April, 1877, 8; *Baltimore Gazette,* 22 April, 1873, 4; *Beadle's Dime Base-Ball Player,* 1872, 33.

80. Altherr, "'The Most Summery, Bold, Free & Spacious Game,'" 80; *Field and Stream,* 29 Aug. 1875, 20.

81. *Wilkes,* 24 July, 1869, 360.

82. *Clipper,* 19 Nov. 1881, 381; *Cincinnati Enquirer,* 23 Jan. 1881, 8; *Buffalo Daily Courier,* 10 March, 1881, 2.

83. *Cincinnati Enquirer,* 4 Aug. 1882, 8.

84. *New York Times,* 6 March, 1871, 6; *Forest and Stream,* 14 Aug. 1873, 8.

85. *Hartford Daily Courant,* 7 Jan. 1873, 2.

86. *Hartford Daily Courant,* 7 Jan. 1873, 2.

87. *Sunday Mercury* (Philadelphia), 31 Oct. 1875, 4.

Chapter 5

1. *World* (New York), 19 Sept. 1875, 2; *St. Louis Globe-Democrat,* 22 July, 1875, 8.

2. *Boston Globe,* 4 Oct. 1875, 5; *Chicago Tribune,* 3 Nov. 1873, 3; 24 Oct. 1875, 12.

3. *Sunday Mercury* (Philadelphia), 4 April, 1875, 4; *Boston Globe,* 14 May, 1875, 5.

4. *Chicago Tribune,* 10 Nov. 1873, 3; *Chicago Times,* 28 June, 1871, 5.

5. *Chicago Tribune,* 18 June, 1875, 2; 28 Sept. 1870, 4.

6. *Chicago Times,* 27 June, 1875, 4.

7. *Chicago Times,* 6 June, 1871, 8; *Wilkes,* 27 April, 1872, 165.

8. *Chicago Tribune,* 18 April, 1871, 3; 28 Feb. 1875, 10.

9. *Chicago Tribune,* 13 Jan. 1871, 4; *Cincinnati Commercial,* 29 Sept. 1870, 5; *New York Tribune,* 30 May, 1871, 8; *Chicago Tribune,* 29 July, 1875, 5; *National Chronicle,* 2 April, 1870, 98; *Chicago Times,* 14 Jan. 1871, 5; *Chicago Tribune,* 27 March, 1870, 4.

10. *Clipper,* 13 March, 1876, 395; *St. Louis Republican,* 7 March, 1875, 8; Wright to William Hulbert, Dec. 29, 1874.

11. *Chicago Tribune,* 20 July, 1875, 5; *Sunday Mercury* (Philadelphia), 25 July, 1875, 3; *Records of the Chicago Baseball Club,* 16 July 1875, 9; 19 Aug. 1874, n.p. Though scholars continue to claim the fear of expulsion from his Boston raid was Hulbert's motivation for setting up the National League, there's virtually no contemporary evidence to support this. Spalding had come close to signing with Chicago in 1873 and 1874, while the *Boston Globe* (28 July, 1875, 8) felt Chicago was well within its rights to sign the players; Lee Allen, *100 Years of Baseball* (New York: Bartholomew, 1950), 30; Voigt, *American Baseball,* 61; *Boston Globe,* 13 Jan. 1873, 8; *Chicago Times,* 5 Jan. 1873, 4; 16 Aug. 1874, 7.

12. *Wilkes,* 9 July, 1870, 324; *Chicago Times,* 1 Nov. 1874, 10.

13. *Chicago Times,* 10 May, 1871, 8; *World* (New York), 3 July, 1870, 1; 6 June, 1871, 1.

14. *Cincinnati Daily Times,* 7 July, 1870, 1; *Chicago Times,* 9 July, 1870, 4.

15. *Wilkes*, 27 June, 1874, 594; *Chicago Tribune*, 30 June, 1874, 5.

16. Spalding, *America's National Game*, 199; *Chicago Times*, 17 Feb. 1871, 4; *Chicago Tribune*, 6 Aug. 1874, 8.

17. *Wilkes*, 13 Sept. 1873, 115; *Sunday Mercury* (Philadelphia), 10 Sept. 1871, 4; *Records of the Chicago Baseball Club*, 18 Aug. 1874, n.p.; *Chicago Times*, 20 June, 1875, 5; *Boston Post*, 14 June, 1875, 3; *Hartford Daily Times*, 25 Aug. 1875, 3.

18. *Chicago Tribune*, 2 Nov. 1875, 12; *Cincinnati Daily Times*, 8 Dec. 1870, 1; *Boston Herald*, 27 Feb. 1881, 8.

19. *World* (New York), 8 Aug. 1875, 8; 18 Aug. 1875, 8; *Clipper*, 27 May, 1876, 67; *Chicago Tribune*, 7 May, 1875, 2; *World* (New York), 25 July, 1875, 8.

20. *Hartford Daily Times*, 7 Oct. 1875, 3; *Chicago Tribune*, 9 Aug. 1875, 3; *Boston Globe*, 25 Oct. 1875, 3; *Chicago Tribune*, 3 Oct. 1875, 9; *Sunday Mercury* (Philadelphia), 28 Nov. 1875, 4; *Field and Stream*, 11 Dec. 1875, 261.

21. *St. Louis Republican*, 5 March, 1876, 10.

22. *Chicago Times*, 6 Aug. 1872, 2; *Records of the Chicago Baseball Club*, 19 Aug. 1874, n.p.; 18 Oct. 1875, 16.

23. Hulbert to H.D. McKnight, Nov. 8, 1881; *Sunday Mercury* (New York), 12 Oct. 1879, 5; Hulbert to unidentified correspondent, Aug. 30, 1875; N.T. Appolonio to Hulbert, June 26, 1878.

24. Hulbert to Campbell Bishop, Sept. 25, 1875; Hulbert to Campbell Bishop, Oct. 25, 1875; *Chicago Tribune*, 28 Nov. 1875, 13.

25. Hulbert to Campbell Bishop, Dec. 8, 1875; *Clipper*, 6 Jan. 1877, 323; *Brooklyn Eagle*, 22 May, 1877, 2; *Cincinnati Enquirer*, 14 Feb. 1877, 2; *St. Louis Republican*, 7 Sept. 1876, 8. Meacham was also the private secretary to the mayor of Chicago; *Cincinnati Enquirer*, 3 Oct. 1878, 8.

26. Hulbert to Charles Chase, Nov. 8, 1875; Hulbert to Campbell Bishop, 4 Dec. 1875.

27. *Chicago Tribune*, 19 Dec. 1875, 13; Hulbert to Campbell Bishop, Sept. 25, 1875; Hulbert to Campbell Bishop, Oct. 15, 1875.

28. *Chicago Tribune*, 4 April, 1880, 9; Hulbert to N.T. Appolonio, March 2, 1874.

29. *Boston Globe*, 24 Jan. 1878, 3; Wright to William Hulbert, Feb. 5, 1875; Wright to William Hulbert, Dec. 30, 1875.

30. *Chicago Tribune*, 14 Sept. 1879, 7.

31. *Field and Stream*, 12 Feb. 1876, 404; Hulbert to Campbell Bishop, Feb. 10, 1876.

32. Hulbert to Campbell Bishop, Dec. 4, 1875; *World* (New York), 12 April, 1876, 6; Hulbert to William Cammeyer, Feb. 12, 1876; Hulbert to Morgan Bulkeley, March 16, 1876; *St. Louis Republican*, 24 Feb. 1876, 8.

33. *Hartford Daily Times*, 5 Feb. 1876, 2.

34. *Chicago Times*, 13 Feb. 1876, 10; *Forest and Stream*, 17 Feb. 1876, 27; *Clipper*, 12 Feb. 1876, 362; *New Haven Register*, 7 Feb. 1876, 4. The National League was so secretive of its proceedings, delegates, on oath, were forbidden to divulge them even to their club directors; *Argus* (Albany), 8 Oct. 1880, 8.

35. *Clipper*, 6 Jan. 1877, 323.

36. *Chicago Tribune*, 4 Feb. 1876, 5; *Clipper*, 25 Oct. 1876, 245. *Forest and Steam* (17 Feb. 1876, 27) also felt the National League was implementing baseball reform "in about as blundering a way as could well be imagined."

37. *Chicago Tribune*, 2 April, 1876, 5; 9 April, 1876, 10; Hulbert to Harry Wright, Jan. 27, 1876; Wright to William Hulbert, May 6, 1876.

38. *New Haven Register*, 28 Sept. 1875, 4.

39. *Hartford Daily Times*, 8 Feb. 1876, 2; 26 Feb. 1876, 2.

40. *Forest and Stream*, 17 Feb. 1876, 27; *Clipper*, 2 Dec. 1876, 282.

41. Wright to William Hulbert, Dec. 30, 1875; *Sunday Mercury* (New York), 7 Jan. 1877, 5; Wright to Ben Douglas, Feb.17, 1875.

42. *Clipper,* 24 Feb. 1877, 378; *Sunday Mercury* (Philadelphia), 13 Sept. 1876, 4; *Sunday Mercury* (New York), 15 Oct. 1876, 5; *Chicago Tribune,* 3 Sept. 1876, 3.

43. *St. Louis Globe-Democrat,* 21 Jan. 1877, 7; *Sunday Mercury* (New York), 22 Oct. 1876, 5; *Clipper,* 21 Oct. 1876, 235.

44. *Clipper,* 3 March, 1877, 387; *Sunday Mercury* (New York), 13 Jan. 1878, 4.

45. Vincent, *Mudville's Revenge,* 153; *Utica Daily Observer,* 25 July, 1878, 5; *Forest and Stream,* 10 Aug. 1876, 11.

46. *Chicago Tribune,* 3 June, 1877, 7; *Indianapolis Journal,* 19 March, 1878, 3.

47. *Chicago Tribune,* 27 Oct. 1878, 12; *St. Louis Globe-Democrat,* 21 Jan. 1877, 7; *DeWitt's Base Ball Guide,* 1878, 38; *Brooklyn Daily Eagle,* 12 Oct. 1877, 3; *Free Press* (London), 15 Sept. 1877, 3; *Lowell Daily Citizen,* 10 Oct. 1877, 2; *Sunday Republic* (Philadelphia), 2 Sept. 1877, 3; *World* (New York), 21 May, 1877, 6.

48. *Chicago Times,* 26 Aug. 1877, 3.

49. Wright to William Hulbert, April 21, 1877.

50. *Sunday Mercury* (Philadelphia), 26 March, 1876, 4; Wright to William Hulbert, April 16, 1877.

51. *Chicago Tribune,* 11 Oct. 1874, 13; Preston Orem, *Baseball (1845-1881) From the Newspaper Accounts* (Altadena, CA: Orem, 1961), 232; Hulbert to Charles Fowle, Sept. 10, 1875.

52. *Wilkes,* 20 March, 1872, 100; *Sunday Mercury* (Philadelphia), 2 April, 1876, 4; Wright to William Cammeyer, April 27, 1874; *Hartford Daily Times,* 22 July, 1876, 2.

53. *St. Louis Globe-Democrat,* 25 July, 1876, 8; *Hartford Daily Times,* 19 April, 1876, 2; *Chicago Tribune,* 24 April, 1875, 7; *Sunday Mercury* (Philadelphia), 9 July, 1876, 5.

54. *World* (New York), 23 July, 1876, 8; *New Haven Register,* 24 July, 1876, 1; Hulbert to Charles Fowle, Sept. 21, 1876.

55. *Clipper,* 23 Dec. 1876, 307; *Chicago Tribune,* 10 Dec. 1876, 7.

56. *Chicago Tribune,* 30 March, 1871, 3; 12 Oct. 1873, 3; *Cleveland Plain Dealer,* 17 April, 1872, 3.

57. *Clipper,* 13 March, 1875, 395; *Chicago Tribune,* 16 April, 1875, 3. The entire Davy Force matter may have been precipitated by the failure of the Keokuks, forcing their delegate on the Judiciary Committee, Trimble, to step down, thus opening the way for Spering; *Sunday Mercury* (Philadelphia), 7 March 1875, 4. Hulbert admitted using this practice of backdating to release James Hallinan in 1878; *St. Louis Globe-Democrat,* 16 Aug. 1878, 5.

58. Hulbert to Charles Spering, 19 Aug. 1875; Hulbert to Charles Bishop, Sept. 25, 1875.

59. Chicago Tribune, 12 Dec. 1875, 12; Hulbert to Charles Fowle, Aug. 19, 1875. Wright (letter to William Cammeyer, March 12, 1875) had also complained about the "Athletics, first, right or wrong" attitude.

60. *Boston Globe,* 4 Aug. 1876, 1; *Courier-Journal* (Louisville), 18 Sept. 1876, 1; 15 Aug. 1876, 1; *Cincinnati Enquirer,* 13 Sept. 1876, 2; *Sunday Mercury* (Philadelphia), 5 Dec. 1875, 4; 19 Nov. 1876, 4; *Cincinnati Enquirer,* 10 Aug. 1876, 8; *Sunday Mercury* (Philadelphia), 10 Sept. 1876, 3; *Chicago Times,* 24 Sept. 1876, 9.

61. *Argus* (Albany), 8 Nov. 1880, 8; Hulbert to Charles Fowle, Sept. 14, 1876.

62. Hulbert to N.T. Appolonio, Nov. 22, 1876, 10; *Chicago Tribune,* 26 Nov. 1876, 7.

63. *Clipper,* 23 Dec. 1876, 307; *Hartford Daily Times,* 19 Sept. 1876, 2.

64. *Chicago Tribune,* 7 Nov. 1875, 12.

65. *Wilkes,* 24 July, 1869, 360; *Chicago Tribune,* 13 Feb. 1876, 12; 4 Feb. 1876, 5.

66. *Brooklyn Daily Eagle,* 31 Oct. 1865, 2; 28 Nov. 1865, 2; 16 Oct. 1866, 2; *Turf, Field and Farm,* 4 Sept. 1868, 580; *Cincinnati Daily Times,* 21 May, 1870, 1; *Chicago Times,* 27 July, 1870, 4.

67. *New York Times,* 28 May, 1871, 8; *Cincinnati Daily Times,* 9 June, 1870, 1; *New York Times,* 11 Aug. 1872, 8; *Daily Gate City* (Keokuk), 2 May, 1875, 4.

68. Wright to Nick Young, March 28, 1873.

69. *Age* (Philadelphia), 8 June, 1869, 1; *Sunday Mercury* (New York), 9 July, 1876, 5; *Hartford Daily Times*, 18 Sept. 1876, 2.

70. *Ball Players Chronicle*, 22 Aug. 1867, 6; *Buffalo Daily Courier*, 5 Dec. 1879, 2; *Courier-Journal* (Louisville), 8 April, 1877, 1; *Chicago Times*, 6 Feb. 1881, 13; *Cincinnati Enquirer*, 16 April, 1879, 2.

71. *St. Louis Globe-Democrat*, 9 May, 1882, 8; *Chicago Tribune*, 27 May, 1877, 7; 22 Aug. 1876, 5; *Cleveland Plain Dealer*, 29 Aug. 1879, 1; *Chicago Tribune*, 7 Aug. 1881, 6. Prostitutes reportedly frequented Cincinnati games; *St. Louis Globe-Democrat*, 12 May, 1878, 7.

72. *Forest and Stream*, 14 Dec. 1876, 310.

73. *Clipper*, 7 Oct. 1876, 219; *Cincinnati Enquirer*, 31 July, 1876, 8; *Chicago Tribune*, 3 Nov. 1877, 3; 14 July, 1878, 7.

74. *Hartford Daily Times*, 2 June, 1876, 2; *St. Louis Globe-Democrat*, 16 July, 1876, 8; *Courier-Journal* (Louisville), 6 June, 1876, 5; *St. Louis Globe-Democrat*, 4 March, 1877, 6; *Chicago Times*, 30 July, 1876, 3.

75. *Clipper*, 14 Oct. 1876, 229; *Chicago Tribune*, 12 Aug. 1877, 7.

76. *Hartford Daily Times*, 21 June, 1876, 2; *Chicago Tribune*, 18 Feb. 1877, 7; 4 Nov. 1877, 7.

77. *St. Louis Globe-Democrat*, 16 July, 1876, 5; *Chicago Tribune*, 9 April, 1876, 10; *Clipper*, 6 Jan. 1877, 323.

78. *Hartford Daily Times*, 2 Aug. 1876, 2; *St. Louis Globe-Democrat*, 26 July, 1876, 8; *Cincinnati Enquirer*, 25 Sept. 1876, 6.

79. *Clipper*, 15 Sept. 1877, 195.

80. Hulbert to J.M. Neff, Sept. 21, 1877.

81. *Courier-Journal* (Louisville), 3 Nov. 1877, 4; *Chicago Tribune*, 9 Dec. 1877, 1. The National League itself never undertook any "full scale investigation" of the Louisville matter as claimed by many scholars; Voigt, *American Baseball*, 72.

82. *Chicago Times*, 21 Aug. 1870, 4; *Buffalo Daily Courier*, 27 Sept. 1878, 2; *Courier-Journal* (Louisville), 25 July, 1876, 5; *Chicago Times*, 8 Aug. 1874, 10.

83. *Chicago Tribune*, 5 Nov. 1876, 10; *Hartford Daily Times*, 14 Dec. 1876, 2; *Clipper*, 6 Jan. 1877, 323; W. A. Halden to John Halden, May 27, 1876; *Chicago Tribune*, 14 Jan. 1877, 2.

84. *St. Louis Globe-Democrat*, 1 Nov. 1877, 8; Hulbert to Bob Ferguson, Nov. 8, 1877; *Chicago Tribune*, 18 Nov. 1877, 7.

85. William Craver to Harry Wright, Nov. 27, 1878; *Chicago Tribune*, 20 June, 1880, 7; *Chicago Times*, 30 June, 1878, 4; *Clipper*, 18 Dec. 1880, 205.

86. *Argus* (Albany), 20 Feb. 1879, 5. Craver won temporary reinstatement from his old club, Troy, in 1878 while Nichols played for a short time with the Resolutes of New Jersey; *Troy Press*, 7 Aug. 1878, 3; *Chicago Tribune*, 21 July, 1878, 7.

87. *Chicago Tribune*, 18 Aug. 1878, 7; *Buffalo Daily Courier*, 10 Aug. 1879, 2; *Argus* (Albany), 31 July, 1880, 8; *Boston Herald*, 30 April, 1882, 8; *Chicago Tribune*, 21 July, 1878, 7.

88. *Chicago Tribune*, 3 Nov. 1878, 12; 2 March, 1879, 12; *Pittsburg Dispatch*, 15 March, 1882, 1; *Cincinnati Enquirer*, 6 Feb. 1879, 8.

89. *Chicago Tribune*, 11 Nov. 1877, 7; *Cincinnati Enquirer*, 16 May, 1877, 8; John Haldeman to his mother, June 6, 1876; *Chicago Tribune*, 3 March, 1877, 7.

90. *Chicago Tribune*, 11 Nov. 1877, 7; 19 Aug. 1877, 7. The *St. Louis Globe-Democrat* (29 Aug. 1877, 3) was so convinced of Devinny's collusion with Louisville it headlined its reports of Louisville's disastrous eastern tour with such near libelous retorts as "Bring on Devinny!" and "A Kingdom for Devinny!"

91. Hulbert to N.T. Appolonio, July 10, 1877; Wright to J.F. Neff, Feb. 8, 1878.

92. *Chicago Tribune*, 11 Nov. 1877, 7.

93. J. E. Findling, "The Louisville Gray's Scandal of 1877," *Journal of Sports History*,

No. 2 (1976), 185; *Boston Globe*, 23 Dec. 1877, 8; *Sunday Mercury* (New York), 4 Nov. 1877, 5; *St. Louis Globe-Democrat*, 23 July, 1877, 8; Hulbert to Bob Ferguson, Nov. 8, 1877.

94. Hulbert to Bob Ferguson, 13 Dec. 1877.

95. *Cincinnati Enquirer*, 25 June, 1878, 8.

96. *Buffalo Daily Courier*, 15 Aug. 1878, 2; *Chicago Tribune*, 12 Oct. 1879, 7; *Utica Daily Observer*, 6 Aug. 1878, 3.

97. *Troy Daily Times*, 30 Aug. 1880, 3; *Chicago Tribune*, 27 Feb. 1876, 9; Wright to Dick Higham, Feb. 10, 1877; *Clipper*, 1 July, 1882, 235; *Providence Evening Press*, 16 Sept. 1881, 3; *Detroit Free Press*, 27 July, 1882, 8.

98. *World* (New York), 8 July, 1878, 8; Spalding, *America's National Game*, 223; *Cincinnati Enquirer*, 4 Feb. 1879, 8.

99. *Buffalo Daily Courier*, 30 May, 1881, 2; *Chicago Tribune*, 25 May, 1879, 7; *Cincinnati Enquirer*, 21 June, 1880, 10; 30 Jan. 1881, 11; *Buffalo Daily Courier*, 7 Feb. 1881, 2.

100. *Buffalo Daily Courier*, 7 Feb. 1881, 2; *Chicago Tribune*, 17 Feb. 1878, 7; *Spalding's Official Base Ball Guide* (Chicago: Spalding & Bros., 1882), 23.

101. *Boston Globe*, 6 Nov. 1876, 3; *World* (New York), 22 Oct. 1876, 2; *Clipper*, 12 Aug. 1876, 154.

102. *Chicago Tribune*, 13 Aug. 1876, 3; *Courier-Journal* (Louisville), 8 April, 1877, 1; *Buffalo Daily Courier*, 15 Dec. 1879, 2; Hulbert to N.T. Appolonio, July 10, 1877.

103. *Chicago Tribune*, 4 Feb. 1876, 5; 16 June, 1878, 7; 7 April, 1878, 7.

104. Hulbert to Robert Townsend, March 19, 1878.

105. *Chicago Times*, 3 Feb. 1878, 3.

106. Wright to William Hulbert, Jan. 18, 1878; Jan. 22, 1878; *Buffalo Daily Courier*, 28 June, 1879, 2; *Cleveland Plain Dealer*, 27 Aug. 1878, 4. Lowell declined to join the National League because its manager "does not care to put his head into a halter that is sure to strangle him"; *Free Press* (London), 14 Feb. 1878, 3; *St. Louis Globe-Democrat*, 3 Feb. 1878, 7.

107. *Chicago Times*, 28 Oct. 1877, 3; *Chicago Tribune*, 6 Jan. 1878, 7; *Sunday Mercury* (New York), 4 Nov. 1877, 5. By 1881 the average expense for a National League game, with salaries, was $500; *Chicago Tribune*, 6 March, 1881, 9.

108. *Indianapolis Journal*, 7 April, 1877, 8; 8 June, 1877, 8.

109. *Indianapolis Journal*, 1 July, 1878, 3; 27 June, 1878, 3; August Solare to Harry Wright, June 14, 1878; *Chicago Tribune*, 29 June, 1878, 5; *Cincinnati Enquirer*, 20 July, 1878, 5; *Clipper*, 2 Nov. 1878, 250; *Cincinnati Enquirer*, 23 July, 1878, 8; *St. Louis Globe-Democrat*, 14 July, 1878, 7.

110. Wright to William Hulbert, Feb. 7, 1878; *Chicago Tribune*, 4 Jan. 1877, 3; *Milwaukee Sentinel*, 2 Sept. 1878, 7; *Chicago Tribune*, 30 June, 1878, 7; 1 Dec. 1878, 7; *Clipper*, 15 Dec. 1878, 298.

111. *Buffalo Daily Courier*, 5 Dec. 1878, 2; *Courier-Journal* (Louisville), 24 Sept. 1876, 1; *St. Louis Globe-Democrat*, 6 Jan. 1878, 7; Wright to Robert Townsend, Dec. 16, 1878; *Cincinnati Commercial*, 15 Sept. 1879, 6; *Clipper*, 20 Sept. 1879, 204; 12 July, 1879, 123; *Chicago Tribune*, 13 July, 1879, 7.

112. *Chicago Tribune*, 11 Sept. 1879, 6; *Clipper*, 20 Sept. 1879, 204.

113. *Clipper*, 10 March, 1877, 394; *World* (New York), 6 March, 1877, 2; *St. Louis Globe-Democrat*, 18 March, 1877, 7; Wright to Morgan Bulkeley, Sept. 13, 1877.

114. *Chicago Tribune*, 24 Dec. 1876, 3; Hulbert to N.T. Appolonio, July 10, 1877; *Clipper*, 15 Dec. 1877, 298; Hulbert to Bob Ferguson, Dec. 13, 1877.

115. *Chicago Tribune*, 22 Sept. 1876, 2.

116. Leiffer, *Making the Majors*, 67; Hulbert to N.T. Appolonio, July 10, 1877; Hulbert to Bob Ferguson, Nov. 15, 1877.

Chapter 6

1. *World* (New York), 13 Feb. 1876, 6.

2. *Boston Globe,* 26 Oct. 1876, 5; 8 Nov. 1877, 5; *Lowell Daily Citizen,* 24 Sept. 1878, 3; *Troy Daily Press,* 2 Aug. 1879, 3; *Springfield Daily Republican,* 24 Oct. 1879, 5; *Worcester Daily Spy,* 26 Aug. 1879, 4.

3. *Sunday Mercury* (New York), 27 Jan. 1878, 3; *World* (New York), 23 Sept. 1876, 2; *Troy Daily Times,* 13 Oct. 1880, 3; *Clipper,* 7 July, 1877, 115.

4. *Clipper,* 27 May, 1876, 67; *Chicago Times,* 4 June, 1876, 4.

5. *World* (New York), 14 June, 1880, 6; *Chicago Times,* 26 June, 1881, 12; *Buffalo Daily Courier,* 7 Sept. 1880, 2; *Boston Herald,* 24 July, 1881, 2.

6. *Sunday Mercury* (New York), 24 March, 1878, 5; 24 Feb. 1878, 5; *Chicago Tribune,* 24 Feb. 1878, 7.

7. *Rochester Union and Advertiser,* 14 June, 1879, 1; *Utica Daily Observer,* 23 Sept. 1878, 2; *Manchester Daily Union,* 15 May, 1878, 3; *Clipper,* 9 Nov. 1878, 258.

8. *Argus* (Albany), 1 April, 1879, 4.

9. *Clipper,* 2 Sept. 1876, 179; 23 Sept. 1876, 205; *Sunday Mercury* (New York), 22 Oct. 1876, 5; *Courier-Journal* (Louisville), 11 Sept. 1877, 4; *Clipper,* 19 Jan. 1878, 338.

10. *Troy Press,* 10 March, 1881, 3.

11. Hulbert to H. D. McKnight, Nov. 13, 1881; Wright to Robert Townsend, March 20, 1878.

12. *Chicago Tribune,* 24 Feb. 1878, 7; *Utica Daily Observer,* 17 Feb. 1879, 3.

13. *Chicago Tribune,* 16 June, 1878, 7; *Boston Globe,* 15 July, 1878, 4; *Chicago Tribune,* 9 June, 1878, 7; *Boston Globe,* 2 May, 1878, 1.

14. *Times* (Philadelphia), 27 Aug. 1882, 2; Bancroft to Harry Wright, Oct. 9, 1878; Bancroft to Harry Wright, Aug. 4, 1878; *Boston Globe,* 18 May, 1880, 1; Wright to Frank Bancroft, Aug. 2, 1879; *Worcester Daily Spy,* 30 Dec. 1879, 4; 21 Jan. 1880, 4.

15. Hulbert to Campbell Bishop, Jan. 22, 1877.

16. *St. Louis Globe-Democrat,* 15 Jan. 1877, 5; Hulbert to N. T. Appolonio, Feb. 2, 1877; *Chicago Tribune,* 25 March, 1877, 7; 16 Sept. 1877, 7.

17. *Buffalo Daily Courier,* 2 April, 1878, 2; *Chicago Tribune,* 7 April, 1878, 7; *Sunday Mercury* (New York), 7 April, 1878, 5.

18. *Chicago Tribune,* 3 Feb. 1878, 7; Wright to T.J. Byron, May 4, 1874.

19. *Clipper,* 5 Jan. 1878, 323; Wright to Robert Townsend, March 20, 1878; Wright to N.S. Sprague, Jan. 17, 1878; Hulbert to J.M. Neff, Feb. 18, 1879; *Troy Press,* 16 April, 1879, 3.

20. *Sunday Mercury* (New York), 7 Jan. 1877, 5; Hulbert to J.F. Evans, May 23, 1879; *Clipper,* 14 June, 1879, 93.

21. *Clipper,* 30 March, 1878, 2; *Lowell Daily Citizen,* 6 June, 1878, 2; *Cincinnati Enquirer,* 14 April, 1880, 2; *Clipper,* 18 Dec. 1880, 309; 1 Jan. 1881, 325.

22. *Chicago Tribune,* 20 Jan. 1878, 7; *Troy Daily Press,* 3 June, 1880, 3; *Clipper,* 4 June, 1879, 93.

23. *Troy Daily Press,* 31 May, 1879, 3; *Argus* (Albany), 26 July, 1879, 4.

24. *Clipper,* 15 Nov. 1879, 269; *Buffalo Daily Courier,* 26 Jan. 1881, 2; *World* (New York), 8 Sept. 1879, 8.

25. *Cincinnati Enquirer,* 24 May, 1878, 8; *Free Press* (London), 26 Aug. 1878, 1; *Buffalo Daily Courier,* 11 July, 1878, 2; *Hornellsville Tribune,* 30 Aug. 1878, 3; *Lowell Daily Citizen,* 5 Dec. 1878, 3; *Manchester Daily Union,* 6 Aug. 1878, 3; *World* (New York), 17 June, 1878, 6.

26. *Rochester Union and Advertiser,* 21 Feb. 1879, 2; *Clipper,* 26 July, 1879, 138; *Utica Daily Observer,* 22 Feb. 1878, 3; *Rochester Union and Advertiser,* 30 June, 1879, 2.

27. *Utica Daily Observer,* 19 Feb. 1879, 3; *Cincinnati Enquirer,* 31 Dec. 1882, 12; *Utica Daily Observer,* 12 July, 1879, 8; *Springfield Daily Republican,* 8 Sept. 1879, 5; *Manchester Daily Union,* 7 July, 1879, 3.

28. *Rochester Union and Advertiser,* 11 Dec. 1879, 2; *Cincinnati Enquirer,* 13 Sept. 1879, 8; 25 Jan. 1880, 10; *Buffalo Daily Courier,* 13 July, 1880, 2; *Washington Post,* 23 May, 1880, 6; *Boston Globe,* 11 July, 1880, 3; *Argus* (Albany), 22 July, 1880, 8.

29. *Chicago Tribune,* 8 Feb. 1880, 7; *Clipper,* 23 Oct. 1880, 245; *Capital* (Wash- ington, D.C.), 11 July, 1880, 8; *Buffalo Daily Courier,* 4 Aug. 1880, 2; *Clipper,* 24 July, 1880, 146; *Argus* (Albany), 24 Aug. 1880, 8.

30. *Chicago Tribune,* 12 Oct. 1879, 7.

31. *Sunday Mercury* (New York), 30 March, 1879, 5; *Cincinnati Enquirer,* 1 July, 1880, 4; *Chicago Tribune,* 10 Dec. 1876, 7; 11 April, 1880, 7; 10 Dec. 1877, 7; *Troy Daily Press,* 9 June, 1879, 3; *Chicago Times,* 23 June, 1881, 6. To avoid ticket refunds, Chicago and Worcester played only one and a half innings in one of their games, a practice so unpopular with the fans a lawyer in Cleveland sued the National League over it; *Troy Daily Press,* 30 Aug. 1880, 3; *Worcester Daily Spy,* 15 July, 1880, 4.

32. *Cleveland Plain Dealer,* 10 Aug. 1878, 4.

33. *Boston Herald,* 13 Aug. 1882, 11; *Cleveland Plain Dealer,* 11 July, 1881, 5; *Chicago Tribune,* 30 July, 1882, 10.

34. *St. Louis Globe-Democrat,* 27 June, 1877, 5; *Troy Daily Press,* 9 Dec. 1880, 3; *Cleveland Plain Dealer,* 8 Dec. 1882, 5.

35. *Chicago Times,* 23 March, 1879, 7; *Chicago Tribune,* 25 Sept. 1881, 12.

36. *Buffalo Daily Courier,* 13 Aug. 1879, 2; *Chicago Tribune,* 15 Dec. 1879, 6; *Cincinnati Enquirer,* 7 May, 1879, 4.

37. *Cincinnati Enquirer,* 26 Sept. 1879, 6; Hulbert to Arthur Soden, Oct. 19, 1879; Hulbert to Si Keck, March 27, 1876; Hulbert to Freeman Brown, Dec. 24, 1879; *Chicago Tribune,* 7 Dec. 1879, 16.

38. *Troy Daily Press,* 17 April, 1879, 3; *Rochester Union and Advertiser,* 3 June, 1879, 2; *Chicago Tribune,* 15 Aug. 1880, 12; *Buffalo Daily Courier,* 12 Dec. 1880, 2. Prior to this, any game a National League club played on Sunday couldn't count in the championship; *Chicago Times,* 1 Feb. 1880, 11.

39. *Cincinnati Enquirer,* 29 June, 1880, 2; 5 July, 1880, 8; 9 Aug. 1880, 7; *Chicago Tribune,* 15 June, 1879, 7; *Troy Daily Press,* 6 Oct. 1880, 3.

40. *Cleveland Plain Dealer,* 9 Nov. 1880, 1; *Chicago Tribune,* 7 Oct. 1880, 5; *Cincinnati Enquirer,* 7 Oct. 1880, 6; *Buffalo Daily Courier,* 7 Oct. 1880, 2.

41. *Chicago Tribune,* 12 Oct. 1879, 7.

42. *Chicago Tribune,* 8 July, 1881, 7; *Courier-Journal* (Louisville), 2 Sept. 1877, 1.

43. *Cincinnati Enquirer,* 5 Nov. 1878, 8; *Chicago Tribune,* 14 Dec. 1879, 12; *Cincinnati Enquirer,* 9 July, 1876, 7; *Rochester Union & Advertiser,* 5 June, 1878, 2.

44. *Chicago Tribune,* 11 March, 1881, 3; *Sunday Mercury* (Philadelphia), 5 March, 1871, 3; *St. Louis Globe-Democrat,* 22 Oct. 1882, 7; 7 April, 1878, 3.

45. *Spalding's Official Base Ball Guide for 1878,* 13; *Clipper,* 10 Aug. 1878, 155; Hulbert to Paul Hines, Dec. 15, 1876; *Sunday Mercury* (New York), 8 Dec. 1878, 5; *Buffalo Daily Courier,* 27 Feb. 1880, 2; *Boston Herald,* 11 Sept. 1881, 2.

46. *Chicago Tribune,* 5 Sept. 1880, 6; *Clipper,* 23 Oct. 1879, 243.

47. *Clipper,* 16 Oct. 1880, 238; *Buffalo Daily Courier,* 7 Oct. 1880, 2; *Cincinnati Enquirer,* 12 Aug. 1880, 8; *Troy Daily Press,* 8 Oct. 1880, 3.

48. *Chicago Times,* 13 Nov. 1878, 4.

49. Spalding, *America's National Game,* 536; *Cincinnati Enquirer,* 27 Aug. 1880, 5.

50. *Providence Evening Press,* 2 Aug. 1881, 4; Hulbert to Albert Spalding, Oct. 8, 1879; Hulbert to Al Reach, Jan. 3, 1882; Hulbert to Arthur Soden, Oct. 10, 1879.

51. *DeWitt's Base Ball Guide,* 1880, 60.

52. *St. Louis Globe-Democrat,* 26 April, 1877, 3; *Chicago Tribune,* 12 Nov. 1876, 7; *World* (New York), 27 July, 1879, 2.

53. *Cincinnati Enquirer,* 4 Feb. 1879, 8.

54. *Providence Evening Press*, 2 Aug. 1881, 4; *Chicago Tribune*, 29 May, 1881, 16; *Cincinnati Enquirer*, 24 Sept. 1877, 8. To get rid of one of their underperforming players, Bill Parks, Boston tricked him into demanding his release by making him a fictitious offer from another club; Tuohey, *A History of the Boston Base Ball Club*, 74.

55. *Clipper*, 8 Oct. 1881, 463; 22 Oct. 1881, 504; *St. Louis Globe-Democrat*, 25 Nov. 1877, 7.

56. *Detroit Free Press*, 2 Oct. 1881, 6; *Chicago Tribune*, 2 Oct. 1881, 10; Hulbert to Freeman Brown, Sept. 8, 1881.

57. *Chicago Tribune*, 12 Aug. 1870, 4; *Buffalo Daily Courier*, 14 Aug. 1878, 2.

58. *Boston Herald*, 3 April, 1879, 4; *Cincinnati Enquirer*, 10 Aug. 1880, 8; *Buffalo Daily Courier*, 28 Sept. 1879, 2.

59. *Chicago Tribune*, 3 Dec. 1876, 7; *Buffalo Daily Courier*, 16 Sept. 1880, 2. The Providence players, after 1882, weren't even permitted to bring personal grievances before their club's directors; *Worcester Daily Spy*, 3 April, 1882, 4.

60. *Chicago Tribune*, 25 Sept. 1881, 12; *Clipper*, 19 Aug. 1882, 349.

61. *Chicago Tribune*, 25 March, 1877, 7; *St. Louis Globe-Democrat*, 3 Aug. 1876, 8; *Worcester Daily Spy*, 9 March, 1882, 4; *Records of the Chicago Base Ball Club*, July 7, 1875, 8; Hulbert to Bob Ferguson, Dec. 13, 1877. By contrast, the St. Louis club, in 1877, was paying $5,000 to rent its ground; *Cincinnati Enquirer*, 8 Nov. 1877, 8.

62. *Chicago Tribune*, 24 Sept. 1882, 9. Chicago had 2,500 advertising posters printed up for itself in 1880, far more than any other National League club; *Cincinnati Enquirer*, 27 Feb. 1880, 8.

63. *Clipper*, 4 Sept. 1880, 187; 11 July, 1880, 6; *Boston Globe*, 29 July, 1876, 5; *Chicago Tribune*, 9 July, 1882, 9; 22 Aug. 1880, 8.

64. *Chicago Times*, 14 Aug. 1881, 5; *Buffalo Daily Courier*, 9 March, 1881, 2; *St. Louis Globe-Democrat*, 11 Nov. 1877, 7.

65. *Chicago Tribune*, 22 Sept. 1876, 7; Hulbert to John Brown, 9 Sept. 1879; Hulbert to Charles Fowle, Sept. 13, 1875; Hulbert to Cap Anson, June 5, 1880.

66. *Troy Daily Press*, 8 April, 1881, 3; *Buffalo Daily Courier*, 20 July, 1880, 2; *Clipper*, 15 Nov. 1879, 269; *Buffalo Daily Courier*, 26 May, 1880, 2.

67. *Chicago Tribune*, 7 July, 1880, 8; 11 July, 1880, 6; *Cincinnati Enquirer*, 22 Aug. 1877, 2; *Chicago Tribune*, 25 July, 1880, 16.

68. *Chicago Tribune*, 28 May, 1882, 16; *Chicago Times*, 5 Oct. 1879, 4; Hulbert to Nick Young, Aug. 25, 1880.

69. *Chicago Tribune*, 9 July, 1882, 9.

70. *Chicago Tribune*, 13 April, 1879, 4.

71. *Boston Globe*, 21 July, 1878, 5; 1 Aug. 1878, 3; *Chicago Times*, 28 July, 1878, 3; *Buffalo Morning Express*, 21 Sept. 1882, 4; *Cleveland Plain Dealer*, 29 Sept. 1882, 5.

72. *Chicago Times*, 3 June, 1877, 4; 10 June, 1877, 4; *Troy Daily Press*, 25 Nov. 1879, 3.

73. Hulbert to Frank Flint, Sept. 6, 1879; *Indianapolis Journal*, 13 Sept. 1878, 8; *Argus* (Albany), 1 Sept. 1879, 8.

74. Hulbert to John Brown, Sept. 10, 1879; Hulbert to Albert Spalding, Sept. 10, 1879; *Cincinnati Enquirer*, 13 March, 1881, 10.

75. Hulbert to N.T. Appolonio, March 17, 1876; *Brooklyn Eagle*, 25 June, 1877, 3.

76. *Courier-Journal* (Louisville), 29 April, 1882, 6; Hulbert to Sid Keck, March 28, 1877; Hulbert to Nick Young, June 11, 1877.

77. Hulbert to Lewis Meacham, June 18, 1877; *Clipper*, 30 June, 1877, 107; *Chicago Tribune*, 24 June, 1877, 7; *Cincinnati Enquirer*, 1 July, 1877, 7; *St. Louis Globe-Democrat*, 20 June, 1877, 3.

78. *Cincinnati Enquirer*, 6 Oct. 1879, 2; 6 Sept. 1880, 8; *Clipper*, 29 Nov. 1879, 282; *Cincinnati Enquirer*, 29 Oct. 1879, 2.

79. *Rochester Union & Advertiser*, 9 June, 1879, 2; *Troy Daily Press*, 25 April, 1879, 3.

80. *Milwaukee Sentinel,* 10 Dec. 1877, 2; Wright to Robert Townsend, March 20, 1878.

81. *Chicago Tribune,* 9 Dec. 1877, 7; *Sunday Mercury* (New York), 19 Oct. 1879, 5.

82. Ben Douglas to Harry Wright, March 22, 1878; Clipper, 5 Jan. 1879, 323; J.M. Neff to Harry Wright, March 24, 1878.

83. Wright to Robert Townsend, March 20, 1878; *Boston Globe,* 21 July, 1878, 5; *Clipper,* 27 April, 1878, 34.

84. *Buffalo Daily Courier,* 15 Dec. 1879, 2; quoted in the *Buffalo Daily Courier,* 9 May, 1879, 2; *Clipper,* 6 Dec. 1879, 291.

85. *Cleveland Plain Dealer,* 10 Oct. 1879, 1; *Cincinnati Enquirer,* 5 Dec. 1878, 8.

86. *Sunday Republic* (Philadelphia), 9 July, 1877, 3; quoted in *Troy Daily Press,* 4 Aug. 1879, 3.

87. *Cincinnati Commercial,* 25 June, 1879, 2.

88. Hulbert to Robert Townsend, March 19, 1878; *Troy Daily Press,* 25 April, 1879, 3; *Chicago Tribune,* 31 Aug. 1879, 7; *St. Louis Globe-Democrat,* 20 March, 1881, 11.

89. *Buffalo Morning Express,* 11 April, 1882, 4; *Washington Post,* 13 June, 1880, 4; *Providence Daily Journal,* 21 Nov. 1879, 1.

90. *Troy Daily Times,* 11 Dec. 1880, 3; Hulbert to Johnson, Sept. 24, 1879.

91. John M. Ward, "Is the Base-Ball Player a Chattel?" *Lippincotts,* vol. 40 (1887), 312.

92. Hulbert to N.T. Appolonio, June 27, 1877; *Cincinnati Enquirer,* 20 June, 1877, 8; Hulbert to J.F. Evans, June 10, 1880; Hulbert to J.F. Evans, June 9, 1880.

93. *Clipper,* 4 Sept. 1880, 187. Hulbert reportedly wanted to rename baseball "The American Field Sport"; *Troy Daily Press,* 24 Sept. 1881, 3; quoted in the *Boston Herald,* 28 Sept. 1881, 2; *Troy Daily Press,* 6 May, 1882, 3.

94. *Cleveland Plain Dealer,* 4 Feb. 1880, 1.

95. *Clipper,* 2 Feb. 1878, 354.

Chapter 7

1. *Chicago Tribune,* 27 Oct. 1878, 12; *Clipper,* 12 March, 1881, 405.

2. *Chicago Times,* 1 Oct. 1881, 7; 8 Dec. 1881, 5; 8 Oct. 1881, 6.

3. *Detroit Free Press,* 17 Jan. 1882, 1; *Troy Daily Press,* 18 March, 1881, 3; *Chicago Tribune,* 14 Aug. 1881, 6.

4. *Troy Daily Times,* 7 Oct. 1878, 3; *Troy Daily Press,* 8 Dec. 1879, 3; *Troy Daily Times,* 4 Nov. 1878, 3; Hulbert to Arthur Soden, Oct. 10, 1879; *Clipper,* 8 Feb. 1879, 362.

5. *Springfield Daily Republican,* 2 Oct. 1879, 5; *Troy Daily Times,* 29 April, 1880, 3; *Cincinnati Enquirer,* 5 June, 1879, 2; *Troy Daily Times,* 20 Feb. 1880, 3; Hulbert to Harry Garfield, Feb. 9, 1880.

6. *Cleveland Plain Dealer,* 4 Feb. 1880, 1; *Capital* (Washington, D.C.), 20 June, 1880, 8; *Clipper,* 7 Jan. 1882, 687; Hulbert to J.M. Day, July 6, 1881; *Clipper,* 16 July, 1881, 266; *Chicago Tribune,* 24 March, 1878, 7. The Chicago press evidently still believed Philadelphia "hated" the National League because of its uncompromising moral stance; *Chicago Tribune,* 17 Feb. 1878, 7.

7. *Chicago Tribune,* 13 July, 1879, 7; J.F. Evans to Harry Wright, Aug. 4, 1878; *Cincinnati Enquirer,* 25 Sept. 1878, 8; *Buffalo Daily Courier,* 15 Dec. 1879, 21; *Chicago Tribune,* 15 April, 1882, 5; *Boston Herald,* 22 Oct. 1882, 12; William Perrin, *Days of Greatness: Providence Baseball, 1875–1885* (Cooperstown: Society for American Baseball Research, 1984), 9.

8. *Cincinnati Enquirer,* 5 Dec. 1879, 2; *Buffalo Daily Courant,* 13 Aug. 1879, 2; *Troy Daily Press,* 16 Sept. 1882, 3; Hulbert to Frank Bancroft, April 7, 1880.

9. *Detroit Free Press,* 12 Sept. 1882; 1; *Clipper,* 12 Feb. 1881, 373; 3 Sept. 1881, 379; *World* (New York), 27 Aug. 1881, 8; Wright to James Mutrie, Feb. 14, 1882; *World* (New York), 27 Aug. 1881, 8; *Buffalo Morning Express,* 31 Aug. 1881, 4.

10. *Sunday Mercury* (New York), 11 Aug. 1878, 5; *Harpers Weekly,* 5 Aug. 1882, 492.

11. *Providence Evening Press,* 7 April, 1882, 3; *World* (New York), 23 July, 1882, 6; *Chicago Tribune,* 3 Feb. 1878, 7.

12. *Troy Daily Press,* 16 April, 1881, 3; *Boston Globe,* 16 Dec. 1880, 9; 12 Dec. 1880, 1.

13. *Cincinnati Enquirer,* 24 Oct. 1882, 2; *Clipper,* 28 Aug. 1880, 178; *Cincinnati Enquirer,* 16 Aug. 1880, 8.

14. *Sunday Mercury* (Philadelphia), 26 Nov. 1876, 4; *Sunday Republic* (Philadelphia), 6 May, 1877, 3; *Buffalo Daily Courier,* 7 Oct. 1880, 2.

15. *Clipper,* 6 Nov. 1880, 26; *Chicago Tribune,* 14 Nov. 1880, 7; 31 Oct. 1880, 11; *Cincinnati Enquirer,* 3 Nov. 1881, 5.

16. *Cincinnati Enquirer,* 3 Nov. 1881, 3; *Pittsburg Dispatch,* 4 Nov. 1881, 5; *Evening Bulletin* (Philadelphia), 29 Oct. 1881, 10; *Courier-Journal* (Louisville), 7 June, 1882, 3; *Times* (Philadelphia), 4 June, 1882, 2.

17. *Pittsburg Dispatch,* 11 Oct. 1881, 4; 4 Nov. 1881, 5. The American Association's only direct tie to the old National Association was its secretary, J. A. Williams, who also held that position in the defunct organization; *Clipper,* 5 Nov. 1881, 532.

18. *Detroit Free Press,* 8 Nov. 1881, 1; *Chicago Tribune,* 18 Sept. 1881, 6; *Chicago Times,* 5 Nov. 1881, 7.

19. Hulbert to H.D. McKnight, Nov. 29, 1881; Hulbert to H.D. McKnight, Nov. 18, 1881.

20. *Pittsburg Dispatch,* 31 Dec. 1881, 7; Hulbert to H.D. McKnight, Nov. 8, 1881; *Pittsburg Dispatch,* 14 March, 1882, 4; *Cincinnati Enquirer,* 6 Nov. 1881, 2; *Detroit Free Press,* 12 May, 1882, 1. The American Association turned down Caylor's idea of reviewing National League expulsions because of the potentially "bad press" it would generate; *Clipper,* 7 Jan. 1882, 687.

21. *Providence Evening Press,* 9 Dec. 1881, 3; Seymour, *Baseball: The Early Years,* 207, 208; *Cincinnati Enquirer,* 8 Jan. 1882, 12.

22. *Pittsburg Dispatch,* 26 April, 1882, 4; 28 April, 1882, 4; *Buffalo Morning Express,* 11 July, 1881, 4; *St. Louis Globe-Democrat,* 12 Dec. 1880, 15.

23. *Pittsburg Dispatch,* 20 Jan. 1882, 2; *Cincinnati Enquirer,* 18 Jan. 1882, 4; *Pittsburg Dispatch,* 28 April, 1882, 4; *Cincinnati Enquirer,* 18 Dec. 1881, 13.

24. *Buffalo Morning Express,* 8 Dec. 1881, 4.

25. *Clipper,* 5 Aug. 1882, 317; *Times* (Philadelphia), 4 June, 1882, 2; *Cincinnati Enquirer,* 10 July, 1882, 8; *Troy Daily Press,* 13 Sept. 1882, 2; *Times* (Philadelphia), 15 Sept. 1882, 4.

26. *St. Louis Globe-Democrat,* 4 Sept. 1882, 3; 25 July, 1881, 7; 15 Aug. 1881, 8; *Courier-Journal* (Louisville), 29 Aug. 1882, 8. Sunday games between amateur teams had drawn large crowds at Cincinnati in 1880; *Cincinnati Enquirer,* 5 July, 1880, 8; 9 Aug. 1880, 7.

27. *Times* (Philadelphia), 3 Sept. 1882, 3; *Troy Daily Press,* 25 Sept. 1882, 3.

28. *Baltimore American and Commercial Advertiser,* 23 July, 1882, 3; *Pittsburg Dispatch,* 19 July, 1882, 2; 29 Sept. 1882, 5; *Cincinnati Enquirer,* 20 Aug. 1882, 2.

29. *Buffalo Morning Express,* 22 June, 1882, 4; *Clipper,* 9 Sept. 1882, 399; *Times* (Philadelphia), 10 Sept. 1882, 2; *Buffalo Morning Express,* 22 Sept. 1882, 4.

30. *Cincinnati Enquirer,* 28 July, 1882, 5; 23 Sept. 1882, 2; *Times* (Philadelphia), 10 Sept. 1882, 2; *Pittsburg Dispatch,* 19 Aug. 1882, 5; *Chicago Times,* 15 July, 1882, 6.

31. Hulbert to H.D. McKnight, Nov. 18, 1881; *St. Louis Globe-Democrat,* 15 April, 1882, 7.

32. *Troy Daily Press,* 20 Dec. 1881, 3; *Chicago Tribune,* 1 Oct. 1882, 9; *Providence Daily Journal,* 7 Dec. 1882, 4; *Worcester Daily Spy,* 11 Oct. 1882, 4.

33. *Detroit Free Press,* 16 June, 1882, 6; *Cleveland Plain Dealer,* 29 Sept. 1882, 5; *Buffalo Morning Express,* 14 Sept. 1882, 4.

34. *Clipper,* 7 Jan. 1882, 687; *Detroit Free Press,* 12 Sept. 1882, 1.

35. *Worcester Daily Spy,* 2 May, 1881, 4; *Buffalo Morning Express,* 10 Aug. 1881, 4.

36. Wright to Arthur Soden, March 22, 1882; *Times* (Philadelphia), 14 May, 1882, 2; *Troy Daily Press*, 18 Sept. 1882, 3; 1 Sept. 1882, 3; 30 Sept. 1882, 3.

37. *Providence Evening Press*, 7 Dec. 1882, 4; *Buffalo Morning Express*, 26 Sept. 1882, 4.

38. *Troy Daily Press*, 26 Sept. 1882, 3. Threats, by both clubs, to pursue legal action over their expulsions also came to nothing; *Chicago Tribune*, 8 Oct. 1882, 4.

39. *Chicago Tribune*, 29 Sept. 1882, 7; *Chicago Times*, 14 Sept. 1879, 3; *Providence Evening Press*, 29 Sept. 1882, 4.

40. *Chicago Times*, 25 Sept. 1881, 11.

41. *Times* (Philadelphia), 31 May, 1882, 3; 21 May, 1882, 2; *Chicago Times*, 23 July, 1882, 6.

42. *Chicago Times*, 25 June, 1882, 8.

43. *Cincinnati Enquirer*, 24 Sept. 1882, 12; *Times* (Philadelphia), 24 Sept. 1882, 2; *Pittsburg Dispatch*, 6 Oct. 1882, 5.

44. *Providence Evening Press*, 19 Feb. 1883, 4.

45. *Cincinnati Enquirer*, 31 Dec. 1882, 12.

A Note on Sources

For all intents and purposes scholarly interest in baseball only began with the publication of Harold Seymour's *Baseball: The Early Years* (New York: Oxford University Press, 1960). This was the first work to treat baseball history in an objective, extensively researched manner, but the work was largely descriptive, rather than analytical, a treatment that has characterized most comprehensive baseball histories since, such as David Voigt's *American Baseball* (Norman: University of Oklahoma Press, 1966), Charles Alexander's *Our Game: An American Baseball History* (New York: Holt, 1991) and Benjamin Rader's *Baseball: A History of America's Game* (Urbana: University of Illinois Press, 1992).

Not until the publication of Melvin Adelman's *A Sporting Time: New York City and the Rise of Modern Athletics* (Urbana: University of Illinois Press, 1986) did baseball become the object of critical, analytical attention, an approach that was also followed with George Kirsch's *The Creation of American Team Sports: Baseball and Cricket, 1838–1872* (Urbana: University of Illinois Press, 1989) and Warren Goldstein's *Playing for Keeps: A History of Early Baseball* (Ithaca: Cornell University Press, 1989). All these works are valuable for understanding baseball's social origins and early development though none extend their analysis beyond the rise of professionalism in the early 1870s.

In recent years there's been a proliferation of specialized publications on pre–1890 baseball, such as William Ryczek's *Blackguards and Red Stockings: A History of Baseball's National Association, 1871–1875* (Jefferson, N.C.: McFarland, 1992), David Nemec's *The Beer and Whisky League: The Illustrated History of the American Association* (New York: Lyons & Burford, 1994) and Stephen Guschov's *The Red Stockings of Cincinnati: Base Ball's First All Professional Team and Its Historic 1869 and 1870 Seasons* (Jefferson, N.C.: McFarland, 1998), but all these well researched and readable works are descriptive, rather than analytical, in their treatment.

As I've noted in this study, there's a conspicuous paucity of original pre–1880 baseball records, though I've extensively utilized the two most important primary sources for this period, the correspondence of Harry Wright and William Hulbert.

The Wright correspondence, contained in the Spalding Baseball Collection at the New York Public Library and available in microfilm from the Society for American Baseball Research in Cleveland, provides important information on the workings of not only Wright's Boston club but also the National Association. Though baseball scholars have frequently consulted this source they have often done so on a selective basis, generally for evidence of the game's growing professionalism, while neglecting its valuable insights into the early years of the National League, especially those contained in letters from correspondents other than Wright.

By far the most valuable source for understanding the circumstances leading up to the formation and early years of the National League are the letters of William Hulbert contained in the Records of the Chicago Baseball Club at the Chicago Historical Society. The correspondence provides a virtual window into the mind of the one man most responsible for laying out the National League's course and direction during its critical early years. Despite their historical value, Hulbert's letters have, surprisingly, been largely neglected by even the most intrepid baseball scholars, a negligence that may perhaps be corrected by their eventual publication, something that would certainly mark a red-letter date in the history of baseball scholarship.

Fortunately the lack of original pre–1880 baseball sources is offset by a plethora of journalistic sources. From the mid–1850s on most of the major sporting weeklies of this era, such as *Porters Spirit of the Times*, the *Clipper, Wilkes Spirit of the Times,* and *Turf, Field and Farm,* carried extensive, if not necessarily insightful, baseball reports. Also invaluable are the baseball specialty weeklies that briefly flourished during the late 1860s, such as the *Ball Players Chronicle* and its successors, the *American Chronicle of Sports and Pastimes* and the *National Chronicle*, as well as the *New England Base Ballist.* A number of general weeklies from this period also contained fairly extensive baseball reports, particularly the New York and Philadelphia *Sunday Mercury* and the *St. Louis Republican.* All these papers provided extensive and, in many cases, extremely detailed baseball coverage from the late 1860s to late 1870s.

Though generally slow to recognize the news worthiness of sporting events, a number of major metropolitan dailies, by the mid–1870s, were providing baseball coverage equal to that found in the best sporting weeklies, among them the *Chicago Tribune*, the New York *World,* the *St. Louis*

Globe-Democrat, the *Cincinnati Enquirer* and the *Boston Herald*. For the antebellum period, I've consulted, in addition to those papers long known for their sporting coverage (the *New York Herald, Brooklyn Eagle* and *Newark Advertiser*), a number of New York dailies largely neglected by scholars, such as the *New York Morning Express, New York Evening Express* and the *New York Daily News,* all of which carried fairly extensive and, in some cases, uniquely informative baseball reports.

Most sports reporting of this period was highly partisan, if not outright biased, in their coverage of local clubs or the leagues in which they played. As a consequence many local controversies were often glossed over or outright ignored. To correct this imbalance I've also consulted numerous papers from second-tier baseball cities, whose sports reporting often provided more critical, behind-the-scenes, revelations of organized baseball's workings. Some of the best for this were the *Buffalo Courier,* the *Troy Press* and the *Pittsburg Dispatch.*

Yet one should by no means presume all the journalistic sources for pre–1880 baseball have been exhausted. Anyone who has perused the baseball sections of the major metropolitan dailies during this period cannot help but be struck by the many baseball quotes and references they carried from numerous smaller, little known, papers of this period, such as the New York *National Standard,* the *Chicago Post & Mail,* and the *Providence Morning Star,* papers that, if we can judge from their often tantalizing quotes, seemed to often express unique, off-the-beltway, perspectives and opinions on the baseball of their time. They remain an untapped, yet possibly valuable, source for constructing a complete understanding of baseball's development during this period.

Finally, a number of baseball annuals from this period were also consulted, among them *Spalding's Official Base Ball Guide,* despite its heavy bias towards the National League, *Beadle's Dime Base-Ball Player* and *DeWitt's Base-Ball Guide,* the last mentioned being especially valuable for its views on the social character of the baseball of that period.

Index